D0214146

# Toward a Deaf Translation Norm

# Studies in Interpret

Melanie Metzger and Earl Fleetwoo

**VOLUME 1**  *From Topic Boundaries to Omis* *on Interpretation*
Melanie Metzger, Steven Collins
and Risa Shaw, Editors

**VOLUME 2**  *Attitudes, Innuendo, and Regula* *of Interpretation*
Melanie Metzger and Earl Fleetv

**VOLUME 3**  *Translation, Sociolinguistic, and* *in Interpreting*
Melanie Metzger and Earl Fleetv

**VOLUME 4**  *Deaf Professionals and Designat*
Peter C. Hauser, Karen L. Finch,
Editors

**VOLUME 5**  *Prosodic Markers and Utterance* *American Sign Language Interpr*
Brenda Nicodemus

**VOLUME 6**  *Toward a Deaf Translation Norm*
Christopher Stone

# Toward a Deaf Translation Norm

# Studies in Interpretation

Melanie Metzger and Earl Fleetwood, General Editors

**VOLUME 1**  *From Topic Boundaries to Omission: New Research on Interpretation*
Melanie Metzger, Steven Collins, Valerie Dively, and Risa Shaw, Editors

**VOLUME 2**  *Attitudes, Innuendo, and Regulators: Challenges of Interpretation*
Melanie Metzger and Earl Fleetwood, Editors

**VOLUME 3**  *Translation, Sociolinguistic, and Consumer Issues in Interpreting*
Melanie Metzger and Earl Fleetwood, Editors

**VOLUME 4**  *Deaf Professionals and Designated Interpreters*
Peter C. Hauser, Karen L. Finch, and Angela B. Hauser, Editors

**VOLUME 5**  *Prosodic Markers and Utterance Boundaries in American Sign Language Interpretation*
Brenda Nicodemus

**VOLUME 6**  *Toward a Deaf Translation Norm*
Christopher Stone

# Toward a Deaf Translation Norm

*Christopher Stone*

GALLAUDET UNIVERSITY PRESS

*Washington, D.C.*

**Studies in Interpretation**
A Series Edited by Melanie Metzger and Earl Fleetwood

Gallaudet University Press
Washington, D.C. 20002
http://gupress.gallaudet.edu

© 2009 by Gallaudet University
All rights reserved. Published 2009
Printed in the United States of America

ISBN 978-1-56368-418-0, 1-56368-418-7
ISSN 1545-7613

Interior design by Richard Hendel

∞ The paper used in this publication meets the minimum requirements of American National Standard for Information Sciences—Permanence of Paper for Printed Library Materials, ANSI Z39.48–1984.

# Contents

Acknowledgments, vii

Introduction, ix

1. Interpreting and Translation, 1

2. Identity and Language, 25

3. Methodology, 58

4. Role and Identity, 76

5. Interpreted/Translated Language Features, 101

6. The Translation and Interpretation Process, 133

7. The Deaf Translation Norm, 165

Appendix A, 175

References, 177

Index, 189

# Acknowledgments

For me finishing a PhD was like swimming the English Channel. Both a BSc and MSc are good training, but nothing like the main event. You can train in the pool and swim some rivers, but these swims are not like swimming the Channel. There are many well-wishers at the beginning and end of the journey, but you swim alone except for your coach in the boat navigating. The coach has a different perspective in the boat from the view you get by being in the water.

Occasionally, you see other swimmers and other coaches in their boats. In the end though, we all swim at our own paces and we, the swimmers, are the ones who have to avoid the jellyfish.

So my first thank-you goes to my head coach, Rachel Sutton-Spence. I would also like to thank my informal coaches: all the members of the Centre for Deaf Studies, past and present, who have taught me and encouraged me, especially Edith Norrman, Gloria Pullen, and Lorna Allsop. Similarly, Professor Bencie Woll for the conversation on the train and the stats spotting, and Professor Diane Blakemore for introducing me to relevance theory.

Thanks also to my interpreter colleagues: Freya McLuckie for always being there; Jo Ross for her support and Scottish news footage; and Zane Hema, Nigel Cleaver, and Marco Nardi for their kind words and kinder drinks. And a special thank-you goes to my old flatmates, Emma and Alfie, and for my family for putting up with my madness. Thanks Mick, Neil, Nat, Matt, and Pete for the parties and for the adventures of homo, mulatto, and the abuser that kept me going—as did the destressing games of badminton and running the downs and towpath.

Thank you to my fellow swimmers: Chamion, Karen, Maria Barbara Lange, Maria, Janie, Galini, Felix, and to PRATL and North West Centre for Linguistics. And thanks to some key supporters: Margo Currie for some book funds, Donna West for listening to my ranting and for being such a great researcher; Elvire Roberts for proofreading and for helping me to make sense of my stuff; and to Robert Adam for proofreading the second time around—mwah.

Finally, and most importantly, I'd like to thank my informants, without whom this project would have been impossible, and a special thanks to the Deaf community for its generosity and for allowing me to enter into a whole new way of being in the world.

# Introduction

This volume looks at the emerging profession of Deaf translators/interpreters (T/Is), from where it has emerged, and how it is enacted in a public space in the United Kingdom (UK). It investigates whether a Deaf translation norm is evolving as increasing numbers of Deaf people work within the mainstream to provide access for their community by translating English into British Sign Language (BSL) for Web sites, public services, government literature, and television media.

My research examines how Deaf and hearing T/Is render English broadcast television news into BSL and whether Deaf T/Is in particular employ certain strategies to present BSL to audiences who, like them, are culturally Deaf and identify as members of the BSL-using community.

## TRANSLATION NORMS

Several factors have contributed to the development of a Deaf translation norm, and they can be broken down into three categories—preliminary, initial, and operational norms (Toury 1995, 53–69). Preliminary norms relate to whether a specific translation policy exists. The historical, community-based preliminary norm was a social practice in the Deaf community. Deaf bilinguals (fluent in BSL and English) were asked by Deaf monolinguals (fluent in BSL and possessing a limited knowledge of English) to translate and explain various events and occurrences. This necessarily depended upon the identity and community membership of the Deaf bilinguals, and although the bilinguals did not need to be audiologically deaf, they needed to have a Deaf identity and be part of the Deaf community (Ladd 2003; Padden and Humphries 1988; see chapters 1 and 4). The Deaf bilinguals supported Deaf monolinguals in a variety of ways, including translating letters and correspondence, providing Deaf monolinguals with information about mainstream society, and retelling or re-presenting information read or gleaned regarding current affairs. These Deaf monolinguals form the constructed audience or "pragmatic other" (Ruuskanen 1996) for whom the BSL text was created (see chapters 4, 5, and 6).

This preliminary norm continues today within the Deaf club (social clubs for sign-language-using deaf people) and Deaf community. There is also now a preliminary norm created by legislation, specifically the Broadcasting Act of 1996 (HMSO 1996, chap. 55, sec. 20). This legislation obligates television companies to provide BSL on television (either as a program presented in BSL or programs with in-vision translation/interpretation).[1] Whereas in the past the Deaf bilinguals and Deaf monolinguals would have exercised some control over what was rendered into BSL in their community, usually within the Deaf club, the introduction of Deaf T/Is in the public sphere (specifically through television but now extending to the Internet and social service documents), much of this macrolevel control is now in the hands of non-Deaf institutions.

Hearing employers decide who to hire (Deaf or hearing T/Is) and what is rendered into BSL (which stories, headlines, Web sites, and public documents). This mediates the degree to which T/Is are able to employ a Deaf translation norm, and while the visible use of BSL in the public sphere can constitute "a counter-hegemonic practice" (Skelton and Valentine 2003b, 128), the act of the institutions in deciding who to employ and what will be signed "colonizes" this particular Deaf cultural space (Ladd 2003, 182).

## Initial Norms

Initial norms govern whether the text created by the translator is rendered into a discourse style or genre already occurring in the target language (TL) and culture, in this case BSL. Alternatively the discourse style represents the language and culture being translated from the source language (SL), in this case English, and marked as "foreign" to the target language and culture. Part of the historical role of the Deaf bilingual following a Deaf translation norm was to create a BSL text in language used and understood by Deaf monolinguals.

The broadcast television news is one of the first mainstream public spaces where the T/Is have been able to follow a Deaf translation norm.

---

1. In-vision translators/interpreters appear on part of the television screen and are not part of the original image. Instead, they are superimposed so that the interpreter takes up part of the screen.

As such, the Deaf T/Is aim to domesticate (Venuti 1998) the BSL text to look like a stand-alone BSL product rather than a translation. The Deaf T/Is create a level of presence counter to current notions of neutrality in translation and interpreting (Rudvin 2002).

## Operational Norms

Operational norms are the microlevel translation decisions concerning the specific texts to be rendered from one language to another. These microlevel translation decisions, identified by the linguistic features of the BSL text, show that fluency within the Deaf translation norm is not concerned with lexical choice; rather, the BSL needs to exhibit specific types of prosodic marking (Sandler 1999b; Wilbur and Patschke 1997; Wilbur 2000). In this case it differs from prosodically marked interpreted language (Ahrens 2005; Shlesinger 1994). The BSL also exhibits cognitive pragmatic enrichments and impoverishments (Sequeiros 2002; 1998).

The prosodic marking manifests as blinks (Sze 2004; Wilbur 1994) and head movements (Jouison 1985). The Deaf translation norm uses blinks and head movements to segment the BSL text into phrase and discourse units (Boyes-Braem 1999, 179). The blinks rates are lower for the Deaf translation norm due to high visual attention (Sze 2004), partly because of the visual demand of watching the autocue (teleprompter) and partly because of presenting a prepared text. The head movements form nested structures that interrelate different idea units, forming a high level of cohesion in the text, and again demonstrating the prepared nature of the text. The cognitive pragmatic enrichments and impoverishments that form part of the Deaf translation norm reduce the cognitive effort required by Deaf monolinguals to understand the BSL text. To achieve this, the Deaf T/Is draw upon native intuitions of the pragmatics of BSL.

## The Deaf Translation Norm Process

The Deaf translation norm within broadcast television news involves a specific process that includes: script reading, watching related video footage (without sound), and presenting the rendered BSL text using an autocue as a prompt rather than listening to the spoken English of the newsreader as a live source of English (as the hearing interpreters). Deaf T/Is are forced to follow this process because they cannot hear the source language, which could account for some of their BSL target language features. Hearing T/Is could follow the same process but choose not to; instead, they listen to the live source of English. The process allows the Deaf T/Is to construct the BSL text without the influence of spoken language prosody and as a performed translation.

## IDENTIFYING THE DEAF COMMUNITY

In the past, one became a member of the Deaf community by being born Deaf or by losing one's hearing at an early age. Cultural identity was then cemented by attending Deaf schools, using sign language, and meeting other Deaf people in "Deaf clubs or at other Deaf social activities" (Ladd 2003, 44). The Deaf T/Is in this study come from multigenerational Deaf families who form the core of the Deaf community. These families have experienced, at least within the home, a Deaf haven from a hearing world. As the guardians of sign language and Deaf history and culture, there exists an expectation that they will preserve and pass on Deaf ways of being in the world to other Deaf people (Padden and Humphries 1988). Selecting the Deaf T/Is from this group enables the exploration of a Deaf translation free from "hearing" institutional barriers.

## THE EMERGENCE OF THE SIGN LANGUAGE INTERPRETING PROFESSION

Throughout history and across the world, whenever sufficient numbers of Deaf people live within a community, sign languages have developed and hearing members of those societies who are able to sign have been called upon to act as T/Is on the Deaf people's behalf (Scott-Gibson 1991). In the UK, sign language interpreting became recognized as a separate profession in the 1970s (Brien, Brown and Collins 2002). With the establishment of interpreter training, examinations, and assessments in the UK, the sign language interpreting profession has expanded to include hearing people as well as Deaf people and hearing members of Deaf families who have a Deaf cultural identify and who have traditionally worked as interpreters for the community either voluntarily or, in recent years, for remuneration.

Despite the emergence of the BSL/English interpreting profession, there have been very few publicly visible interpreters from the "core" of the Deaf community (that is, Deaf people from Deaf families). This contrasts with most minority spoken-language T/Is, who come from within their communities (Alexander et al., 2004). In many situations it does not seem feasible to the mainstream that a Deaf person could work as a T/I. Yet in conference settings, STTR can provide scrolling English for Deaf T/Is (for example, the ASLI conference 2008) in the form of verbatim speech-to-text reporting or live subtitling. Deaf T/Is are doing more Web translation in Europe and North America, and the vice president of the World Association of Sign Language Interpreters (WASLI) is a Deaf interpreter. Clearly, these opportunities create the possibility for greater acceptance of Deaf T/Is through greater visibility.

## Sign Language Interpreting and Television

Signed languages are unwritten languages, and, therefore, until the advent of film they were not recordable or transmittable across geographical location and historical time (Gannon 2004). Now, technological advances mean visual languages can be recorded for personal use, for the public record, and for public broadcast (Ladd 2003, 53–56).

The first television program in the UK to use BSL as its primary language was *For Deaf Children* in the 1950s (Ladd 2007, 6). The first news program was *News Review* in the 1960s, and it contained thirty minutes of weekly news, current affairs, and a Deaf news story deemed relevant to the Deaf audience (ibid.). External groups wanting to maintain power over the BSL-using Deaf community tried, with success, to limit the public presence of sign language on the television.

*See Hear*, a weekly news magazine program for Deaf and hard of hearing people, has been on BBC 1 since 1981. In the past, there was a monthly feature called "Behind the News" that gave in-depth information about current events to fill in the knowledge gaps a Deaf audience might have. Another Deaf program, *Listening Eye* (which became *Sign On)* was shown on Channel 4, from 1981 to 1998 (Ladd 2003, 55) and it also included news and debates on current affairs. All of these programs provide examples of BSL news discourse.

With the introduction of the Broadcasting Act of 1996, more mainstream programs, including current affairs programs, popular programs, and soap operas, have been presented in, or translated into, sign language. As a result, a variety of Deaf and hearing T/Is have been employed to undertake this work. BBC News 24 has interpreted news on weekdays in the morning (7:00–7:45 A.M. and 8:00–8:20 A.M.) and lunchtime (1:00–1:45 P.M.). There are also examples of daily BSL Web news (for example, Deafstation)[2] emerging.

In 1981 *See Hear,*[3] the Deaf magazine program of the BBC, created the first full-time T/I job. Deaf people started working in television as presenters in 1979, working from autocue and subsequently translating/interpreting the news, including some regional BBC lunchtime news, some regional six o'clock news and some regional weekly news reviews.

One of the few domains where we find examples of all three groups of interpreters working is in television (Steiner 1998). This allows the exploration of the similarities and differences between a Deaf and non-Deaf culturally centered perspective. It is also possible to explore notions of power in rendering from a majority language and culture to a minority language and culture.

Traditionally, training has not included any Deaf community models for translation or interpreting, because these have been hidden. There are, however, adaptations made to mainstream models when applying them to sign language interpreters (Gresswell 2001; Leeson 2005a). Although there are descriptive accounts of what sign language interpreters do (Cokely 1992; Metzger 1999; Napier 2002), to date no one has explored the types of translation activity Deaf people have undertaken throughout history. There are no descriptions of Deaf-led community based translation and interpreting models.

With automated speech-to-text technology available by using a laptop and the keyboard to type a "live" rendering of the BSL into English, community interpreting is possible. But the employment of Deaf T/Is in the public sphere other than television is limited to circumstances where a Deaf client uses another signed language (Boudreault 2004), has idiosyncratic language use, or has a learning disability (in this case the Deaf client uses a form of BSL hearing interpreters find hard to understand, and the Deaf interpreter works between two visual modes).

BSL has evolved from being the language of face-to-face communication to being used in television broadcasts, both by Deaf and hearing people. Anecdotally, the Deaf community reports that more and more people

2. http://www.deafstation.org/
3. Personal communication Edith Norrman, May 1996

are exposed to BSL without meeting the community (Denmark 2002). They also report that more and more people are learning BSL without having ever met a Deaf person; and more and more people become T/Is by following training routes, rather than by mixing with the community to gain acceptance and approval before working as T/Is. This leads to the hearing T/Is having no exposure to the Deaf translation norm. This research explores and enables the training of Deaf T/Is to include a Deaf translation norm.

*Chapter 1*

# Interpreting and Translation

This research examines the differences between Deaf and hearing translators/interpreters (T/Is), and the analysis falls into two main categories: analyzing the target language (TL) as a stand-alone piece of linguistic data and comparing the source language (SL) and the TL as translated or interpreted data. A variety of literature addresses both of these points, and this study explores them from the perspective of translation studies, interpreting studies, and relevance theory.

The terms "interpreting" and "translation" are not synonymous within the translation and interpreting field. Extensive research has been undertaken within translation studies, and only in recent years has interpreting studies attempted to establish itself as an equal (Pöchhacker 2004). Interpreting is often seen as a field within the area of translation, confirmed by the preface of a prominent interpreting studies reader: "The idea of devoting a separate volume to Interpreting Studies, rather than relegating it to a subsection of Lawrence Venuti's *Translation Studies Reader*, was not immediately evident, but was readily espoused in consultations with Advisory Editor Mona Baker" (Pöchhacker and Shlesinger 2002, ix).

While translation and interpreting are concerned with the rendering of one language into another, differences exist due to the form and time constraints. Frishberg (1990, 18) identifies the difference saying translation refers to written texts and interpretation refers to the "live and immediate transmission" of discourse, either spoken or signed. In both cases the source or original language or text (SL) is translated or interpreted into a target language or text (TL).

In the UK Deaf T/Is translate to camera (TV news, Web sites, etc.) working from an autocue of written English. This falls between the Frishberg distinction of the form of the SL and TL for interpreting since the SL is written, but the TL is not. An alternative distinction is one of time: the decision making process in translation is usually one subject to review, revision, and a longer time, whereas for interpreting it is instantaneous. Kade (cited and translated in Pöchhacker 2004, 11) defines interpreting as, "a form of Translation in which a *first and final rendition in another language* is produced on the basis of a *one-time presentation* of an utterance in a source language" (emphasis in Pöchhacker).

Within broadcast news, scripts are often given the day before the broadcast to the T/Is. This gives the T/Is an opportunity to read and re-read the SL, resulting in a greater than one-time presentation of the SL text before rendering it into BSL. The T/Is can read and ascertain the intention of the whole text; in interpreting, the SL utterance is broken into short units for rendering (Shlesinger 1995, 194).

BSL has no written form, and since no way exists of editing a recorded form of the language (although sections of a longer text could be refilmed), a performance or presentation element very similar to interpreting remains. Even though we can compare the SL with the TL product, investigating the reasoning behind the translation itself provides one way of exploring competency. If the TL BSL is a translation, we can analyze the level of preparedness by looking at prosodic features. The process of the translation or interpretation can also be examined by think-aloud protocols to see whether the T/Is physically rehearse the TL product before creating the final TL live.

## INTERPRETING AND TRANSLATION STYLES

The interpreting field draws heavily from theories in translation studies and although some researchers have focused on various aspects of the interpreting process and SL-to-TL text comparisons, etc., a strong influence from the translation field remains. Linguistics has been used to try and measure the accuracy of translation. Catford (1965) measured shifts from one category to another in a translation: for example, does an adjectival phrase in the SL become an adjectival phrase in the TL and thus achieve formal equivalence or become an adverbial phrase and perhaps achieve textual equivalence? Cokely (1986) within sign language interpreting research also formally analyzed "additions" or "omissions" according to the SL focusing on linguistic transfer between languages, without looking at whether information was being delivered in a culturally sensitive way that was appropriate for the audience.

This token-for-token approach is often used to judge fidelity, but one must question what one is being faithful to, either single linguistic units or a greater communicative goal. Although the form plays some part in rendering a TL text as, "it is the linguistic form of the source text where many clues to meaning are found" (Janzen 2005, 71), in recent years, the general trend in translation studies has been toward cultural, rather than linguistic transfer (Hatim 2001, 10, 44).

Hatim writes, "the 'cultural turn' in translation studies has shifted the focus to the study of ideology as a shaping force . . . and to translation as re-writing within such trends as [for example] the gendered practices of feminist translation" (2001, 10). The move toward cultural rather than linguistic transfer encompasses not only sense-for-sense interpretation (Seleskovitch 1978), but also the adoption of the need for the T/I to be accountable for the wider informational content and culturally loaded information in a SL message.

Cronin (2002) also discusses the cultural turn in interpreting, translation, orality, and colonialism. He opens up the field of interpreting to consider much of the recent moves in translation studies within a context of translation and interpreting rather than the product solely as a scientific object for enquiry. Within a colonized context it is the voice of the oppressed group that wishes to be heard. We need to consider language differences such as the primary orality of a group of people whose language has no written form. We also need to consider how the T/Is position themselves with respect to the different language groups they work between and of which they are members.

Furthermore, within the area of ideology, Hatim (2001) writes there are two emerging trends, the ideology of translation and the translation of ideology. This research examines the ideology of translation from the perspective of translations favoring hegemonies. Specifically, the work focuses on the Anglo-American tradition where foreign texts, when translated into English, are normalized with foreign cultural references changed to be culturally appropriate for the home audience. This adoption of a transparent and fluent style works in favor of the dominant and powerful target culture. The translation of ideology "focuses on how ideology is conveyed in and through the use of language" (Hatim 2001, 11) and will be explored in greater depth in chapter 5.

Hatim also explains that although linguistics is capable of informing the study of translation, for example, by examining cross-linguistic variation and language typology, more than one discipline can be brought in to widen the scope and goals of this type of analysis. These disciplines include sociolinguistics, pragmatics, text linguistics, and discourse analysis. This gives us a good background from which to work, and Hatim

(2001) discusses many different schools of thought and theory in relation to translation studies from the 1960s to the present. His diagram (43) provides a useful way to examine different models of equivalence and their orientation to the source or target language (refer to fig. 1.1 for a modified version).

In figure 1.1, the theories on the left-hand side of the triangle are orientated toward the SL and attempt to analyze or hold the translation accountable to it. Those on the right-hand side of the triangle hold the translation accountable to the TL. Amongst the feminist translators this involves in some cases a quite radical intervention. Hatim (2001, 53) gives an example of a traditional translation versus a feminist translation by Linda Gaboriau.

> This evening I'm entering history without pulling up my skirt.

> This evening I'm entering history without opening my legs.

The feminist translation makes the implication in the SL explicit. This explication fulfills the political aims of the feminist translator since it does not euphemize the exploitation of women throughout the ages. This is made clearer within the feminist translation style as the reference is a line about women. We might see similar explication by Deaf T/Is if a story refers to Deaf people or contains an explication of the Deaf experience. A mainstream audience might not understand nor desire an explicit translation that documents some of the atrocities carried out on Deaf people in the name of eugenics and oralism that a Deaf translator could make explicit.

On the left-hand side of the triangle in figure 1.1 we see notions of translation explored with a SL focus. Catford's approach is described earlier. Nida's focus was on the readers of the TL responding to the text in the same way as readers from the SL culture when reading of the SL. Koller included both Catford's formal equivalence and Nida's dynamic equivalence within the five frameworks of equivalence he proposed, which included denotative equivalence, connotative equivalence, and text-normative equivalence. Beaugrande extended the narrow focus of other scholars to the notion of text as the unit for translation rather than word or sentence renderings, and while Venuti is also interested in text as the unit of translation, his focus is on ensuring that the reader is reminded that the source text and culture is foreign to the TL reader.

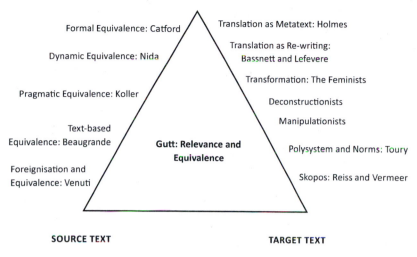

Formal Equivalence: Catford

Dynamic Equivalence: Nida

Pragmatic Equivalence: Koller

Text-based
Equivalence: Beaugrande

Foreignisation and
Equivalence: Venuti

**Gutt: Relevance and
Equivalence**

Translation as Metatext: Holmes

Translation as Re-writing:
Bassnett and Lefevere

Transformation: The Feminists

Deconstructionists

Manipulationists

Polysystem and Norms: Toury

Skopos: Reiss and Vermeer

**SOURCE TEXT**             **TARGET TEXT**

FIGURE 1.1. *Translation studies as a whole*

On the right-hand side of the triangle in figure 1.1 we see different notions of translation explored in relation to the TL. Holmes acknowledges the difficulties in translating (predominantly) literature and poems. He looks toward creating a TL that considers a network of correspondences because of the shifts encountered when translating from SL to TL that fit to a greater or lesser extent. Bassnett and Lefevere took this further by moving to a cultural level whereby the translation had to take on board the network of cultural symbols within which the translation was situated. This was followed with the idea of translation as production and not reproduction, as demonstrated by the feminist translators, and similarly with the notion of the TL being a response to the SL by the deconstructionists. Toury was interested in applying polysystems to look into the ideologies behind what was chosen to be translated, and manipulationists explored this theme in greater depth. They were interested in issues of the perpetuation of ideas about the SL being sacrosanct rather than allowing the TL to be a stand-alone product. Finally Skopos theory looked at the intended function of the TL within the TL culture and accepted that this function can be different from its function with the SL culture. Relevance theory (RT) occupies the center of the diagram, since RT provides a framework for equivalence measured by the cognitive effort of understanding rather than against the SL or TL, and will be explored in greater depth later as a central framework for this research.

When considering translation strategies, Hatim (2001, 87) describes them as a complex relationship between

1. A concern with the notion of "register" and issues related to the use and the user of language (this is within the source language orientation);
2. A concern with "intentionality" and other aspects of pragmatics such as speech acts, implied meaning and relevance;
3. A concern with the wider notion of "culture," with the focus shifting to the status of text, genre, and discourse in the translation process (this is within the target language orientation).

These three factors are examined by investigating the interplay between the direction in which the T/Is are working (from or into first language) and the decisions that the T/Is make when constructing the TL.

## Culture and Intentionality

Two factors needing consideration are intentionality and culture. RT explores how T/Is use contextual assumptions to make something optimally relevant to their addressees. These contextual assumptions include cultural knowledge and intentionality (what the speaker intends the addressee to understand as being communicated), and they are clearly culturally bound.

This research explores differences between the TL of Deaf and hearing T/Is in order to identify a Deaf translation norm. Pragmatics will be used to examine the types of translation shifts occurring between the SL and the TL, and it will provide a theoretical framework for the notion of cognitive cultural contact, which Stolze (2004, 43) defined as: "The two culture systems establish contact within the translator's mind: in other words, her cognition as an expert reaches out into two different cultures and into various discourse fields."

This will be understood in terms of pragmatic enrichment and impoverishment (Sequeiros 2002, 1998) discussed later. The shifts made will be analyzed in accordance with implied meaning and relevance. Insights can be gained into the cultural and linguistic transfer, and the ideology behind these transfers or shifts, by analyzing the texts of the Deaf T/Is (from the TL culture) and hearing T/Is (from the surrounding SL culture), and comparing these texts with interview data.

When discussing empirical research in translation studies, Hatim (2001, 154) acknowledges that four factors need to be considered.

1. The range of translators represented in a corpus
2. The level of expertise
3. Directionality (whether the translator is working into or out of the mother tongue)
4. The spectrum of textual practices represented (genre, text type, discourse)

The level of cultural information (expressing an intention) that can be included in a translation may depend upon which culture the T/Is come from. It also depends upon the skill of the individual T/Is to be able to identify and incorporate such information. Directionality acknowledges that T/Is are able to work in different directions, but naturalness is something I compare against native (linguistic and cultural) intuitions. Some of the judgments on intentionality and cultural relevance could differ depending on whether one is working in one's mother tongue, irrespective of whether these decisions affect comprehensibility.

The T/Is in this research are either Deaf / Deaf (hearing) with their first language (L1) as BSL and second language (L2) English; or hearing with L1 English and L2 BSL. They all work in television, some of the Deaf T/Is also work in Web cast news, Web, and DVD translation. A discussion of their level of expertise can be found in the methodology section. Factors three and four are relevant to the research design; directionality of rendering (L1 to L2, or L2 to L1) is one of the principal factors being researched and can be explored by examining the translation ideology the Deaf T/Is discuss in interviews and the manifestations of this ideology in the TL.

The spectrum of texts is limited to broadcast news; this information-giving medium enables an analysis of how the T/Is situate themselves: either as passive conduits or active and empowered agents within television interpreting. Some of the data may be prepared translation by the T/Is from a script. Other pieces of data will have T/Is interpreting, that is, rendering unseen information they have had no time to prepare.

By examining the TL product and its blinking phenomena, and the process the T/Is undertake creating the TL, their preparedness can be seen. The level of preparedness shows the degree to which the T/Is give themselves the agency to construct an optimally relevant TL. Optimal relevance is achieved by expressing the communicative intent the T/Is perceive is being made manifest in the SL in a culturally appropriate way in the TL.

## INTERPRETING, TRANSLATION, AND EQUIVALENCE

One of the central themes of both translation and interpreting is equivalence, both in terms of its conception and realization in the TL vis-à-vis the SL and/or vice-versa. As seen earlier (refer to fig. 1.1), equivalence can be judged as something orientated toward the SL or toward the TL. Equivalence can also be seen to be solely linguistic, or pragmatic, or cultural—or a combination of all of these. Generally the term "'formal equivalence'" is used when a specific feature present in the SL is also present in the TL, and "functional equivalence" describes when there exists some difference between the SL and TL, but the translation functions in the same way as the SL (Pöchhacker 2004, 141). For example,

SL He put his hands in his pockets

TL Il a mis *les* mains dans *ses* poches

        *b*              *a*

In TL *a*, the translation is word for word (exemplifying formal equivalence), while in TL *b* the third person possessive *his/son* is changed to the plural definite article *the/les* (exemplifying functional equivalence). In French this functions in this context in the same way as the English SL, since the possessive *ses mains* would only be used if he put his hands in someone else's pockets!

Shlesinger (1995, 195) notes, "formal equivalence is (essentially a matching of surface forms commonly referred to as 'literal translation')," as opposed to "functional equivalence (essentially a matching of the ways in which the text will be used and understood)." This is also a theme Napier (2001) examines with sign language interpreters, using the terms "literal" and "free" interpretation, although these can be understood to mean the same as formal and functional equivalence. That is not to say that in some instances languages present things in the same way and so a surface-form translation fulfills a functional equivalence. The aim of this research is to use all three criteria of equivalence, linguistic, pragmatic and cultural, as defined by the Deaf T/Is through ethnographic interviews, to explore a Deaf translation norm from their perspective.

Ruuskanen (1996) provides a useful way of conceptualizing functional equivalence. She examines translators' construction of their audience, which she calls "the pragmatic other." In her analysis, translators construct their notion of equivalence by imagining who their audience will be. Ruuskanen discusses the preparation of a TL text within the context of the commission one is given. If the SL is a piece of technical language intended for medical doctors, the translators would construct their pragmatic other including that knowledge. The equivalence would then be judged by whether the technical text is understood and seen as appropriate by the medical doctors. If the same technical text is translated for a lay audience, the pragmatic other would be different, and as such the TL would be different. If the audience sees the text as appropriate for the context, it will have achieved equivalence even though the TL is different from that of the medical doctors.

Within Web/narrowcast/broadcast translation/interpretation, this functional notion of equivalence is useful as the audience is not present. The T/Is must make judgments about who will be watching and how they will render the SL into the TL to achieve functional equivalence for that audience. This functional equivalence implies that for a different, constructed pragmatic other, the SL will be rendered differently into the TL.

Gutt (2000, 377) discussed equivalence in terms of "faithfulness." Here the notion does not rely upon equivalence with respect to either the SL or the TL. Instead, Gutt uses RT to examine the goal of faithfulness to the intentionality of central premises while re-writing or representing these notions in pragmatically appropriate renderings of the TL. Gutt (in Pöchhacker and Shlesinger 2002, 390) cites Namy.

> When the French Polytechnicien, addressing his American counterpart, says: "Quelle est la proportion de main d'oeuvre indirecte que vous appliquez à l'entretien du capital installé?" should the interpreter say "What is the proportion of indirect labor you apply to the maintenance of the fixed capital?" or should he say, "How many people do you employ to keep the place clean and maintain the equipment?"

He goes on to explain when listening to an interpretation, the audience "needs to be able to recover the intended meaning instantly." The motivation being to ensure the TL utterance is optimally relevant and therefore requires the least amount of effort from the audience for comprehension.

To represent intentionality requires both competence in the pragmatics of the language and cultural competence. Cultural competence also manifests itself in the contextual assumptions at play, including the contextual assumptions the T/Is use to construct the pragmatic other they have readily available within the shared cognitive environment. In this study, these assumptions are made when viewing the language (via autocue) and video footage at the time of the rendering of the SL into the TL.

As described in detail later, the Deaf community has some level of competence in English as well as BSL. If the T/Is ascribe some level of bilingualism to the audience, this will then be used to judge whether an apparent surface-form equivalence might meet functional equivalence, as long as linguistic (polysemically appropriate rendering) and pragmatic faithfulness are also manifest in the surface form. Consider the following example.

English: a green expert

BSL: PERSON-CL IX GREEN EXPERT

If the audience were aware of environmentalists being called "greens," this would be sufficient information for the audience to understand the BSL without excessive cognitive effort. If not, then this could fail to be functionally equivalent.

## Pragmatics and Relevance Theory

Pragmatics is the study of language in use and how people understand language in different contexts. Aspects of pragmatics include analysis of conversation (Grice 1981; 1978; 1975), speech act theory (Searle 1979; Austin 1962) and implicature and explicature (Carston 2002; Blakemore 1992). Pragmatic theory also examines the interaction between the inference system and the linguistic code used to understand direct and indirect meanings of language (Sperber and Wilson 1995, 1986). Although several of these aspects are important to this study, RT, a cognitive theory of pragmatics, gives insights into equivalence.

> When . . . interconnected new and old items of information are used together as premises in an inference process, further new information can be derived: information which could not have been inferred without this combination of old and new premises. When the processing of new

information gives rise to such a multiplication effect, we call it relevant. The greater the multiplication effect, the greater the relevance. (Sperber and Wilson 1995, 48)

RT enables the examination of how information is processed by T/Is from one language into another. The interpreted language shows the types of information the T/Is find relevant, through their representation of the SL in the TL, and we are able to look at the types of transfers the T/Is make with respect to the SL. The following section reviews the different models proposed to explain how people understand language in context, including RT and ideas of enrichment and impoverishment. Finally, the section shows how RT has been applied to translation in the works of Gutt (1991), Hickey (1998), and Sequeiros (2002, 1998).

## Code-Based and Inference-Based Comprehension Models

There has been a gradual shift in understanding how people comprehend language. The message model (de Saussure, 1922, [1916] 1974) is an early model used to explain how interlocutors understand language. It was based on the following idea: thoughts are generated by a central thought process; these thoughts are encoded into a transmitted linguistic signal; this signal is perceived by a hearer, decoded, and the thought is received.

Authors have argued the linguistic code does not contain enough information for this simple message model to work (Sperber and Wilson 1995, 1986; Blakemore 1992, 1987; Grice 1975). The linguistic code underspecifies the information needed by the audience in order to fully understand what is being said. Hence Grice (1981, 1978, 1975) developed the concept of the cooperative principle; the idea that in conversation we aim to be a useful interlocutor because we have expectations about the rules of conversational communication. From this idea he developed nine maxims of conversation deemed to rule conversational interaction and first introduced the idea of relevance (Grice 1975).

His idea of relevance focused on the inference system and inference-based communication, relying not only on the surface form of a message but what underlying meaning there might be to that message. The surface form of the meaning is often called literal, and message meanings not following this surface-form meaning are taken to be nonliteral. A classic example of nonliteralness is irony, as when a speaker says, "Why don't you take all day?" Within the context of criticizing someone for taking a long time, we know that to understand this utterance we need to derive more than its surface-form meaning. There could be a variety of clues, including the expectation that the task being undertaken by the addressee should not, literally, "take all day." In this case the addressee is supposed to infer from the utterance something other than its literal meaning.

Although many theorists (Bach and Harnish 1979) used this inference-based model to augment the code-based model, Sperber and Wilson (1995, 1986) use Grice as a starting point to focus on inferential communication, examining relevance in "psychologically realistic terms." Grice started examining *identifying* "what is said," and RT started to address *how* "what is said" is identified (Carston 2004, 13).

## Relevance Theory

This theory of pragmatics is grounded in information processing and cognitive theories of linguistic communication with its central tenet: "the aim of information processing is to recover as many contextual effects as possible for the least cost of processing" (Blakemore 1992, 34).

Human beings use certain "behaviour which makes manifest an intention to make something manifest–*ostensive* behaviour or simply *ostension*" (Sperber and Wilson 1995, 49). This is a general property of human interaction; the desire to point out information and to communicate this information has been intentionally pointed out. The hearer uses inference to understand there was an ostension; a coded communication such as language can be used to strengthen this ostensive-inferential communication, where ostensive-inferential communication can be defined as,

> *Ostensive-inferential communication*: the communicator produces a stimulus which makes it mutually manifest to communicator and audience that the communicator intends, by means of this stimulus, to make manifest or more manifest to the audience a set of assumptions. (Sperber and Wilson 1995, 63)

Within linguistic communication, the processing effort the hearer makes to understand an utterance needs to be considered to be worth making. This effort is seen as worthwhile when overt communication is occurring; ideally in this situation, the speaker is deemed by the hearer to be optimally relevant. The speaker intends the hearer to believe she (the speaker) is being optimally relevant when she speaks, and two principles bind RT.[1]

Cognitive Principle of Relevance

Human cognition tends to be geared to the maximization of relevance.

(Wilson and Sperber 2002, 254)

Communicative Principle of Relevance

Every ostensive stimulus conveys a presumption of its own optimal relevance. (Wilson and Sperber 2002, 256)

There exists a risk when communicating a speaker's intention in an optimally relevant way that it might not be believed by a hearer. A speaker can misjudge the information she is giving her audience by providing too little or too much information for the communication to be successful. RT does not ignore this possibility, but rather accepts the risks present in linguistic communication. This overt linguistic communication occurs in the context of a psychological construction coming from several sources: the immediate environment or information, the expectation, and general cultural assumptions. Sperber and Wilson (1995, 16) outline, "A central problem for pragmatic theory is to describe how, for any given utterance, the hearer finds a context which enables him to understand it adequately." The goal of RT is to identify how contexts are selected and used in utterance comprehension (Sperber and Wilson 1995, 20). These contexts can be cumulative, such that environmental factors, cultural assumptions, expected future outcomes, and previous and present linguistic code could be used collectively to understand an utterance.

## Explicature and Implicature

One of the most important ideas underpinning RT is the underdeterminacy of language; it never fully encodes the information we wish to communicate. Some of information is communicated explicitly (by explicature) and some implicitly (by implicature). Explicature is taken to be an "explicitly communicated assumption," that is, "an assumption

---

1. This follows the convention adopted by Sperber and Wilson (1986) where the communicator is assumed to be female and the audience male.

communicated by an utterance *U* is *explicit* if and only if it is a development of a logical form encoded by *U*" (Sperber and Wilson 1995, 182).

By combining the logical form of an utterance (decoding the linguistic information) with assumptions (pragmatic inferring from the context), the hearer is able flesh out the semantic representation (Blakemore 1992).

It's snowing [IN KATHMANDU]. (Carston 2002, 323)

In this example, the logical form is understood and then the utterance enriched with a location shown in parentheses. The semantic representation becomes, "it is snowing in Kathmandu." If the speaker intended to communicate the location, and the hearer understands the speaker to have intended to communicate this information, then the ostensive communication is successful. Depending upon the contextual assumptions in the shared cognitive environment (the speaker and the addressee being in Kathmandu or having previously mentioned Kathmandu) successful communication is possible.

Varying degrees of explicitness exist within explicature: how explicit the linguistic code is affects the level of inference, making the utterance (or explicature in this case) more explicit. In the example above (it's snowing), there could also be a temporal as well as location explicature.

It's snowing [IN KATHMANDU] [AT THE PRESENT TIME]

The quantity of the information present in the linguistic code reduces the amount of explicatures needed and increases the degree of explicitness. We need to bear in mind there is a "possible difference between the proposition expressed by the speaker and her explicature(s): the proposition expressed may or may not be communicated; only when it is communicated is it an explicature of the utterance" (Carston 2002, 117). That is to say if the speaker intends to communicate P by saying utterance U, P is an explicature if the hearer understands U to have communicated P. This constitutes successful ostensive communication without which the explicature would not exist.

Implicature on the other hand is, "when the speaker could not have expected his utterance to be relevant to the hearer without intending him to derive some specific contextual implication from it, then, and only then, that implication is also an implicature" (Sperber and Wilson 1981, 284). The following example from Blakemore (1992, 123–124), where the hearer has to access the context (5) and to deduce the contextual implication (4), expresses this. [The numbers are those used by the author.]

(2) A: Did I get invited to the conference?

(3) B: Your paper is too long.

(4) Speaker A did not get invited to the conference.

(5) If your paper is too long for the conference you will not be invited.

The answer in (3) B is enriched by an explicature: your paper is too long [for the conference] and there is the specific contextual implication (the implicature) (5). It is not clear whether the enrichment happens prior to or subsequent to the implicature, but both are present in this utterance.

Sperber and Wilson developed useful concepts within a relevance framework (1995). They argue that no language utterance is ever completely explicit, and more contemporary works support this idea (Talmy 2000a, 2000b; Fauconnier and Turner 2002; Fauconnier 1997). The linguistic code of an utterance always underspecifies the assumptions associated with that utterance. The RT definition of explicature and implicature (derived from explicit and implicit), however, is not what would commonly be understood by these terms. Wilson (2005, 1130) gives useful examples of both explicatures and implicatures.

Identification of explicit content (explicatures):

1. John left *the party*. ('political groups', 'festive gathering')
2. The teachers told the students *they* needed more holidays. (reference resolution)
3. I met *no-one* in town. ('no-one I knew', 'no-one interesting')
4. Your father will be here *soon*. (resolution of vagueness)
5. The sky is *blue*. ('partly/totally', 'blue of a certain shade/blueish)
6. You will be there tomorrow. (request, bet, prediction)

Implicit context (implicatures):

7. This book is as good as any the author has written. (good? mediocre? bad?)
8. Some of the lectures were interesting. (scalar implicatures)
9. a. *Jim*: Have you read *Relevance*?
   b. *Sue*: I don't read difficult books. (indirect answers)
10. I'm hungry. (indirect speech acts)
11. Bill is a giant. (literal/metaphorical/ironical)

These types of inferences affect T/Is, since it is necessary for them not only to access the full propositional form in the SL but also to decide how to represent it in the TL. It is of course possible for there to be an error on the part of the hearer (in this case the T/I) who would make decisions about rendering what he has understood a speaker to mean. This being the case, one would expect the greater the explicature in the SL linguistic code, the less likely it is the T/I will make an error in the TL. The problem might well be that the speaker is not mindful of the translation process and as such assumes it is a two-way interaction (between the speaker and addressee) rather than a three-way interaction (between the speaker to the T/I and then T/I to addressee). This could mean she assumes the T/I has the same knowledge about the subject as her audience, which might not be the case.

## RT and Translation

For Gutt, RT enables "an empirical account of evaluation and decision-making" (1991, 21) with respect to equivalence and the relationship between the source and the target text. What is of interest for this study is Gutt's treatment of covert translation, which he describes as being "where the translated text is intended to function like a target language original" (1991, 45). The TL has all traces of the SL removed from it. Having a minority language TL with majority language SL traces removed from it, supports Venuti (1997) as outlined above, which picks up from the ideas of Schleiermacher (1813) [cited in Munday (2001)].

> Either the translator leaves the writer alone as much as possible and moves the reader towards the writer, or he [sic] leaves the reader alone as much as possible and moves the writer toward the reader.

Venuti supports the idea of moving the reader toward the writer, and this suggests creating a covert translation. It maintains cultural and linguistic difference and does not reinforce and re-impose the hegemonic values, language, and culture on the minority audience. Within RT there are different types of language use, "descriptive" and "interpretive," and these can account for "loose talk." If someone says, "Bill is a gangster," this can mean literally that Bill is a gangster and would be a descriptive use of the language. Alternatively, it can give Bill some of the attributes of being a gangster, and this would be an interpretive use of the word (Gutt 1991, 33–37).

Gutt suggests that many acts performed by bilinguals are called translations, with the main difference being whether the SL is descriptively or interpretively used. In some situations the original text could be used as a guideline rather than a source text to be followed faithfully. Again Sperber and Wilson's RT (1995, 1986) can be applied to the TL and the shifts occurring in the translation process because the TL has to be relevant enough to make it worth the addressee's while to process the ostensive stimulus. If the Deaf audience has to spend too much cognitive effort on understanding the TL, the T/Is are not fulfilling their purpose, that is, translating the English SL into a BSL TL and creating equality of access for the Deaf audience.

## Enrichment and Impoverishment

Sequeiros (2002) analyzes both pragmatic additions enriching the TL and pragmatic omissions impoverishing the TL with respect to the SL text. Sequeiros defines enrichment as, "A process of completion of the logical form (i.e. the semantic representation encoded by the utterance) whose aim is to arrive at the proposition expressed, which may or may not be one of the set of thoughts explicitly communicated by the utterance" (2002, 1070). And he defines impoverishment as, "given a particular proposition (i.e., thought) expressed by an L1 (Language 1) utterance, the linguistic rendering in L2 (Language 2) may encode less than the L1 as a result of a process which will be called *interlingual impoverishment*" (2002, 1070).

Initially it is useful to look at intralingual examples, that is examples of the process of the completion of a logical form to arrive at the propositional form within a language. Wilson and Sperber's (1993, 293) notion is that, "If the linguistically encoded information is too vague, or too incomplete, to yield an adequately relevant interpretation, it will be enriched using immediately accessible contextual assumptions, to the point where it is relevant enough."

Sequeiros uses the idea to further expand upon this idea of pragmatic enrichment. We know not all information is linguistically encoded, for example in a conversation the speakers could say,

Speaker A: Will Aoife be long?

Speaker B: She is with Richard.

Here the logical form of the utterance made by Speaker B is not sufficient to answer Speaker A's question. If however, the situation is such that Speakers A and B know Aoife is a student, Richard is her tutor, and

Richard only ever spends a short time with his tutees, then Speaker A can use this information to make a relevant interpretation of the logical form to create the propositional form. The T/I then has to decide how to represent the enriched logical form (the propositional form) in the TL to be relevant to the audience as the speaker intended. If we now look at interlingual enrichment (and impoverishment) then according to Sequeiros, "An utterance is a case of interlingual enrichment if its semantic representation is the intended enrichment of the semantic representation of an utterance from another language" (2002, 1078). In other words, if the translator explicates the TL on the lines of the full propositional form rather than following the logical form this would be a case of interlingual enrichment. Similarly if the TL became less implicit this would also be an example of interlingual impoverishment. Sequeiros (2002, 1077) states,

> The logical possibilities between the two languages seem to allow four different cases as regards explicitness/implicitness:
>
> A  Translation *more* explicit because of (enrichment):
>    i.   Linguistic differences between two languages
>    ii.  A choice of the translator on some other grounds
>
> B  Translation *less* explicit because of (impoverishment):
>    i.   Linguistic differences between two languages
>    ii.  A choice of the translator on some other grounds

Sequeiros further details four areas of enrichment: temporal enrichment, thematic enrichment (agent, source, and possessor), enrichment based on discourse relations, and enrichment based on implicatures. These four areas of enrichment build on his previous work on impoverishment (Sequeiros 1998) and give a useful taxonomy of the types of pragmatic shifts that may occur in translation and can be used to compare the types of shifts the two groups of T/Is perform.

The temporal shifts afford the TL utterance an additional time unit, which can be understood to have been intended in the SL. For example, "now" can mean this second, or this minute, or this hour, or this afternoon, or today, etc. When the translation is explicated, it pragmatically enriches the TL so the TL is closer to the intended propositional form of the utterance than the logical form of the SL. An example:

d. I HAVE HAD LUNCH [*TODAY*] (Sequeiros 2002, 1072)

This would be the same as BEEN LUNCH in BSL, where the addressee explicates the temporal context of the utterance.

Thematic enrichment explicitly states the agent of an event in the TL when compared with the SL. The impoverishment occurs when the agent is purposefully lost and becomes implicit in the TL. The TL is still understood, and the implication should not be an error but a decision made by the translator for reasons of naturalness and efficiency over effectiveness.

A cada impulso sonaba un diminuto crujido [SL text]

*With every push it crackled a little* [suggested translation]

*With every gust of wind it crackled a little* [TL text]

. . . the degree of explicitness has been changed . . . [the] interlingual enrichment [is] based on information which had not been linguistically encoded in the original but merely suggested, but which is linguistically encoded in the translation. (Sequeiros 2002, 1081–82)

The source thematic enrichment occurs when the TL makes explicit the point of origin of an event or entity.

El agua salía hirviendo, y eso compensaba la falta de sol y de aire.

*The water* [from the tap] *was boiling hot, and this compensated for the lack of sun* [light] *and* [fresh] *air.* (Sequeiros 2002, 1083) [my additions indicate enrichments]

The possessor thematic enrichment occurs when the TL builds into the linguistic code the possessor of an entity described in the utterance. Even though this may be a grammatical necessity, it still falls within a strict definition of enrichment with respect to the SL.

Ruti sonrió con melancolía. Le puso una mano en el hombro.

*Ruti smiled sadly and put his hand on the old man's shoulder.*

The English version includes the possessor of the shoulder, namely, the old man and also the possessor of the hand, namely, Ruti. These two pieces of information are merely suggested in the Spanish original. (Sequeiros 2002, 1084)

This example highlights different motivations for the construction of the TL text. The hearer of the Spanish will enrich the logical form of *Le puso una mano en el hombro* to mean Ruti's hand and a man's shoulder as this is how Spanish linguistically encodes the possessive. In English the possession is explicitly marked in the linguistic code so the translation into

English requires that a possessive be used. While the process involves an enrichment of the logical form from the Spanish, the translator has no choice in how this is translated with regards to the possessive markers, although the addition of *old* relies on contextual assumptions in the text. As described, there are different categories of enrichments and impoverishments, shifts that the interpreter or translator can choose to make and those that are obligatory.

The enrichment shifts based on discourse relations occur when the TL makes explicit the connections between two clauses or utterances.

El calor pegajoso le humedecía la camisa, adhiriéndosela al cuerpo.

*The sticky heat made his shirt damp, so that it clung to his body.*

. . . the Spanish has two clauses . . . . Between the two clauses there is a discourse relation [sic] relationship of consequence. . . . This connection is left implicit in the original but in the translation it is encoded linguistically by adding the connecting expression *so that*. (Sequeiros 2002, 1085)

This enrichment shift from Spanish to English would not be necessary from BSL to English, although there could be a need for a causal connective such as BECOME. It is also important to examine the features one would expect from an unwritten language (Ong 1982, described later). As BSL is an active language, events generally occur in chronological order and follow a logical order of cause and effect, all of which may create translation shifts toward both enriched and impoverished forms.

A further category may have to be developed, as the previous categories do not cover the situations when the contextual assumption is due to visual information and the potential for BSL to linguistically encode locational information.

CAR DRIVE CL-MOVE-LEFT-HAND-SIDE-OF-ROAD

*the car is driven on the left hand side of the road*

This type of enrichment could be grammatically obligatory, as the TL has to encode a less ambiguous lexical item than the SL. The news headline where the English uses the word *balloon*, meaning hot air balloon, and the Deaf T/I translates this as HOT-AIR-BALLOON provides another example. No superordinate sign covers these two English contexts, which can be understood to mean either hot air balloon or "party" balloon depending on contextual assumptions.

The RT notion of relevance is assessed in terms of cognitive effects and processing effort.

1.  Relevance of an input to an individual
    a.  Other things being equal, the greater the positive cognitive effects achieved by processing an input, the greater the relevance of the input to the individual at that time.
    b.  Other things being equal, the greater the processing effort expended, the lower the relevance of the input to the individual at that time. (Wilson and Sperber 2002, 252)

If the goal of the T/I is to maximize the TL relevance for the target audience, then the TL will be constructed in such a way that it *is* relevant to the audience rather than just *seeming* to be relevant to the audience. Optimal relevance then becomes,

An ostensive stimulus is optimally relevant to an audience if [if and only if]:
    a.  It is relevant enough to be worth the audience's processing effort;
    b.  It is the most relevant one compatible with communicator's abilities and preferences. (Wilson and Sperber 2002, 256)

In relevance terms, ease of understanding is viewed within a framework such that comprehension is described as,

Relevance-theoretic comprehension procedure
    a.  Follow a path of least effort in computing cognitive effects: Test interpretive hypotheses (disambiguation, reference resolutions, implicatures, etc.) in order of accessibility.
    b.  Stop when your expectations of relevance are satisfied. (Wilson and Sperber 2002, 259)

In the example when HOT-AIR-BALLOON is used to translate the word *balloon*, the BSL is a translation of the pragmatically enriched form (the fully intended propositional form). The T/I's motivation for this translation comes from the fact that BSL specifically encodes a difference between "blow-up balloon" and "hot air balloon," but the consequence is that the audience requires less cognitive effort to understand the TL; there is no need to disambiguate the term balloon since the most explicit semantic representation is encoded linguistically. There remains a need to resolve the reference, that is, which hot air balloon is being referred to, and this is where an interaction occurs between either the SL or the TL and the information being shown on the screen.

The final category, pragmatic shift based on implicatures, differs from those described above. Sequeiros notes, "This is a case where the translator has included an implication of the original text in the target text thereby translating not only what was said but also what was implied" (2001, 1086). These translation shifts extend beyond mere enrichment of the original. Sequeiros sees this as unacceptable—not because what is linguistically encoded in the TL is more narrowly specified in the propositional form than the SL, but because of explicating an implicature when the level of possible enrichment moves away from the intended propositional form.

| | |
|---|---|
| Happily for the self-command of both Heyward and Munro they knew not the meaning of the wild sounds they heard. | Afortunadamenta para Munro, y Heyward, no entendían el significado de los salvajes gritos que oían, *pues de lo contrario dificilmente huberan podidio dominar su renovado dolor.* |
| | (Cooper, The Last Mohican) |

The translator has added an implication of the first clause to the Spanish text . . . which was not present in the original version.

Pues de lo contrario difícilmente hubieran podido dominar su renovado dolor.

*Since otherwise they would hardly have been able to control their renewed suffering.*

This translation goes beyond a mere enrichment of the original. (Sequeiros 2002, 1086)

One important factor to add is that both Gutt and Sequeiros examine written translation from a RT perspective. In this study, the written English SL is shown to the T/I before broadcasting, but as BSL is an oral language, an editable, written TL cannot be constructed. Any constructions of the TL are used in preparation for the task, and then either a live broadcast or a recorded broadcast takes place. When the TL is broadcast live, the preparation and BSL practice supports the production of the text but cannot remove the performance factor.

## THE PROCESS OF TV TRANSLATION/INTERPRETING

The theories previously outlined can be considered within the context of television interpreting. Sperber and Wilson (2002, 14–15) provide a cognitive, linguistic way of thinking about the interaction between the T/I and the audience.

> In particular, an individual A can often predict:
> a. which stimulus in an individual B's environment is likely to attract B's attention (i.e., the most relevant stimulus in that environment);
> b. which background information from B's memory is likely to be retrieved and used in processing this stimulus (i.e., the background information most relevant to processing it);
> c. which inferences B is likely to draw (i.e., those inferences which yield enough cognitive benefits for B's attentional resources to remain on the stimulus rather than being diverted to alternative potential inputs competing for those resources).

The news broadcasts examined are summary headline news or news-week review programs totaling 23 minutes, 25 seconds. The summary headlines are translated after the main news has been delivered and occur as a summary of three or four main news stories. Similarly, the news-week review has the whole program translated, but happens at the end of the week and reviews the main news stories of the week.

The news is subtitled, giving the Deaf audience access to the news stories in English before they see it rendered into BSL. Therefore, the bilingual audience already has some knowledge of the news story before the translation occurs. It is fair for the T/Is to assume their translations may not be the first time the audience has come to know the news story; however, it is the first time the audience has seen the news story in BSL.

Before the translation occurs, the T/Is receive the English script and have some time to prepare how they will approach the translation. For the headlines, in the studio the T/Is also see the videotape footage that has run during the initial broadcast of the story. For the news-week review, the T/Is see the video footage that will be running in the background while they are rendering.

BSL is a visual language and has some nouns and verbs differentiated according to visual motivations (Sutton-Spence and Woll 1999, 164). This builds upon the work of Mandel (1977). Taub (2001) explores these ideas in greater depth in American Sign Language (ASL) and discusses visual motivation in ASL and other signed languages.

> [T]he meaning of *tree* and the associated visual image do not *determine* the signs' forms, as they are all different – but neither are the forms unrelated to the meaning. Instead the forms all bear different types of physical resemblance to the image of a tree. The nature of these forms, given their meaning, is neither arbitrary nor predictable but rather *motivated*. . . . In using the *motivation*, I intend that two conditions be met: that one can observe a *tendency* rather than a strict rule, and that one can attribute the tendency to some *reason* external to the linguistic system (ibid., 8–9).

The videotape footage enables the T/I to select the appropriate, visually motivated, lexical items for the news.

In choosing a visually motivated lexicon, the linguistically encoded information in the script is modified by actual iconography or isomorphism to render the SL into the TL. The choosing of appropriate visually motivated lexicon is not a voluntary decision by the T/I, as often this is merely a disambiguation of a superordinate or polysemic noun into BSL so the TL is factually correct (for example, hot air balloon). The path movements of verbs, however, can be motivated by the desire for naturalness rather than accurate propositional representation.

The limited amount of time for the broadcast maximizes the need for a succinct and relevant TL. Since the news stories recapitulate previously broadcast news items, the T/I is able to select old and/or new information from the SL and the videotape footage, and represent relevant information in the TL to the audience using visually motivated implicature (for example, metaphoric use of space) and explicature (disambiguated nouns and polycomponential verbs [Schembri 2003]), as well as culturally specific contextual assumptions that influence the TL.

## SUMMARY

Different theoretical approaches have been discussed in order to understand how translations and interpretations are related to and understood when compared with the original texts. Different translation norms also have been discussed in order to examine what is translated, how it is translated, and the specific linguistic and cultural analyses applicable to translational activity. Relevance theory (Sperber and Wilson 1995; Wilson 2005) provides a useful context for understanding some of the themes raised in the interviews.

# Chapter 2

## Identity and Language

The issues of identity, fluency, and language are pivotal in understanding the different features T/Is bring to translation and interpreting. This chapter examines notions of bilingualism within the Deaf community for both Deaf and hearing people born into the community, as well as those who are outsiders, to provide a way to explore and discuss how identity influences translation and interpretation. Notions of translation, power, and politics will be explored to highlight how they relate to notions of equivalence; the ideas of authorship and gatekeeping also will be explored. Finally, specific issues of text linguistics and cohesion will be addressed, highlighting areas where first language competence may be evident.

The fields of translation and interpreting studies examine cultural bias in the SL and the TL, representation of minority voices, and authorship (Hatim and Mason 1990; Venuti 1995). The relatively recent emergence of Deaf people interpreting on television has encouraged some debate by Deaf broadcasters and their allies about whether hearing interpreters should be working in this area at all (Duncan 1997). Interestingly, there has been scant interaction with the Deaf community to elicit their views on the validity of the interpreting seen on television, even though this is a public display of their language and culture. Although the community is a collective community (Smith 1996), no attempt has been made to achieve consensus on who should be undertaking BSL interpreting and translation on television. Likewise, no move has been made to try and give a voice to the Deaf community or their collective understanding of how their language should be represented on television, on the Web, and in the translation of public service documents.

Anecdotally, some Deaf T/Is have said television should be the sole domain of Deaf T/Is as it is an accessible situation for Deaf people to interpret, because of the use of the autocue (teleprompter). The claim that only Deaf T/Is can provide an appropriate (linguistically and culturally sensitive) translation into BSL provides one dimension of this debate. It is important to examine the issue of identity and levels of bilingualism with this in mind.

Although the Deaf community is a bilingual community, not all members of the community have a high degree of fluency in English (Woll 2000, 71). Their first or preferred language is BSL, and their fluency in English can vary. In fact, some Deaf people could be described as semilingual in that they do not have full fluency in either BSL or English, where semilingualism is the condition of not being able to fully express one's emotions or of not being fully affected by a given language (Winsa 1998, 128; see also Hinnenkamp 2005 and Skutnabb-Kangas 1981). Despite evidence that D/deaf children have higher levels of English literacy with even moderate fluency in a signed language (Strong and Prinz 1997), oralism (education of D/deaf children using speechreading and speech production) still persists. Not only does this education deny deaf children (depending on their hearing loss) access to acquiring the only natural face-to-face communicative language they can perceive (a visual one),[1] but it also denies them the choice of socializing within both the hearing and Deaf worlds in their adult lives (Zaitseva, Pursgrove, and Gregory 1999).

Although all Deaf people experience the world visually (when not using hearing aids), we might expect to find language differences arising from their age of acquisition of sign languages, their degree of deafness, and their exposure to the Deaf community. As mentioned earlier, Deaf children with Deaf parents have exposure to the language from birth, and this typically can be different from D/deaf[2] children of hearing parents (Harris 2001).

## Early versus Late Acquisition

Mayberry (1995) compared the different linguistic abilities of Deaf people who have acquired sign language as a natural first language from their parents, early learners of sign language, and late learners of sign language. She found that native users of ASL made semantic lexical intrusion

---

1. Written English is perceivable in the form of notes and subtitles but cannot be naturally acquired without tuition.

2. Here D/deaf is used because it is not guaranteed that a deaf child born to a hearing family will become Deaf in terms of using a sign language and mixing in the Deaf community.

errors in a shadowing task while nonnative late learner ASL users made predominantly phonological errors. Similarly Newport (1984, 1990) reports that native signers were better able than nonnative late learners to produce and comprehend complex morphological structures in ASL. Although there are two possible subgroups within the Deaf group of T/Is—native BSL users and later learners—only Deaf T/Is who are native BSL users were involved in this study.

## Balanced Bilingualism

Most hearing BSL/English T/Is have spoken English as their first language. They belong (to a greater or lesser extent) to the majority hearing culture, and their experience of the world stems from that of the majority hearing culture. However, Deaf (hearing) T/Is, have Deaf parents and were exposed to BSL and the Deaf community from an early age. This implies that some of the Deaf (hearing) T/Is are native users of BSL and to some extent may approach the state of balanced bilingual (Romaine 1995), whereas those who learned BSL as second language as adult learners have a different level of bilingualism.

The concept of a balanced bilingual is an archetypal notion that may only exist on paper rather than in the real world (Grosjean 1998, 132). A balanced bilingual would be someone who has equal fluency in both languages in all knowledge domains or situations of language use. Generally bilinguals use their two languages in different situations, and this language use can be influenced by the language or languages used in mainstream society and by the people around them. To be a balanced bilingual in BSL and English would require that English and BSL be used in equal amounts at home, at work, and socially. For Deaf bilinguals, their home language and language of face-to-face communication is BSL, and English is used for written communication and reading printed text and television subtitles. The extent to which a hearing child who has Deaf parents who are BSL users, is bilingual and bicultural has not been researched in depth.

Romaine (1995, 11) gives comprehensive descriptions of bilingualism and describes different stances and definitions. Romaine also discusses the degree of bilingualism of individuals and suggests four categories of proficiency for assessment of A and B languages: listening, reading, speaking, and writing (ibid.,13). This needs to be modified for sign languages having no written or sound-based form, so these would become producing and receiving sign language. In the production and receiving of sign language, proficiency would be assessed by elements such as correct pronunciation/articulation of BSL lexicon, appropriate prosody, grammatical knowledge, appropriate pragmatic use of language structures, stylistic range, control of register, appropriate lexical choice, etc. Romaine remarks,

> In principle there is no necessary connection between ability in one level and another. For example, a bilingual might have good pronunciation, but weak grammatical knowledge in one of the languages or vice-versa. Or a bilingual might have excellent skills in all the formal linguistic aspects and perception in both written and spoken medium but is unable to control the stylistic range. However, in practice there are some interdependencies (1995, 13).

Romaine also writes of the difficulties trying to assess bilingualism and trying to categorize bilinguals as balanced or dominant bilinguals. This mainly arises because of the status of languages and their subsequent use in different situations in society. This concurs with Grosjean (1997, 165), who explains, "Bilinguals usually acquire and use their languages for different purposes, in different domains of life, with different people. Different aspects of life require different languages."

This suggests that not all Deaf (hearing) people are balanced bilinguals. Their home language is BSL (and perhaps English with hearing siblings). The language they use at school is English (whereas the school language of Deaf peers is BSL at least some of the time in a Deaf school). When watching television at home the language is spoken English rather than subtitles.

## Translator and Interpreter Bilinguals

As a challenge to the notion of balanced bilingual for all bilinguals, Grosjean (1997, 166) notes,

> If a language is spoken with a limited number of people in a reduced number of domains, it may be less fluent and more restricted than a language used extensively. If a language is never used for a particular purpose, it will not develop the linguistic properties needed for that purpose (specialized vocabulary, stylistic variety, some linguistic rules, etc.)

He introduces the concept of restricted domains under his "complementary principle." Under this title he discusses the bilingual individual before training as a translator or interpreter and also raises the idea that few bilinguals are totally bicultural. This, he says, affects the bilingual's language in such ways as a lack of vocabulary or stylistic varieties in one or more of their languages. That being the case, there are specific goals interpreter training aims to accomplish.

> Interpreter bilinguals, unlike regular bilinguals, will have to learn to use their languages (and the underlying skills they have in them) for similar purposes in similar domains of life, with similar people. That is something regular bilinguals do not often need to do. (1997, 168)

Deaf and hearing T/Is have to reflect upon their language use and ensure they have language skills in both languages for the areas within which they work. This is not something that naturally occurs and regular bilinguals "may not know the translation equivalents in the other language" (ibid., 167).

As yet there is little specific training for Deaf T/Is, although there has been training for hearing T/Is in the UK for twenty years or more in a variety of different forms (Scott-Gibson 1991). The construction of the TL product of the Deaf T/Is is something that has evolved through practice rather than the result of training, in contrast to the experience of hearing T/Is. But this requires the Deaf T/Is to rise above the level of regular bilingual to interpreter bilingual.

Grosjean also discusses language characteristics of "interpreter bilinguals" and the types of linguistic features seen when they work as T/Is, such as: loan translations,[3] nonce borrowings,[4] and code-switching,[5] etc. These types of shifts may be higher for T/Is if they are working into their nonnative language and culture, demonstrating that directionality is important, even for apparently "balanced" bilinguals. These shifts may also be less prevalent when language is prepared rather than interpreted, with processing happening online. This has particular relevance to Web/broadcast translation/interpretation because the scripts and texts are given to the T/Is before the rendering occurs, so that some level of

---

3. Where the morphemes in the borrowed word are translated item by item (Crystal, 1997, 227)

4. Naturalizing a source language term by adapting it to the morphological and phonological rules of the target language (Grosjean 1997, 175)

5. Reproducing the sounds heard in the source language (Grosjean 1997, 175)

preparation is possible over and above that which is possible for simultaneous interpreting.

## THE BILINGUALISM OF PARTICIPANTS

This study did not measure the level of bilingualism of the T/Is involved. The five Deaf T/Is in the group all come from Deaf families, have acquired BSL as a natural first language, have grown up in the British Deaf community, and have British Deaf culture as their first culture. English language competence is not measured for the Deaf group. The Deaf T/Is work regularly in media situations and as such are deemed by their employers (at least) to be functionally fluent in English within this context.

All but one of the seven hearing T/Is in this study have hearing parents, have English as a natural first language, and have grown up as part of the hearing majority with British culture as their first culture. All of the hearing BSL/English T/Is have been trained to become interpreter bilinguals and have achieved BSL to the full professional level of the national occupational standards.[6] Much the same as the situation with the Deaf T/Is, these T/Is are deemed to be functionally fluent in BSL within this context. The research data come from three sets of participants.

1. Interviews with Deaf T/Is from Deaf families. The Deaf T/Is' L1 (first or native language) is BSL and their L2 (second or nonnative language) is English. The study used video footage of their interpretation from English to BSL.
2. Interpretation of English to BSL from a Deaf (hearing) T/I.
3. Interpretation of English to BSL from hearing T/Is from hearing families (L1 English and L2 BSL).

The Deaf T/Is would be considered core members of the Deaf community, the Deaf (hearing) T/I would be considered part of the community situated between the Deaf T/Is and the hearing T/Is. The hearing T/Is would be considered, at best, peripheral to the community.

For Deaf T/Is the primary experience of the world is visual. The bilingual skills of both Deaf (hearing) and hearing T/Is without this primary visual experience will necessarily be different from the Deaf T/Is (Bishop

6. http://www.cilt.org.uk/standards/tistandards.htm

and Hicks 2005). This ontological state affects their work in the television studio when working from English to BSL. The directionality for the Deaf T/Is is from a written language, presented in a multimedia environment into a visual language. The Deaf T/Is are able to draw on their uniquely visual experience when translating/interpreting, but the Deaf (hearing) and hearing T/Is will be influenced by their experience as hearing people.

A critical finding of this study concerns T/Is working into their first language and culture and those working into their second language and culture, and includes the power dynamic of translating a majority language and culture into a minority language and culture. This is the first study within a BSL/English translation/interpreting context to address how notions of culture and power act on translation and interpreting.

## TRANSLATION AND INTERPRETING IDEOLOGY—
## THE SEARCH FOR EQUIVALENCE

Interpreters and translators have been used throughout the ages to facilitate communication and trade between groups that do not speak or write the same language (Hermann 1956). They have also been used by majority cultures to oppress, manipulate, and control minority cultures and languages (ibid.). The oldest recorded use of a T/I was in 2500 BC in ancient Egypt under King Neferirka-Re. In ancient Egypt T/Is were used in trade and to ensure that the "barbarians" who did not speak Egyptian obeyed the king (ibid.). It is arguable that neocolonialism can be facilitated by T/Is in modern times in much the same way as T/Is have been used in antiquity to exercise power (Bassnett and Trivedi 1999).

### Translation and Power

Venuti (1998) places the onus on the translator to accept every translation and interpretation as a political act that embodies the ideology of the translator. This means that the politics of individual T/Is influence the TL, and their ideology is as much informed by the cultural identity of the T/Is as by their fluency in the TL.

Within this context it is important to note that in the Deaf community, hearing family members, priests, teachers, and social workers have acted (and still act) as T/Is (Scott-Gibson 1991). This highlights the power these individuals and groups had over the Deaf community. Their power can be broken down into three different types.

1.  Those acting as T/Is have power by virtue of being in a position of power within the community.
2.  Those acting as T/Is, including Deaf (hearing) family members and hearing people, have power by virtue of being members of the mainstream majority.
3.  In their capacity as T/Is, they are able to exercise power in controlling the information that an individual or the community receives, as illustrated by the anecdotal stories of T/Is telling Deaf people they will "tell them later."

However, Deaf people have also acted as translators in Deaf communities since the nineteenth century; those who were better at reading English have always supported those who were not. These Deaf people provide an example of translators from the minority community rather than from the majority community. Although these Deaf T/Is held power over other Deaf monolinguals in at least being able to be gatekeepers to information, their roles also might complicate the idea of the historical Deaf community being a collective culture (Ladd 2003). That is not to say there have not been gatekeeper T/Is within the community, and it would be important to look for evidence of this in future studies, including the number of Deaf adults schooled by way of oralism at Mary Hare Grammar School for the Deaf who now hold powerful positions (Ladd 2003, 138).

## The Erosion of Deaf Choice

Professional sign language interpreters emerged in the early 1980s (Scott-Gibson 1991). For the first time, the role of interpreters became distinguished from the role of social workers, or other majority-culture authority figures. A potentially emancipatory move for Deaf people, interpreters were expected to adhere to a code of ethics and not become involved in all the aspects of Deaf people's lives, unlike missioners and social workers. Metaphors of an interpreter being like a telephone or conduit were prevalent at that time (Roy 1993).

This professionalization also brought more people from the majority culture into the community to work as interpreters. Unlike in minority spoken language communities, this meant most of the interpreters were community outsiders (Alexander et al. 2004). In terms of power and control, the Deaf community has historically exercised some control over who was selected as an interpreter in some contexts. Anecdotally, suitable Deaf (hearing) and hearing people who socialized in the community would be chosen to interpret in different settings, for example, asking someone if they would come with them to the doctor's. Those who were not chosen were not deemed to be appropriate (and might never be deemed so) or not yet ready to interpret.

The creation of a separate profession has gradually eroded the control Deaf people have over who is chosen to become an interpreter. In some areas UK legislation specifies that only those interpreters listed in the national registers of communication professionals working with Deaf and Deaf-blind people, the NRCPD (formerly CACDP) directory should be used to interpret (PACE Code C 2005, 94). And many best-practice guidelines indicate an interpreter should be drawn from NRCPD, SASLI, or ASLI directories. But as with spoken-language minorities, friends and family are often trusted because of shared understandings and notions of obligation (Edwards et al. 2005). The increase in Deaf intermediaries registered with the home office and "Deaf interpreters" affiliated with ASLI in DIN (the Deaf Interpreter Network) provides more evidence of these relationships.

Some institutional situations will not allow for friends or family to be brought in to translate, so a professional who may not be considered appropriate by the service user could be contracted to provide an interpreting service. With government funds being made available for communication support within employment, whereby Deaf and disabled employees apply for access to work funds to pay for interpreting support and specialist equipment to ensure equality of access, some control might be regained. Since there is no stipulation that the people undertaking communication support need to be registered, qualified, or trained interpreters, Deaf people are free to choose whomever they'd like. To some extent market forces can also address the balance (those interpreters who are seen as appropriate are contracted for work), but since demand far outweighs supply, choice remains limited.

Deaf people now have to rely more heavily on the hearing interpreter becoming immersed in Deaf culture prior to working as an interpreter. The decline of traditional routes for Deaf people in choosing who is sanctioned to be interpreters means that mainstream institutions, rather than the Deaf community, make this judgment. Community members only have power to decide who will interpret for them on a personal level, where they have some degree of agency in the decision making process, or in the administering of funds paying for the interpreter's services, although this may be something that is UK specific.

## THE POLITICS OF TRANSLATION

Translation and interpreting scholars discuss the idea of an ideal translation. This extends to an ideal interpretation if we accept that there is at least a core commonality between translation and interpretation, even if neither is a subset of the other. Álvarez and Vidal state in their preface,

> Contemporary studies on translation are aware of the need to examine in depth the relationship between the production of knowledge in a given culture and its transmission, relocation and reinterpretation in the target culture. This obviously has to do with the production and ostentation of power and with the strategies used by this power in order to represent the other culture. (1996, xx)

Highly relevant to the situation of Deaf and hearing T/Is working in broadcast media, the issue of cultural identity is also important when considering the Deaf community in the UK. The relationship between the knowledge produced and its reinterpretation in the target culture (Deaf culture) needs to be considered because of the power potentially exerted by hearing people and interpreters of the news. The relationship of the translator to the culture producing the knowledge is also important, as described by Temple and Young.

> For people who do not speak the dominant language in a country, the idea that language is power is easy to understand. If you cannot give voice to your needs you become dependent on those who can speak the relevant language to speak for you. (2004, 164)

Neutrality does not exist: information cannot just be relayed without seeking equivalence and understanding the power vested in the interaction. The relationship between power and the cultural identity of the T/I manifests itself in the TL text.

### Hegemony and Assimilation in Translation

Venuti (1998) discusses the idea of ensuring the text is translated with a degree of foreignness such that the "otherness" of the source language is at least noted by the reader. If the foreignness of the SL text is removed from the TL text, then the reader fails to appreciate that the text relates to another culture. Venuti highlights how most of the translation activity in the world occurs from minority languages into the powerful majority language of American English. His core motivation relates to the power differentials between these languages. If the TL texts are domesticated, then difference is lost and the translator marginalizes the minority culture and reinforces the values of the hegemony.

The underlying value propounded by Venuti is one that preserves difference: a readership whose language is a majority world language should be reminded of the different cultural context of the original text, thereby reducing the power of the hegemony. Within the reverse context of translating from a majority language into a minority language, I would suggest that the minority TL should be domesticated and appear as naturalistic as possible, in order to reduce the impact of the majority language and to reinforce minority values and difference. This is especially important in the Deaf community because the community has, to some extent, been metaphorically colonized by non-Deaf people trying to eradicate signed languages and Deaf community values (Ladd 1998, 2003). Mason, cited in Venuti, discusses the skewing of a Spanish text in the English translation.

> Thus, "antiguos mexicanos" ("ancient Mexicans") is rendered as "Indians," distinguishing them sharply from their Spanish colonizers; "sabios" ("wise men") as "diviners," opposing them to European rationalism; and "testimonias" ("testimonies") as "written record," subtly privileging literary over oral traditions. (1998, 2)

It can be seen as being politically advantageous to minorities to ensure American (or British) monolingual readers of translated texts are aware that the events they are reading about happen in a different local reality than their own. Rather than the foreign becoming domesticated, some difference is maintained while being mindful to avoid exoticism. For the Deaf community wanting to preserve its cultural views and values, preserving mainstream majority values in the minority TL would also be seen as undesirable.

## Nonexistent Neutrality in Translation and Interpreting

Clearly there could be political reasons for the skewing of text when working from one language to another. Several authors (Inghilleri 2003;

Rudvin 2004, 2002) explore this idea of neutrality and "skewing" in terms of identity, allegiance, and membership of a collective community. Metzger (1999, 21–24) enters into some discussion of neutrality in signed language interpreter research and introduces the idea of the interpreter paradox akin to the sociolinguistic idea introduced by Labov (1973). While identifying the potential for the interpreter to influence the interaction, she does not explore how these interactions relate to minority and majority communities and the accompanying power issues.

Rudvin (2002) discusses the idea of interpreters and their interaction with respect to dominant cultures and languages and the cultural identity of the interpreter. The historical tradition of interpreting within courts is one of word-for-word translation, or surface-form SL to TL transformations.[7] She analyzes non-Western traditions of the exercising of justice and different ways of presenting information that are seen as valid within those cultural norms but that would be seen as untruthful or invalid in a Western cultural context.

Any surface-form transformation of the SL and the TL does not take into account cultural differences between the SL culture and the TL culture (Baker 1992). Since these differences are encoded within linguistic forms, their relevance needs to be unpacked (or enriched) and converted into appropriate discourse styles. In light of this, Rudvin (2002) urges interpreters to move away from a positivistic view of neutrality, some token-for-token transformation that cannot exist within human interaction, and toward operating in a way that embraces both the SL and the TL cultures and the cultural values of their service users.

### Deaf Interpreters' "Presence"

As members of the Deaf community, the Deaf T/Is have a non-majority cultural identity—unlike their hearing counterparts (unless they also come from a minority community).[8] Similarly, the Deaf (hearing) T/Is have greater exposure to mainstream culture than the Deaf T/Is. This identity (non-Deaf, Deaf (hearing) or Deaf) informs the types of translation/interpreting decisions made. These decisions can be made in light of

---

7. http://www.acebo.com/papers/verbatim.htm

8. ASLI fees and salaries report 2005/6: ASLI reports 89.1 percent (106 respondents) of ASLI members as white British.

the perception of the audience and also taking into account how a topic would be discussed within the community rather than within the cultural references of mainstream society.

The historical Deaf community is a collective community, and as such its allegiance is to the minority community rather than the individual-istic values of the majority society (Smith 1996). Although this can be contested with the present-day heterogeneous Deaf community (Skelton and Valentine 2003a, 2003b), the Deaf T/Is in this study are from multi-generational Deaf families that adhere to traditional notions of collective identity. The TL has to be produced in a way that minimizes the effort of the audience, and as a member of the collective it is important to adhere to the group or community goal. We can measure the translation or interpretation against the audience's comprehension. In this way the Deaf T/Is are less likely to fall into the trap of thinking they operate in a "neutral" way (Leeson and Foley-Cave 2004) since their aim is to create a TL where their presence is seen.

However, institutional constraints placed on how T/Is work in broad-cast media are similar to the institutional constraints interpreters face in other domains. Inghilleri (2003) considers interpreters within an asylum-seeking context and discusses the need for the interpreters to ensure the believability of the interviewee by constructing their narrative as to be believable to the interviewer. This requires the interviewee to be per-ceived as a victim by the target audience within target cultural norms to be granted asylum or refugee status rather than constructing the story in a way that is believable and valid in the source language and culture but that may not look persecutory to the UK official.

This is mirrored by BSL T/Is working within a broadcasting context, although the power dynamic operates in a different direction. In the con-text of asylum-seeker interviews, where the person's history must be seen as valid within a majority context, there is no room for any of Venuti's suggestions for a translation preserving difference—rather there is the need for domestication. The person's history must be domesticated so the "authenticity" of the account can be judged from an institutional per-spective, that is, from the domestic viewpoint. This parallels the situation in the broadcasting context for BSL T/Is.

In this context, the audience not only comprises the Deaf target audi-ence, but also a mainstream audience that sees the in-vision T/I. The T/Is must construct a product acceptable to both the Deaf and the main-stream audiences in terms of cultural expectation (Woll 2000), such as using fewer grammatical facial movements and translating at a speed perceived by the mainstream audience (which is ignorant of the TL) to be appropriate for this medium.

In summary, tension exists between creating a TL that preserves the spirit of Venuti's idea and the situation in which the translation occurs. The TL should preserve difference and be constructed in a way seen as culturally appropriate within the TL culture and also be unmarked by SL references. Yet for T/Is working into BSL on television, the TL is also viewed by the SL audience, which holds expectations of how broadcast information, people, and characters should be represented. The T/Is therefore have to produce the TL in a way that does not offend the majority audience's cultural sensibilities. This power dynamic mirrors those found in colonial contexts where the colonized mediate their behavior and translation against the ever-present backdrop of the colonizers.

## DEAF CULTURAL EQUIVALENCE

The search for equivalence provides a central theme to both translation and interpreting studies. Equivalence can be measured in a variety of ways. Some authors approach equivalence from a linguistic perspective and look for word for word, phrase for phrase, noun phrase for noun phrase, and verb phrase for verb phrase equivalence (for written translation, see Catford 1965, and for signed language interpretation Cokely 1986). While this approach is useful from some positivistic notion of being able to statistically analyze the presence or absence of units in the TL with respect to the SL, this approach does not necessarily account for differences with SL and TL norms or different language typologies.

### Sense for Sense Rendering

By moving toward an understanding of sense for sense translation and interpreting (Seleskovitch 1978, 2002), we move away from the search for equivalence at the surface form of the language. It is important to understand the idea units contained within the SL and render them in the TL in an appropriate way. This is an idea that has been suggested for centuries starting with St. Jerome in the fourth century (Munday 2001).

Napier suggests that for BSL/English interpreting a sense-for-sense, or "free" style, is preferred by interpreters and Deaf people, but that within a university context both styles might be used to good effect (2001). This free style ensures the TL contains the SL idea units expressed in a culturally appropriate way for the consumer. It also ensures that the TL has an equivalent effect on the consumer or audience. Equivalence then becomes judged by comparing the cultural relevance of the SL and the cultural relevance of the TL.

Take the example, "he rang the doorbell" translated to IX PUSH-DOOR-BELL LIGHT-FLASH. Deaf people do not use sound-based doorbells but have doorbells with visual alerts, commonly wired to house lights and causing the lights to flash when the doorbell is pushed. Here the mainstream context of the doorbell ringing is domesticated to a "natural" BSL utterance where, in a Deaf context, the doorbell flashes.

A counter argument exists that the translation should be IX PUSH-DOORBELL ALARM-RING++ or even just IX PUSH-DOORBELL. Both of these translations provide an understanding of the action. One represents the activity of the man going to a hearing person's (someone from the majority society) house, and the other leaves the context ambiguous. While these renderings do not reinforce Deaf experiences, they may well represent the actual event. Deaf people are aware of mainstream contexts, they live in a "hearing" world, and many Deaf people have hearing parents. As such it cannot be assumed that a cultural shift is required or desired. A definition of how cultural equivalence can be understood from a Deaf perspective within broadcast news, where the news is interpreted from the majority language into the minority language, becomes important to ascertain.

## Constructing Equivalence

The T/Is make decisions like any other interpreter or translator (Baker 1992; Leeson 2005a). A translator's decisions take into account a variety of different factors, including how texts might be best represented in the TL. Toury (1978/1995) addressed this idea by explaining that we can draw upon a standard type of discourse style or norm for the genre being translated. If this produces a text that is domesticated, then the BSL appears within a multimedia environment and the information précised by the journalists will create a different text from that of the one created by a BSL journalist. To naturalize this information in the TL, some power must be appropriated by the T/Is. These editorial decisions shift the authorship of the text from the scriptwriter to the T/Is.

Additional issues relate to the visual nature of the BSL T/I who appears on the right-hand corner of the screen. Since the T/I is visible, there is greater pressure to take on responsibility for the authorship of the TL (or to be more of a journalist and less of a T/I) than there would be for an unseen T/I. (Unseen insofar as for a written text, the translator will always be unseen, and for an interpretation of spoken language within media contexts, the interpretation is heard without the interpreter being seen.) The Deaf community easily recognizes T/Is, and notices their community membership immediately. This fosters a desire to be judged by the community as having created "good" BSL and creates a dynamic in the search for equivalence.

As described earlier, some models of analysis measure equivalence in terms of word-for-word or phrase-for-phrase parity (Cokely 1992, 1986; Catford 1965). This measurement of equivalence denies the human experience of communication by reducing it to surface-form realizations of language without reference to how language is used to communicate. To take an earlier example, "he rang the doorbell" consists of a pronoun, a verb, a determiner, and a noun. The grammatical relationship to one another is noun, noun phrase, verb phrase, and sentence. In the BSL translation IX PUSH-DOORBELL LIGHT-FLASH consists of pronoun, verb, and verb. While these sentences contain the same idea units, they are not seen as equivalent in Catford-ian terms.

## Authorship in Translation

Many alternative philosophies are applicable to translation and interpreting, hermeneutics being one applied by Stolze (2004). This philosophical tradition of the understanding of knowledge comes from a personalized interpretation and can provide a humanistic approach to both translation and interpretation. To this end, Stolze (2004, 43) argues, "translation is an open process towards an optimal solution, responsive to orientation, motivation and revision. This includes a change of viewpoint—from a relationship between texts to the translator's perspective." Stolze allows equivalence to be defined in terms of personal understanding and authorship, congruent with the situation in which the broadcast news T/Is find themselves.

More importantly, within the context of Deaf and hearing T/Is, Stolze argues,

Translators do not stand "between cultures" (Bassnett 2000, 113), but they are rooted in one culture, and by having access to the other, they cognitively reach out into both. The two culture systems establish contact within the translator's mind: in other words, her cognition as an expert reaches out into two different cultures and into various discourse fields. (2004, 43)

Equivalence is achieved by the translators (or interpreters) drawing on their understanding of not only the text, but also their knowledge of how this information is represented culturally in a relevant way and in an appropriate register or discourse style. In this case, a translator aiming to domesticate the TL, and who does not have that language as a first language, will always need to consult with a native informant, not so much for any notion of linguistic equivalence, but rather for cultural domestication. Subsequently, some scholars believe that T/Is should only work into their "mother tongue" or A language to maximize idiomatic naturalness as the level of intrusion that can happen with a B language can be high (Donovan 2004).

This idea of equivalence also relies on the T/Is having an idea of the audience for whom they are translating or interpreting. The Deaf community, while small, is not a homogeneous community (Ladd 2003; Skelton and Valentine 2003a, 2003b). The T/I has to make some decisions about the audience and the cultural background its members will have (Leeson 2005b). These decisions ensure that information is represented in a way deemed appropriate, both in terms of cultural reference and discourse style. The T/Is need to establish cultural contact between their understanding of the culture of the audience watching the news and their understanding of the culture that has created the news they are rendering into BSL. This is achieved by finding an equivalent rendering within the target culture within the cultural space available.

## Subtitles

The issue of subtitles is important when considering the dynamics of the relationship of the T/I to the audience. Adams (cited in Gutt 1991) mentions *semilanguage peoples* as those who know some of the source language and yet are not bilingual, although they have native fluency in their first language. This describes the nature of some of the Deaf audience; all Deaf people have some knowledge of English because of their education, but many would not consider themselves to be bilingual. The semilingual

Deaf may read subtitles as well as follow the translated version of the news. While this habit may not be the constructed pragmatic other the T/Is are translating for, their power in the situation to criticize and hold the T/Is accountable might strongly influence the target language product.

If the aim is to domesticate the TL product, this domestication happens in relation to the target audience that the translator constructs. Within the context of television, the T/I must construct the audience, as it is unseen. The unseen audience, also called the "pragmatic other" (Ruuskanen 1996), will be discussed in greater depth in the chapter 5. But any notion of equivalence (linguistic or cultural) must be judged against the audience or readership expected to be "reading" the TL text. Being rooted in one culture and yet cognitively reaching into both cultures still means the T/I must try to ensure the TL s/he creates is relevant to the readership, or is domesticated for a group of people from a subset of a potential audience.

## Intercultural Communication

The issue of cultural equivalence correlates to intercultural communication within the translation (and interpreting). When working from one language to another language, culturally laden utterances within a text may or may not survive the process of translation/interpreting (Gutt 2005). For example, when a Deaf person talks about their school days and uses the term DEAF SCHOOL, the concept is difficult to convey. While this often means a state boarding school, a mainstream audience could understand an interpretation such as "residential school for the Deaf" to mean a terrible institution where Deaf children were segregated from society.

However, Deaf residential schools are often cherished by Deaf people and felt to be a place where Deaf children can gain a positive identity. This is in contrast to the assimilative "mainstream" model of a hearing-impaired person who aspires to be hearing (Ladd 1998, 113–146). Therefore, the implied information of the term in BSL might need to be made explicit, so the audience understands the intention of the speaker. This bridges the information from one community to another and would be an example of successful intercultural communication.

## Reaching the Audience

The T/I plays a role within the intercultural communication process and makes a decision as to whether information is carried into the text "foreignizing" it, that is, whether the T/I marks a concept as different by using nonstandard language, normalized to adhere to the target language culture (Venuti 1998; Robinson 1997), or whether the T/I provides some kind of explanation.

The example of DEAF SCHOOL could be interpreted as a loan translation, "Deaf school" or "Deaf residential community school," both of which would be a foreign concept for an audience with no knowledge of the Deaf community. If the interpreter wanted to normalize the concept, the translation could become "state funded boarding school," with no mention of Deaf because Deafness is not a "normal" concept for a mainstream audience. And as stated previously, a "naturalized" TL text might not be desirable, since this translation does not wholly represent the idea units contained with the notion of DEAF SCHOOL.

## Causing the Audience to Reach

Venuti has explored this idea of maintaining difference. He states, "The economic and political ascendancy of the United States has reduced foreign languages and cultures to minorities in relation to its language and culture" (1998, 10). He tends to translate works considered marginal in the U.S. mainstream language community and so, in accordance with his political agenda contesting the hegemony of English, explores how texts can be "foreignized" to mark them as different from the TL culture. The audience appreciates the marked text since it does not originate from the United States and therefore increases intercultural awareness by communicating different cultural norms. Venuti considers the role of translators and interpreters within colonial and postcolonial contexts and the role they play in communicating minority cultural values within those contexts.

Ladd (1998) analyzed the Deaf community and introduced the concept of Deafhood as a postcolonial construction. Ladd identifies the traditional colonizers as the oralists and social welfare systems. In the present day he sees this manifested in such organizations as Signature (formerly CACDP— the council for the advancement of communication with Deaf people) and those who organize the mainstreaming of Deaf children. These colonizers acted as gatekeepers of the Deaf community to the outside (mainstream) world. They used English as their dominant language to maintain power over Deaf people and in education to deny the deaf[9] pupils language (BSL),

---

9. I use the lowercase deaf rather than Deaf because without access to their language, culture, and history these pupils cannot become Deaf.

by forcing Deaf people to speechread and speak, resulting in deaf pupils being denied their cultural and historical heritage.

This history places the mainstream motivations for translation and interpretation into an assimilating historical context. If actions are not taken to ensure the preservation of difference, then the language status of BSL and the worldview of Deaf communities continues to be assimilated. With this in mind, the issue of foreignizing or normalizing the text becomes relevant for T/Is working from and into BSL. The translation decisions the Deaf and hearing T/Is make about the audience (or pragmatic other) and the degree of gatekeeping these decisions may contain should be examined in terms of what (and how) the news stories are interpreted. It is relevant whether the T/Is adopt the style of educator, bringing English knowledge to the audience, or information-sharer constructing information in BSL regardless of the English text.

## Gatekeeping in Translation

Vuorinen (1995, 161–162) says of news translation (researching into English to Finnish news), "The gatekeepers decide what messages or pieces of information shall go through a particular gate and continue their journey in the channel and what not ("in" or "out" choices), and in what form and substance these messages are allowed to pass." Vuorinen focuses on the gatekeeping that occurs within large news houses. Here, many international stories are translated for a different audience and the process of editing is "part and parcel of normal textual operations performed in any translation" (1995, 170).

On a smaller scale, the T/Is interpreting into BSL also perform *in* and *out* choices. But as Shoemaker (1991) notes, the gatekeepers (T/Is) are still constrained by the organization they work for and the format of the broadcast. For instance, the T/Is have no control over which stories are to be translated.

Also of interest within intercultural communication is Schäffner and Adab's (1995, 325) discussion of hybrid texts where languages and cultures come into contact.

A hybrid text is a text that results from a translation process. It shows features that somehow seem "out of place"/ "strange"/ "unusual" for the receiving culture, i.e. the target culture. These features, however, are not the result of a lack of translational competence or examples of "translationese," but they are evidence of conscious and deliberate decisions by the translator.

This highly pertains to a minority community situated within a majority community. Although Deaf people do have access to English, they do not have access to English in the same way as other hearing people from other minority language groups. Other minorities have access to hearing English spoken in a variety of different situations, whereas Deaf people generally have access to written English only, from subtitles or on the Internet, etc. While Deaf people live in a "hearing" world, mainstream culture is still different from Deaf culture. A need for some intercultural mediation between mainstream and Deaf British culture remains.

Without a firm grounding in Deaf culture, hearing T/Is may not have or be familiar with the frame of reference of the receiving (target) culture. This can lead to the type of calquing (the "out of place" features as mentioned above) described by Schäffner and Adab (1995). The hearing T/Is make "conscious and deliberate decisions" the audience understands and that are not marked linguistically but show the T/I to be hearing or a bilingual individuals with the TL as their L2 (Halverson, 2003). The linguistic and cultural heritage of the Deaf T/Is gives them a greater resource to draw upon.

In summary, part of the shifts that happen when translating or interpreting the television news are those that act as instances of intercultural communication. These shifts happen so that the text can be normalized or domesticated to the constructed other. English oralists, for instance, can be considered to be the colonizers of the Deaf community; the Deaf T/Is from multigenerational Deaf families may gatekeep information so the TL reinforces Deaf cultural norms. The Deaf T/Is from multigenerational families understand the information in the SL and attempt to render it into culturally appropriate BSL. The grounding the Deaf (hearing) and hearing T/Is have in Deaf culture can lead to a hybridized text, marking it rendered by a T/I who is Deaf or hearing depending on their choices.

Within a postcolonial context, not all Deaf people (and their offspring whether Deaf or Deaf (hearing)) maintain a level of resistance against assimilation by assimilatory educational practices and colonial powers and institutions. But those of multiple generations have greater resources to draw upon both as family units and due to their relationships with other family units (nationally and transnationally), and are able to maintain some continuity with a historical Deaf translation norm.

Textual features might occur within both the SL and the TL when looking at the notion of "translationese." Clearly, the institutional limits applied to the T/Is restrict their choices in language output. It is useful to see whether these restrictions prevent the T/Is from domesticating the TL. In order to do this, it is important to identify text features of both English and BSL and then analyze how these features may differ.

## TEXT LINGUISTICS

This research examines the different outputs of the different T/Is at the text or discourse level. This textual analysis includes the analysis of intonation and thematic development or information flow. Both hearing and Deaf T/Is use these devices to develop cohesion and the dependence of meaning throughout a text. The specific devices used by Deaf and hearing T/Is might be different and these differences could indicate different translation/interpretation styles.

Cohesion is "the network of lexical, grammatical, and other relations that provide links between various parts of a text" (Baker 1992, 180); these are the surface connections that establish interrelations in a text (ibid., 113). Matthews (1997, 59) explains cohesion is "the connection between successive sentences in texts, conversations, etc., in so far as it can be described in terms of specific syntactic units." Cohesion manifests itself differently in English and BSL.

Within this context it is important to recognize that unlike English, BSL is an unwritten language. Unwritten or "oral" languages exhibit different features that influence the organization of the discourse and how different parts of the text are related to one another. Ong (1982, 36) uses a taxonomy to describe the "characteristics of orally based thought and expressions." He lists nine characteristics for oral (as in "unwritten") cultures.

1. Additive rather than subordinate
2. Aggregative rather than analytic
3. Redundant or "copious"
4. Conservative or traditionalist
5. Close to the human life world
6. Agonistically toned
7. Empathetic and participatory rather than objectively distanced
8. Homeostatic
9. Situational rather than abstract

In terms of cohesion, it makes sense that different sentential relations occur because of points one and three above, that is, information is not constructed with subordinate clauses but rather uses additional sentences to add relative clauses, and some of these will contain repetition of information that would be/could be seen as redundant were the language written.

Constructed action (CA) and constructed dialogue (CD) are linguistic resources in signed languages (Metzger 1995) where a narrator either linguistically reconstructs the actions of another or the utterance of another or others. These features can also be use metaphorically when some actions or thoughts of nonhuman entities are anthropomorphized to license CA or CD (Quinto-Pozos 2007). These features could be examples of points five and seven in Ong's list.

Ong also describes how the use of a written system influences the thought processes of people. The discourse features used by Deaf T/Is, whose first language, BSL, has no writing system, might differ from hearing T/Is in the ways described by Ong for oral cultures. There are two different types of orality: the primary orality, including oral histories and poetry, of oral cultures, and the secondary orality of literate peoples, including telephone calls and conversational storytelling. Primary and secondary orality are different (Cronin 2002; Ong 1982) because secondary orality incorporates elements of the written and oral modes (for a greater treatment of this topic please see Furniss 2004).

Deaf T/Is are able to use their primary orality to their best advantage when working from English to BSL in a way not available to hearing T/Is who possess secondary orality skills. This is arguably true even of Deaf (hearing) T/Is whose first language is BSL, by having fluent spoken and written English where the orality is secondary and where, for example, the editability of written English facilitates subordination.

Since the news stories are written and then read aloud, they are ostensibly written/literate texts delivered orally. This does not make the English texts examples of either primary or secondary oral texts, but rather edited, subordinated, and succinct literate texts.

## Cohesion

Halliday and Hasan (1976) list the main areas of English cohesion as reference, substitution and ellipsis, lexical cohesion (reiteration and collocation), and conjunction—these are all textual devices.

Reference typically denotes referring to something, but in this instance, it refers to a device that points to something either previously mentioned in a text or something to be mentioned explicitly later in the text. For example, if someone says, "The milkman delivers milk to number 3. He delivers milk to number 40 too," the pronoun *he* refers back to *the milkman* and provides a link between the first and the second sentence of the text. Different speakers could have said the two sentences and the reference would still point to *the milkman*. This textual relationship is expressed in BSL by the use of space.

> The space around and on the signer's body is exploited at all levels: formationally similar signs may contrast only in location; verb agreement is marked using spatial position; and discourse topics are distinguished from one another by where the signs are articulated. (Padden 1990, 118)

A locus (which is "a point on the body or in signing space" Liddell 1990, 176) is established, and then this is referred to again by an indexation or a pointing of the index finger. Similarly,

> Loci can be used for anaphoric purposes like demonstratives in spoken languages. To fulfil their function, spoken language demonstratives depend on the receiver's memory of the temporal structure of discourse. Similarly, loci depend on the receiver's memory of the spatial and temporal structure of the discourse to fulfill their reference-tracking function . . . loci reflect discourse-dependent semantic-pragmatic features of the referents which may contribute to making it easier for the receiver to remember and sort out the different referents. (Engberg-Pedersen 1993, 143)

The uses of loci, however, have also been found to function as discourse markers and episodic boundary markers (Stone 2001). Substitution is where an item or items are replaced by something else. For instance, "The milkman delivers milk to number three. He does to number forty too." In this example *delivers milk* is replaced or substituted with *does*; English commonly uses *do*, *one*, and *the same*, as substitutes for item(s) (Halliday and Hasan, 1976). In BSL we see a similar use of SAME, MILK MAN MILK IC-HANDJ NUMBER 3 NUMBER 40 SAME.

However, a T/I could use the verb DELIVERS (which would be a handling classifier verb C-hand to show the shape of the milk bottle moving through space to place the cylindrical object in the location of number three and number forty) repeated rather than substituted: MILK MAN MILK IC-HANDJ NUMBER 3 IC-HANDK NUMBER 40 SAME. In this example, the subscript letter i represents the location at the interlocutor's body, and the letters j and k represent different locations in the signing space. Ellipsis occurs when an item or items are omitted.

A: The milkman delivers milk to number three.
B: To number forty too.

The speaker B omits *the milkman delivers milk*; this phrase is ellipted. Again we can see similar structures in BSL too with,NUMBER 40 SAME.

Baker (1992, 187–188) raises how the distinction between reference, substitution, and ellipsis is blurred, and cites an example from Hoey (1991), following the question, "*Does Agatha sing in the bath*"? The following responses could be given (the cohesive device is given in between the parentheses).

1. No, but I do (substitution)
2. Yes, she does (ellipsis)
3. Yes, she does it to annoy us, I think (reference)

Taking the example above and changing *sing* to sign, the following responses in BSL (equivalent to responses one through three above) are appropriate.

1. NO BUT IXi (ellipsis)
2. RIGHT (ellipsis)
3. RIGHT S-HAND-L(base hand)- S-HAND-R-(open to)-5-HAND (ellipsis)

A gloss of three being, "*Right (vee) the-joke's-on-us*."

All of the responses would come under ellipsis; concurring with the point Baker raises when she says these devices may be used differently in different languages, a point also noted by Shlesinger (1995, 193).

Clearly, textual cohesion is an important feature of a text. It is not necessarily important to compare the differences in cohesion between the SL and the TL, as different languages use different devices more or less frequently. What is important within this study is to compare the use of these devices between the Deaf and hearing T/I within the TL to see what differences occur and how cohesive texture is given to the TL translation.

## Spatial Cohesion in Sign Languages

While the cohesive features described by Halliday and Hasan (reference, substitution and ellipsis, lexical cohesion [reiteration and collocation], and conjunction) are important, there are also cohesive features of sign languages unique to the visual mode that need to be examined. Sign language has been seen to use a variety of different features for the organization of discourse.

Metzger and Bahan (2001, 135) explain, "In signed discourse, cohesion can be found not only lexically and grammatically, but also spatially." They also cite Winston (1992, 136) and state, "spatial mapping plays an extremely important role in the structuring of discourse and in involving addressees in making sense of the discourse that they see."

Winston (1995, 91) defined spatial mapping as "a process of building mental representations through the use of physical sign space." This use of space,

> creates two types of cohesion: immediate and distant. When a signer first maps an entity, there may be repeated, immediate pointings to that map in the following utterances. The signer may maintain this map for few to several utterances. It may then be ended, not to appear again in the discourse, or it may be suspended, re-appearing at intervals throughout the discourse. While head movements also used in spoken language comprehension (Hadar, Steiner, and Rose 1984), these are not directly coordinated with a three-dimensional space of the vocally articulated language as there is none, creating distant cohesion (Johnson, 1995, 94).

Johnson (1985) describes the movement not only of the manual elements of the sign and their articulators, but also how movements of the

| Torso | lean-back-left _____ |
| Head | tilt-back-left _____ |
| Hands | IX-(over left shoulder) THINK-NOTHING WOMAN RIGHTS |

*Translation: in the past we did not think about women's rights*

| Torso | lean-forward-right _____ |
| Head | tilt-forward-right _____ |
| Hands | NOW WOMAN RIGHTS SOCIETY SEE IMPORTANT |

*Translation: nowadays women's rights are valued by society*

FIGURE 2.1. *Example of spatial cohesion in BSL*

head and neck, and the torso, are used to create meaning in sign language discourse. The head, neck, and torso allow for the use and referencing of space to create structure in discourse related to the spatial mapping used manually in sign languages (see fig. 2.1).

Winston (1995, 101) also discusses the relevance of spatial mapping in comparative discourse frames and lists several features, "including pointing with the hands, torso, head and/or eyes." For example, when asked if hearing parents and Deaf people have the same view on cochlear implants for their children the response could be,

NO PARENTS IX-L WANT CHILDREN IMPLANT HEAR NEG DEAF DIFFERENT THEIR-R

*no parents want their children to have cochlear implants so they can hear whereas Deaf people have a different view*

Where the index left (IX-L) establishes one group, and the other group for comparison is established by the direction of the movement THEIR in the right-hand signing space. Time is mapped in a similar way, as are performatives such as constructed action or dialogue (Winston, 1991). For example, when asked about women's rights in the Victorian era and the modern day, a response was given in figure 2.1. Here you see a diagonal plane used for temporal comparison and the movement of the torso and head also co-occur in constructing this comparison. The use of spatial mapping by both Deaf and hearing T/Is can be analyzed by looking at the nonmanual realization of this by head movements.

The possible differences in usage by Deaf and hearing T/Is are of further interest. As Winston (1995, 110) notes, spatial mapping is a powerful marker of discourse structure and can manifest itself at both the morphemic and syntactic levels. Most importantly, since this feature is optional, Deaf and hearing T/Is may use it differently to reflect the underlying semantic relationships of the source language.

Currently, there is much debate as to whether some iconically motivated aspects of signed language are gestural rather than linguistic (Liddell 2003, 2000; Liddell and Metzger 1998). The difficulty in categorizing gesture and language within signed languages is that both occur with the same articulators and much research needs to be done to tease these apart. While some of the ways signed languages encode spatial information might well be gestural, this would still be culturally specific (McNeill 1992; Kendon 1988) and the possibility remains that the less encultured

T/Is (Deaf (hearing) and hearing) would be less able to produce cultural appropriate gestures when compared with Deaf T/Is from multigenerational Deaf families.

## Superarticulation in Sign Languages

The features above such as head, torso, and eyes are parts of sign language prosody and used as cohesive devices (Jouison 1985). These prosodic units are marked not only by head, torso, and eye movements, but also by blinks (Wilbur 2000) and will be explored later. These units can be seen in the examples above where the contrastive units are contained within different prosodic units.

Both blinking and head movement behavior in the BSL TL texts will be analyzed. By looking at both features, in terms of their co-occurrence at boundaries and individual occurrence at constituent boundaries, a more complex understanding of the use of nonmanual features in translated texts can be gained.

Sandler (1999a, 205) compares intonational tunes in spoken languages and argues that sign languages have facial expressions paralleling intonation, tones, and tunes, which she terms as *superarticulation* (linguistic features co-occurring with the articulation of the phonological part of the language) *arrays* (as there often appears to be more than one facial movement occurring at the same time). These facial expressions include brow raises, head nods, eye gaze changes, the use of the mouth, and the position of the tongue, and can be seen in figure 2.2. For instance, for the phrase, "I ate the cake up completely" where X represents a blink and O—▶o the open to close movement of the mouth.

| (29) | | [[cake]$_p$]$_I$ | | [I eat-up deplete]$_p$]$_I$ | |
|---|---|---|---|---|---|
| brows | | up ——— | | | |
| eyes | | squint— | | X | X |
| cheeks | | | | | |
| mouth | | O—▶o | | lip sputter | |
| tongue | | | | | |
| head | | forward | | tilt——————— | |
| mouthing | | 'cake' | | | |
| hold | | = | | = | |

FIGURE 2.2. *Example taken from Nespor and Sandler (1999)*

Sandler discusses the use of a variety of nonmanual components contributing to the sign language arrays. A single facial articulation is discussed as the signed language equivalent of a tone, and the systematic combination of these tones create the tune or superarticulatory array. This multiple articulatory system has the potential to add more specific and greater variance in meaning than its corresponding two-tone intonational system in spoken language. Other research suggests blinks are consistent markers of clause boundaries (Nespor and Sandler 1999; Sandler 1999a; Wilbur 1994) although there is no absolute consistency (Johnston et al. 2007). This is addressed in terms of prepared and unprepared utterances in Sze (2004).

Veinburg and Wilbur (1990) discuss the superarticulatory array used in conjunction with negative headshakes. They conclude that the timing of the negative headshake is important and in most cases starts before and finishes after the syntactic constituent. These negative headshakes appear to be the same as the negative omens described by Steiner (1998), fulfilling a larger discourse role of indicating a contrasting discourse unit. The research analyzes the timing of the superarticulatory array for both the Deaf and hearing T/Is to see whether nonnative T/Is exercise the same level of control over the segmentation of discourse units.

Wilbur (1999), Sandler (1999b), Boyes-Braem (1999), and others discuss the idea of superarticulation and arrays under the scope of prosody. Their research introduces the concepts of intonational phrases (IP) and phonological phrases (PP) and the role that superarticulation plays in sign language syntax, focus structure, and discourse.

The notions of intonational and phonological phrases are based in prosodic phonology, which requires formal syntactic knowledge of a language; this research has not been undertaken on BSL to date. Boyes-Braem has undertaken a similar study of Swiss German Sign Language examining prosodic phrasing. While not formally identifying the units as IPs and PPs, she was able to distinguish between phrase and discourse units, as shown in figure 2.3 for the phrase, "I will not go to that store, me never!"

The [chin up------] marks the boundary of P-unit 1 and the [chin up + head back-----] marks a D-unit containing P-unit 2 and P-unit 3. Some head movements also occur at a lexical level as shown in figure 2.4.

| | Sentence 1 | | | Sentence 2 |
| --- | --- | --- | --- | --- |
| | P-unit 1 | P-unit 2 | P-unit 3 | |
| manual signs | I SAY | I NOT STORE I GO-TO (right) | NEVER! I | THEY ... |
| *mouthings* | [*sagen / say*-----] | [*Geschäft / store*-----] | [*niemals / never*---] | |
| mouth shape | [corners down--] | [tongue out] [corners down-----------] | [neutral...] | |
| position of head | [chin up-------] | [chin up + head back-----------] | [neutral...] | |
| eye shape | [eyes closed-----] | [eyes half closed -----------] | [open...] | |
| eye blinks | # | | | |
| duration | 20 video frames 0.40 sec. | 58 video frames 1.16 sec. | 55 video frames 1.10 sec. | |
| Direction of Torso movement | [from position left of neutral] | [ to position right of neutral ] | [change direction to move back to the left of neutral] | [change to move towards neutral ...] |

FIGURE 2.3. *Example taken from Boyes-Braem (1999)*

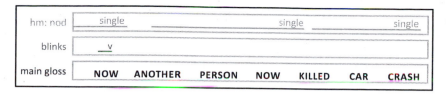

| hm: nod | single | | single | | | single |
|---|---|---|---|---|---|---|
| blinks | v | | | | | |
| main gloss | **NOW  ANOTHER  PERSON** | | **NOW** | **KILLED** | **CAR** | **CRASH** |

FIGURE 2.4. *Example of lexical and phrasal head movements from Deaf T/I headlines*

*Another person has been killed in a car crash.*

The head movement, incorporating some torso movement, above the sign NOW seen in figure 2.4, is lexically motivated and acts as a discourse marker (Stone 2001; Roy 1989). The example shows echo phonology (Woll 2001) of the head, where the head mirrors the movement of the hands. With the sign NOW, the hands move down and then are held in that position; the lexical head movement mirrors this by moving down and being held, that is, performing a single nod. The next head movement is to the left and marks the subject followed by head movement to the right, marking a predicate. These units remove the need for a formal linguistic analysis of BSL for this analysis.

## Blinking

Wilbur has shown there are two different categories of blinks in ASL. Sze (2004) found Wilbur's categories for linguistic blinks (lexical blinks, which are voluntary blinks, and boundary blinks, which are involuntary) failed to explain all of the blinks in naturally occurring Hong-Kong Sign Language (HKSL). Sze gives a tentative classification of five different blink types.

1. Physiological
2. Boundary sensitive
3. Co-occurring with head movement
4. Voluntary
5. Hesitations and false starts

Type one is not linguistically motivated and type five should not occur as often, if at all, if the language is prepared. Type four blinks, voluntary blinks, play a greater role either semantically or lexically, although not exclusively, and so they are not involved in sentence and discourse structure.

The boundary sensitive blinks occur between a variety of grammatical structures including subject predicate, predicate predicate, noun verb, and sentence. Sze also suggests that, as blinks can occur with other features including head nods, this activity could also be sensitive to grammatical boundaries.

## Blinking as an Indication of Preparedness

Wilbur used prepared sentences and Sze recorded spontaneous signing, and the differences provide a way of analyzing the level of preparation or unpreparedness of the TL produced by the T/Is. This analysis can also highlight whether there are issues of primary and secondary orality at play; those T/Is able to reproduce an oral text with fewer disfluencies are more likely to have both greater levels of fluency in the language and primary as well as secondary orality.

Sze also notes a difference between the types of blinking in monolingual monologue and dialogue situations. She attributes this to an inhibition of blink due to a higher visual demand in conversation than in a monologue. If this happens in natural data then we can assume that an audience would understand a TL who displays similar features, fewer blinks, or has a greater conversational quality and therefore creates greater rapport. Even though these features may well be unconscious aspects of language use, higher levels of fluency will ensure that these features occur at natural boundaries; there is less likely to be interference from L2 phrase and discourse units.

## Cohesion in Translation/Interpretation

Baker (1992) discusses the devices described above as features a translator needs to be aware of when translating from one written text to another. For idea units to be accurately rendered, the interrelationship of the ideas needs to be accurately rendered too. Individual sentences form only part of the information that is being conveyed by the SL. Interpreters need to maintain this awareness.

Shlesinger (1995) also uses Halliday and Hasan's taxonomy to examine shifts in cohesion in simultaneous interpreting for English to Hebrew interpretation. She focuses on the presence or absence of cohesive devices chosen randomly throughout the TL with respect to the SL. The interpreters in her study interpret the same text twice, so that the effects of prior knowledge and text cohesion could be analyzed. Since the T/Is within the broadcast news have access to scripts, they also have prior knowledge of the SL text (refer to chapter 4 for further discussion).

Signed languages use spatial prosodic cohesion that is different from spoken languages.

*because their daughter had been bullied at school*

| | | | | | | | |
|---|---|---|---|---|---|---|---|
| hp: tilt side | | | | | | | left |
| hm: nod | | single | single | single | | | single |
| blinks | | v | | | | | v |
| main gloss | INE | THROUGH | DAUGTHER | BEEN | BULLY | SCHOOL | IX |

FIGURE 2.5. *Example of use of spatial prosodic cohesion in BSL*

Figure 2.5 shows how the head nods overarch the subject, temporal marker, verb, and noun phrase, whereas the head tilt to the left (the same side as the IX) overarches the verb phrase.

This research examines the head movements of the TL for different types of prosodic phrasing both at a phrasal and discoursal level, analyzes whether there are differences between the hearing and Deaf T/Is, and notes any of these differences.

## Chapter 3

# Methodology

In this study, two phases of semistructured interviews were carried out with five Deaf T/I informants. The five Deaf T/Is were interviewed (approximately 45 minutes per interview) to gain a Deaf perspective of translation /interpretation. In the first phase, questions were asked as a starting point for eliciting Deaf-centered responses. In the second phase, the thematic categorization of their responses was given to the Deaf T/Is to ensure appropriate understandings and elicit a greater depth of understanding (refer to the section below). This enabled a Deaf-centered focus to the analysis of the translation /interpretation data.

TL data was collected from broadcast news of four of the five Deaf T/Is interviewed (14 minutes, 26 seconds) and an additional four hearing T/Is (8 minutes, 59 seconds) to investigate linguistic and translational similarities and differences in the Deaf and hearing output of the TL.

Think-aloud protocols (TAPs) were also carried out by three of the five Deaf T/Is interviewed (10 minutes, 58 seconds), one Deaf (hearing) T/I (3 minutes, 59 seconds), and one hearing T/I (3 minutes, 30 seconds) to examine the rendering of the same source texts by different Deaf and hearing T/Is: the results were used to further investigate and categorize linguistic and translational similarities and differences by using translations of the same SL. Only one Deaf (hearing) T/I and one hearing T/I (both with experience of interpreting the television news) were able to take part within the timescale.

A variety of methodologies were used to explore the different features of the Deaf translation norm, as seen in table 3.1. Interpreters H01 to H05 were recorded from television and, as they were not interviewed, were not asked to provide pseudonyms.

## CRITICAL ETHNOGRAPHY AND SEMISTRUCTURED INTERVIEWS

First, one-to-one interviews with Deaf T/Is were made in order to gain a deeper understanding of their motivations and understandings of a Deaf

TABLE 3.1. *Matrix of T/Is in the Data from Interviews, Broadcasts, and TAPs*

| T/Is | Interview | Headlines | Weekly Review | TAP |
|---|---|---|---|---|
| | Clark | | | |
| | Kim | Kim | Kim | Kim |
| Deaf | Rebecca | Rebecca | Rebecca | Rebecca |
| | Georgina | Georgina | Georgina | Georgina |
| | Kat | Kat | Kat | |
| Deaf (hearing) | | | | Arthur |
| | H05 | | | |
| | | H01 | | |
| hearing | | H02 | | |
| | | H03 | | |
| | | H04 | | |
| | | | | David |

translation norm. Since this Deaf-led research explores themes relevant to Deaf T/Is, no Deaf (hearing) or hearing interpreters were interviewed during this stage.

To ensure the interviews gathered rich descriptions, semistructured ethnographic interviews were carried out. The initial themes raised in the interviews came from casual conversations with Deaf T/Is, from reflections on their work, and their reflections on my work, and from my own reflections. Further topics raised within the interviews guided the research process and ensured its relevance to the Deaf T/Is and to the Deaf cultural framework.

## Critical Ethnography

Ethnographic research aims to study and to represent cultures from within their own frames of reference (Spindler and Spindler 1992). The six tenets of critical ethnography (Lather 1986; Simon and Dippo 1986) are: respondent validation, triangulation, typicality, judgment sampling, reflexivity, and catalytic validity.

*Respondent validation* ensures informants recognize and agree with the way their account is represented by reporting the interviewer's understanding of an informant's account to the interviewee for correction. *Triangulation* cross-references findings between informants and studies them for reoccurring ideas, comments, and themes. *Typicality* requires informants to be typical of the group under investigation. *Judgment sampling* is a purposive approach used to ensure the sample group under investigation is typical. *Reflexivity* concerns situating oneself as the researcher in the study and being cognizant of how one's life experience, opinions, and values influence the interpretation of the findings. Finally, *catalytic validity* ensures information is disseminated among the group studied so they are empowered to overcome power imbalances within their situations and wider societies. This qualitative research methodology aims to be rigorous by framing the information in terms of the informants' themes and information, while also being reflexive about the ontology and epistemology of the researcher (Cook and Crang 1995).

## Deaf-Led Research

Scholars in Deaf studies (Ladd 2003; 1998; West 2001; Young 1995) have successfully used critical ethnography as a framework for researching and exploring cultural views. In attempting to ensure this research was Deaf-led or Deafhood-informed, comments from the semistructured interviews of the five Deaf informants were categorized to generate grounded theories (Strauss and Corbin 1990). After categories and themes were generated, Deaf informants then were asked to ensure that the themes were framed within cultural references understood by them. This facilitated triangulation, respondent validation, and catalytic validity. These themes were further explored by think-aloud protocols (Jääskeläinen and Tirkkonen-Condit 2000) and by examining television data of Deaf and hearing T/Is.

## Reflexivity

Reflexivity enables the information presented to be understood within the context of individual researchers, their characters, and their life experiences. It also brings a greater awareness of the cultural lenses through which the researchers view their analyses.

I am from a hearing family and initially learned BSL as a second language by volunteering for a Deaf children's playgroup at the university where I earned my first degree. I socialized with the Deaf community during my four years there. I attended interpreter training at the University of Bristol's Center for Deaf Studies (CDS), studying two years with Deaf peers (one-third of my student contemporaries were Deaf) and upon graduating I worked as an interpreter for a year in Uganda, living in a house with only Deaf people. Working as an interpreter since 1997, many of my friends are Deaf; Deaf people also see me as a hearing professional working in the Deaf community.

My first exposure to Deaf people working as interpreters was at the CDS, when Deaf people interpreted for visiting lecturers. In Uganda, initially I relied on my Deaf manager, Gloria Pullen to interpret from BSL to Ugandan Sign Language (USL) and initially vice-versa. Throughout my ten months in Uganda, even after I had functional fluency in USL, my Deaf colleagues often acted as language mediators, re-presenting my TL moderated for rural Deaf people.

I have worked alongside Deaf interpreters in a variety of situations, including the broadcast news, and seen different approaches to the reformulation of information. I have also stood in for my Deaf colleagues, although I was only asked if Deaf T/Is were unavailable. I believe this is because the group of Deaf T/Is knows me; they know I gained a rich cultural exposure by living in a Deaf household. I regularly mix with Deaf people and have Deaf friends and this is seen as an important part of being an interpreter *of* the community rather than *for* the community. I believe I have gained a level of trust from my Deaf colleagues.

I am honored by the trust I receive from Deaf informants and believe some of their insights have been presented to me directly because of this trust. The Deaf T/Is also wanted to facilitate change for themselves, in their working conditions and the access the Deaf community has to mainstream television programming. I have ensured my informants that they would be kept up to date with this project. They trust me to represent their views accurately. My informants trust me as an ally and an advocate because they have witnessed me giving time, information, and skills to the community, which highlights reciprocity (Mindess 1999); this trust is not afforded to all "hearing" interpreters.

Some recent work by Allsop (personal communication, January 2005) suggests that members of the Deaf community identify a difference between "our" interpreters and "their" interpreters, that is, interpreters who are considered part of the community and follow culturally appropriate norms as opposed to those who work for institutions providing access for those institutions. Rudvin (2002, 2004) and Inghilleri (2003) explore similar notions, as discussed previously, and the trust I have from my informants stems from me being seen as one of "our" interpreters by the Deaf community.

The motivations behind my research concerns some of the tensions (Naples 1996) found in translation/interpretation work. I hope to identify some of the differences in the language production of hearing interpreters as perceived by Deaf service users, with meta-awareness. I achieved this by interviewing the Deaf T/Is who use interpreting services and have a meta-awareness because of the T/I work they do. These findings should be able to be fed into interpreter training programs to improve the production of non-Deaf interpreters.

Finally, while I have attempted to reflect the opinions and descriptions of the Deaf T/Is, some themes and topics seem of vital importance to me in the political struggle of Deaf T/Is. In attempting to recognize the heterogeneity of the Deaf T/Is, I may use some quotes to represent the opinion of one informant rather than many; these quotes form part of the intersubjective truths that make this project a blend of my understandings of the informants, the informants' validation of my understandings, and examples I have thought important, which may be given greater emphasis than my informants might have given them. The application of RT is my understanding of the information expressed by my informants with respect to some of the different types of translation decisions made by the Deaf and hearing T/Is. While RT has been described to my informants, the decision to use it is wholly mine.

This reflexive account is by no means comprehensive, and by its very nature provides my subjective account of my own subjectivity. The account omits elements I have consciously and unconsciously avoided. It is an attempt to increase the transparency of this project, but ultimately the readers will decide the level of transparency achieved and understand this project through those decisions.

## SEMISTRUCTURED INTERVIEWS

The ethnographic interviews were carried out in the language of the informants (BSL). Establishing this cultural space gave importance to the Deaf T/Is terms of reference in relating and representing their worldviews of the tasks before them. The location of the interviews was chosen in the hope it would maximize the cultural centeredness of the space for the

Deaf T/Is (Macfarlane 2002) and as somewhere the Deaf T/Is considered a "homeland," rather than in the television studio.

In the first interviews, the retrospective ethnographic (Bernard et al. 1984) topics were:

- what is a Deaf interpreter?
- what is the role of an interpreter?
- should hearing interpreters try to emulate Deaf people/interpreters?
- do you watch Deaf in-vision interpreters?
- is television interpreting like international sign interpreting?

In all the interviews, the ideas and language of the Deaf T/Is were reflected back to the informants to gain richer and deeper explanations of important points (Spradley 1979, 67). Topics raised by informants in previous interviews were raised with other informants within each phase, gaining access to cultural meanings, triangulating information, and gaining a "thick" description of Deaf T/Is' accounts of translation and interpreting.

As the researcher, I take full responsibility for choosing the additional topics from the interviews that seemed most relevant as part of the search for *"inter-subjective truths"* (Cook and Crang 1995, 11). In acknowledging there is no absolute truth, critical ethnography uses a balance between the judgments of the researcher/learner and the judgments of the informants/knowers.

Fortunately, the informants are knowledgeable about the research process and understood the need for me to focus on specific areas of the data. Ideally, there would be sufficient time and availability of my informants for me to return to them repeatedly until no further information or understandings could be gleaned on the topics. This is what is referred to as the point of saturation.

> [T]here usually comes a point in the research process where the range of arguments which *can* be made concerning a particular matter *has* been made. . . . This is termed the point of *theoretical saturation.* (Cook and Crang 1995, 12)

My regular contact with the informants allowed me to achieve saturation of some of the ideas and concepts from both the formal (interviews) and informal (unplanned) interactions. Even so, this project cannot fully represent all of the information present in the interviews.

I am responsible for any misrepresentation or inadequate prioritization of the data. Presenting these data so the informants have the power to change the information and how it is disseminated is vital to achieve full catalytic validity.

Catalytic validity was partially achieved through presentations of some of the data given in the presence of some of the informants while the project was taking place. The presentations were also filmed so informants were able to see my categories and provide feedback on my understandings between the first and second phases of the interview process. My informants were given a preliminary, written English report of my findings to fulfill both respondent validation and catalytic validity.

While information has been made available, and I have provided feedback regularly to my informants (albeit in an unstructured and unplanned way), not all of the informants have read or watched all of the information made available to them. This could be seen as a strength in terms of the trust my informants have in me, but it is also an indication of the lack of time these working professionals have to review all of the documentation.

## Informants and Sampling

The informants are Deaf T/Is who regularly work within the media, presenting news footage live from English (via autocue) to BSL. They have between four and ten years experience, and all work in the same geographical area. All of the informants have chosen the names that they wish to be known by in this research.

The Deaf interpreters were purposively selected (Arber 2001, 61–62) for typicality: they all come from Deaf families and have BSL as their first and native language; they would all consider themselves to be culturally Deaf; and they have meta-awareness of the task they are undertaking, including knowledge of the linguistics of BSL from formal education and work at the university level.

## The Interviews

The interviews were filmed on VHS videotape with the questions and responses transcribed into English in the first phase of interviews. The translations of BSL were undertaken so the English was comprehensible and as close as possible to the form of the informants' original language.

One of the problems of translating one language to another is the voice of the originator can be lost (Venuti 1998). Respondent validation was therefore of paramount importance, and in this research the process is aided by the informants being bilingual. They have been shown the reports of their accounts in the first-phase interviews and have been shown how both the first- and second-phase interviews have been understood and represented in this study.

The topics were introduced one at a time with the responses of the informants providing the direction of the dialogue. I responded to the points raised by the informants, dropping topics if they were not seen as important, and following up on the comments of the informants to arrive at the references of the Deaf T/Is themselves.

Each interview was influenced by the previous interview; the topics raised by other informants were also raised and triangulated (Cohen et al. 2000, 236), reducing the level of cultural translation by the informants (Spradley 1979, 80–82). Initially, some of the Deaf T/Is had difficulty seeing me as a learner and being confident in their roles as teachers. By introducing topics from other informants, I was able to seek further validation of my understandings and shift the roles of researcher and informant further toward learner and knower.

## Translation Issues

Video recording the interviews and then translating them into English in first phase of the coding moved my analysis a greater distance from the raw data than merely analyzing the data in the original language. When translating the data, I tried to ensure the original phrasing of the SL was preserved, so as not to alter the order of the themes discussed by the informants in their responses. I also used a descriptive translation style for the interviews, although there were times when this could have obscured the meaning in English. At these times, I used a sense-for-sense translation style.

The translations are marked as foreign by some of the syntax and word choice, so the reader is mindful of viewing a "foreign" language and culture through an English translation. This adds a layer of abstraction away from the original language, but it enabled me to use MAXQDA software for the initial phase analysis. In the first phase, VHS tapes made analyzing the interviews in BSL time consuming, and as such there could have been over reliance on the English translations of the interviews.

The second phase interviews were filmed using a DV video camera and imported via iMovie onto an apple computer. The interviews were partially analyzed by watching them on the computer, and chapters were added to the video before burning them onto DVDs, which made the footage easily searchable using a DVD player. The coding and theme categorization then happened in the language of the interviews (BSL), staying closer to the meanings of the original language.

The English translations of the first interviews were imported into MAXQDA, which was subsequently used to code the interviews. The translations were typed into .rtf files and imported into the qualitative data-analysis software. Open coding was used so the properties or dimensions of the categories could be explored (Strauss and Corbin 1990, 69). In open coding, the nouns and verbs of a conceptual world are used as specific instances of more general categories. In this study, the news companies would be examples of the category of institutions. The descriptions of these categories (generally adjectives and adverbs) are taken to be the properties of these categories. So in this example, the news companies were described as "hearing."

The interviews were categorized into three main themes, representing broad categories important to the Deaf informants: community membership (cultural competency), the Deaf interpreter's role, and language competency.

The use of memos or code notes enabled comments to be written about the coding of the interviews. The memos were short notes in English keeping a record of my thoughts about the comments and tacit knowledge presented by the Deaf informants in the interviews. These were attached to the coded segments and the codes themselves, as were the questions that occurred during the coding process.

The memos enabled a greater level of conceptualization of the data (Strauss and Corbin 1990). By detailing the thoughts I had concerning the interviews, I was able to explore inconsistencies in my thinking and my changing perspectives on the data. This level of conceptualization facilitated the achievement of reaching the final set of categories.

## Respondent Validation

One of the things to strive for when constructing intersubjective truths is whether or not the picture painted by the researcher/learner is something with which the informants/knowers identify. My regular contact with the informants during the study greatly supported the process. I could share my categorizations and thoughts during this contact and receive feedback on whether I was accurately representing the values, beliefs, and motivations of the Deaf T/Is.

One of my informants acted as a principal informant; I still work regularly with this informant who was interested in my findings at all research stages. Our conversations and the explanations or confirmations of my ideas were invaluable and have enabled me to see greater connections in my data. This relationship emerged throughout the course of my research rather than being something I planned for, and for which I am grateful, as, without this contact, my understandings would not have been as rich or as valid from a Deaf-led perspective.

Toward the end of this project I presented my findings in a seminar at which my informants were present. This allowed for further respondent validation and adjustments and changes to be made. However, the project is ultimately a "positioned and intersubjective" (Cook and Crang 1995, 12) one, and the understanding shared by my informants and myself. I cannot withdraw myself from my findings, which represents the truths that Deaf T/Is and I jointly found through mutual negotiation.

## Linguistic Analysis

The linguistic analysis pertained to both broadcast television data and the TL from think-aloud protocols (detailed later). Deaf and hearing T/Is rendered local television news broadcasts into BSL. These were recorded from two locations in the UK. Two different formats were recorded: headlines (both lunchtime and evening news) and news-week reviews.

The T/Is render the final summary of the headlines of the local television news into BSL. Previously reported stories are summarized at the end of the news broadcast. Typically, three or four news stories are summarized within one minute. These final headlines (as opposed to opening headlines) are rendered live into BSL, and I used recordings of these headlines for my analysis. The scripts were available for the T/Is on their arrival at the studio up to twenty minutes before broadcast.

In contrast to the final headlines of the local news broadcast, T/Is translate/interpret the whole of the news-week review program. The news stories on these programs were longer than the final headlines, with each story typically being two to three minutes in duration. The scripts were available at least several hours before the weekly broadcast.

The Deaf T/Is work regularly in both headline and news-week review formats, whereas the hearing T/Is only work regularly in the news-week format. Because of this, I only have one example of a hearing T/I working in the headlines format. Having one hearing T/I working in the headlines format allows for the comparison of T/Is working between shorter and longer preparation times. It further allows for some triangulation against the ideal translation style explained in the interviews. It also allows a comparison between Deaf and hearing T/Is who regularly work in the longer format.

## PARTICIPANTS

The four Deaf T/Is are native users of BSL and have Deaf parents who attended schools for the Deaf. The four Deaf T/Is were drawn from the five interviewees. The hearing T/Is are all trained interpreters who learned BSL as a second language and come from hearing families, although one of the hearing T/Is has a Deaf older sibling. All of the interpreters, both Deaf and hearing, are women.

The age range of the participants is between forty and fifty years old for the Deaf T/Is and is between thirty and forty years old for the hearing T/Is. They have been working as T/Is on the news for four to ten years. The hearing T/Is have been working as interpreters for seven to ten years and on the news specifically for two years. The length of experience demonstrates that the T/Is are not novices and the types of translation decisions they are making are indicative of those made by experienced professionals.

### Glossing

Video clips were recorded from television and captured from a mini-DV camcorder to QuickTime files on a Mac PowerBook G4. SignStream™ was used to gloss the linguistic content of the video. As the manual realization of the sign was not analyzed, the gloss incorporates the mouthing (Sutton-Spence and Day 2001) and the manual signs, that is the manual sign BRITAIN with mouthing "brish" and FLY with mouthing "airway" are glossed as BRITISH AIRWAYS. Any regional variations of signs were ignored and meaning-based glossing was used.

The analysis examined the nonmanual features of the language, specifically blinks and head movements (Sze 2004; Wilbur 1994; Jouison 1985), as described previously, to explore the phrasing similarities and differences between Deaf and hearing T/Is. It also enabled the identification of prepared or spontaneous TL texts according to their different blinking features. The preparedness of the TL allows us to assess whether the TL is a translation or an interpretation.

In order to analyze the phrasing of the TL texts, it becomes important to identify the temporal relationship between the manual and nonmanual articulations. This was achieved using SignStream, where the manual glosses and nonmanual features are attached to the beginning and ending of frames in the QuickTime files of the television and TAPs data.

Blinks lexically or semantically motivated are voluntary blinks. These tend to have a longer duration than involuntary blinks (Sze, 2004). For example:

| hm: nod | single | | single | | single | single |
| blinks | v | | | v | | |
| main gloss | AL | AWFUL | FROM-HEAD-DOWN | | AWFUL | |

FIGURE 3.1. *Example of voluntary blink*

In the gloss the *hm:nod* line represents the head movements, the *blinks* line represents blinks, and the *main gloss* represents the manual component of the BSL. The voluntary blink begins while the sign AWFUL is being articulated and continues until the beginning of the next articulation of the sign AWFUL. This voluntary blink is semantically motivated and intensifies the awfulness of the injury inflicted on the victim from the head down and all over her body. Blinks occurring at the end of a sign or in between signs are boundary sensitive blinks and involuntary. For example:

| hm: nod | | | single | | |
| blinks | v | | v | | v |
| main gloss | IX | COUNCIL | PLAN | TRUE | OPPRESS |

FIGURE 3.2. *Example of boundary sensitive blinks*

Here a blinks occurs after COUNCIL PLAN, the subject and then TRUE OPRESS, the predicate.

As Wilbur (1994) and Sze (2004) categorize blinks according to their occurrence in relation to the whole or part of a manually articulated sign, it is important to specify when manual signs have been determined to start and to finish and when blinks are determined to start and to finish in this study. The start of a sign is taken to be when the target handshape[1] starts to be formed while moving toward the target location. The sign is not taken as finished until either the target handshape of the next sign is starting to be formed or the orientation of the palm starts to move toward the target of the next sign. In the case of a return to neutral position as a discourse marker, for example, NOW, IX, etc. (Stone 2001; Roy 1989), the sign is taken to be finished when the neutral handshape (typically the lax 5-handshape) has started to be formed.

The start of the blink is taken to be the first video frame when the eyes are closed. The end of the blink is taken to be the first video frame when the eyes open. The start of the head movement is taken as the first frame where the head is moving upward in the vertical plane away from the previous position of the head. The end of the head movement is when the head is no longer moving downward (that is, the frame after the end has the head in the same position). If the head were down the only possible movement is up. In this case, the head moves from the low position up. When the head movements include sideways motion, the start and end points are measured. The beginning point is taken to be the movement away from neutral and the end point is the first of the nonmoving head movements from neutral (Jouison 1985).

There are times when there are two layers of head movement: the head moves downward in the vertical plane and while in the down position moves sideways in the horizontal plane. The head then moves back to center and then back up to neutral. These are counted as a head movement within a head movement. Some of these movements occur because lexical items have associated movements and some perform phrase and discourse functions (Boyes-Braem 1999) as described later.

Reliability of the coding was established by asking a Deaf native BSL research assistant to code 25 percent of the data. She was given the

1. Handshape is one of the phonological parameters of sign languages along with location of articulation, movement, and palm orientation (Brennan et al., 1984; Brennan, 1990; Brentari, 1998).

descriptions above and asked to follow those descriptions when coding. The number of glosses for signs were counted and compared. Similarly, the number of blinks and their positions were compared. Finally, the number of head movements and their positions were compared. In each case there was a high score of 80 percent or more.

## THINK-ALOUD PROTOCOLS

The think-aloud protocols (TAPs) elicited the decisions the participants made (Jääskeläinen and Tirkkonen-Condit 2000; Danks 1997) when creating their BSL TL text. The four stages of the TAPs allow the triangulation of results from the interviews to be achieved by comparing the process and decisions made throughout the TAPs with those described in interviews. This also enabled some analysis of ideal translation goals and how they are mediated by operational constraints. As the translation was from written English to BSL (an unwritten, visual language), the TAPs were videoed using a DV camera. The video footage of the completed TAPs was then imported into iMovie and segmented using iDVD for the analysis.

There were five participants, three Deaf T/Is and two hearing T/Is. The three Deaf T/Is were all Deaf adults from Deaf families with BSL as their first (and preferred) language and written English as their second language. These three Deaf T/Is were interviewed as part of the first study and some of their broadcast television work was recorded for the linguistic analysis in the second study. They ranged in age from between forty to fifty years old, and they each have between four to ten years experience working on the television news.

One of the hearing T/Is grew up in a Deaf family with BSL as the home language and is therefore Deaf (hearing). The other hearing T/I is an adult learner of BSL with English as his first language. They ranged in age from between forty to fifty years old. They have between ten to thirteen years experience working as interpreters, and between two to seven years working on television news. While one of the hearing T/Is has less experience working in television, he has at least as much experience working as an interpreter.

All of the Deaf T/Is are women, and both of the hearing interpreters are men. This differs from the data collected from the television broadcast news where all the participants are women. One example of a male hearing T/I was collected for the broadcast data. While gender differences might produce some differences in manual lexical items, I assume that the prosody of the language will not be affected.

## Material

The script for the TAPs was taken from a recent Scottish local news broadcast. None of the participants are from this region and had no previous knowledge of the news. The information spoken by the newsreader was transcribed from the videotape and produced as a script for the participants. The news broadcast contained three short stories and one long story totaling 3 minutes, 20 seconds. The short stories were narrated by the newsreader, and a newsreader introduced the long story and then shifted to a reporter and two interviewees.

Of the three short stories, the first news story concerned a former soldier who had gone on hunger strike; the second story concerned three antinuclear protesters; the third story concerned a public enquiry into the sinking of a fishing vessel. The longer story was concerned with a nonnative species of seaweed invading Scottish waters. (For the scripts of the stories, see appendix A.)

The news footage demonstrated two different ways in which information could be presented: either an anchor introduces and/or presents news stories from behind a news desk to camera, or a reporter voices-over prerecorded video footage and interviews people (either prerecorded or live). In the interviews, the Deaf T/Is said that while the presentation of the different types of news stories ("presenter" and "signer") end up with the Deaf T/Is being labeled differently, they are essentially the same task. Therefore, in the TAPs the T/Is were asked to sit and render the stories for the camera. No distinction was made between the different presentation styles of the television news footage.

## The TAP Process

During the first stage, the participants were given the scripts and filmed from that moment on. They were asked to verbalize all of their thoughts regarding the scripts, and to make a first attempt at rendering the written English into BSL. This enabled an analysis of the types of enrichments and impoverishments that T/Is make, based solely on the English source language.

The second stage of the TAPs involved showing the participants the associated video footage from the news clip shown alongside the news when broadcast locally. The news footage includes visual information about the news stories and contributes to the cognitive environment of the T/Is and the audience. The T/Is were then asked if any of the visual information would change their original renditions. The analysis of the changes to the TL because of the video footage provides information about whether this knowledge brings about a significant change in the cognitive environment from the T/Is' perspective. These changes relate to enrichments and impoverishments with respect to the SL.

The third stage of the TAPs was for the T/Is to render the script into BSL. The Deaf T/Is were shown the script on a laptop where the script was simulated like an autocue; the script was in large white font on a black background. In order to remove some of the pressure the T/Is would have experienced in a television studio, they were asked to render one story at a time. They were also told they could take as much time as they needed to render the scripts.

The Deaf T/Is followed the autocue and were shown the full script for each story. The video footage was not played at the same time, which removed the time pressure on the rendering. By showing the video footage and requesting the T/Is to reflect on any changes in their renderings of the English before asking them to perform their rendering, the T/Is were allowed to have all of the necessary information and not feel under pressure from the speed of the video footage.

The hearing T/Is were given the opportunity to either follow the autocue or to hear the spoken English (by having the video footage playing) in order to interpret each story. Both of the hearing T/Is chose to interpret the spoken English, as this was the system they were both familiar with. Both the hearing T/Is were told they could take as long as they needed for each story, and the stories were played one at a time. This meant they had a few seconds lead into each story. The story was then played and stopped as soon as the complete story had been read by the newsreader. The interpreters were allowed to finish their interpretation before the next story was played.

The fourth and final stage of the TAPs involved retrospection. The T/Is were shown the translations/interpretations they had done. They were then asked to comment on the TL, whether upon reflection they would change anything, and if so why this would be changed. The T/Is also commented on what would have helped them in the first place to improve their translation.

Ideally participants/informants should be familiar with the process before using TAPs to collect data (Li 2004), but time constraints prohibited this. The participants proffered different amounts of information, but the four-stage process (including retrospection of the rendering process) and the TL product countered the lack of familiarity. Using both TAPs and retrospection allowed for a rich description of the participants' accounts.

## Analysis of the Translation Shifts

The news footage has been examined for pragmatic enrichment and pragmatic impoverishment occurring between the SL and the TL identified above. The BSL translations were glossed (in the same manner as described earlier) and compared with the English source text. As a gloss is an abstraction from the actual data, the video footage was referred to when there was any doubt in the glossing informing decisions of whether a translation shift had occurred or not.

All of the news footage and TAPs footage of the Deaf, Deaf (hearing), and hearing T/Is was analyzed for translation shifts. The total time of the translated footage can be seen below in table 3.2. Pragmatic enrichment and impoverishment are measured with respect to the SL. If the TL has been made more explicit than the logical form linguistically encoded in the SL, this is interlingual enrichment; if the TL is less explicit than the SL, then this is interlingual impoverishment (Sequeiros, 1998, 2002).

TABLE 3.2. *Data Length*

| Data Type | Length of Data (Seconds) |
| --- | --- |
| Deaf headlines | 347 |
| Hearing headlines | 71 |
| Deaf weekly review in-vision | 420 |
| Deaf weekly review anchor e | 99 |
| Hearing weekly review in-vision | 468 |
| Deaf TAPs | 658 |
| Deaf (hearing) TAPs | 239 |
| Hearing TAPs | 210 |
| Total | 2510 |

These shifts are purely expansions or contractions of the linguistic form of the utterances, made because of contextual assumptions, to arrive either closer to or at the intended propositional form as described in chapter 1.

The next three chapters analyze the data. Chapter 4 explores the data from the interviews; specifically focusing on the perception Deaf T/Is have of their roles. This includes their identity, how this interacts with competing understandings of the job they perform on television and the translation they do in the community, and some exploration of the institutions within which they work.

## Chapter 4

# Role and Identity

Several themes on the role and identity of T/Is emerged from the interviews. The Deaf T/Is described their role within broadcast news. They described the types of language decisions they would make in an ideal situation, and they described some of the limits and constraints within which they find themselves working. This is important to the Deaf T/Is because of the emerging profession of Deaf T/Is and their desire for this profession to adhere to Deaf community notions of translation, interpretation, and collectivism. The language decisions and the constraints are reported alongside the relevant results from the television recordings and the TAPs.

### ROLE: INTERPRETER, TRANSLATOR, OR NEWSREADER

One of the main issues concerns the role the Deaf T/Is perceive themselves to have. Rather than assuming that all T/Is took on the role of an interpreter, one of the topics within the semi-structured interviews considered the difference in roles between Deaf and hearing T/Is. The responses highlighted a difference in the role the Deaf T/Is afford themselves and the historical reasons for this difference. The Deaf T/Is are able to collaborate with their hearing colleagues in the news studios, and they are co-newsreaders who use translation as a part of their job. The exception to this role happens when a report is shown and no one is available to collaborate with. In this case, they act solely as translators.

The Deaf T/Is in this study question whether they would label themselves as "interpreters," "translators," "presenters," or "newsreaders." Some of this questioning arises from the lack of choice in self-labeling. While labels are given in the credits, the roles they perceive are different from the ones ascribed by the institution. They perceive themselves to make different decisions about their translation when compared with hearing interpreters. This awareness informs the discussion of the role the Deaf T/Is undertake and a suitable label for this role.

The television companies label the Deaf T/Is either as "presenters" or "signers." When the Deaf T/I is sitting with the hearing presenter (anchor) following the autocue, the company label is "presenter." When they stand in front of a Chroma-Key background (typically a blue or green screen), and the video footage is superimposed on the background to create the background plate, the company label is "signer." Both of these situations can be found in the weekly review for Deaf T/Is.

There is an asymmetry in operation vis-à-vis the job description ascribed. The companies never use either the term translator or interpreter, and "signer" focuses on the language used rather than the function the professional is undertaking, for both Deaf and hearing T/Is. The T/I is signing using sign language, and the hearing person is talking using spoken language, but the hearing person is not called a "talker."

In one format the Deaf T/Is (as presenters) are acknowledged as being present and introduce themselves and the hearing anchors. They present some of the news stories and can even engage in some interaction with the hearing anchor in BSL. The Deaf T/Is in this role have had access to the script beforehand, have prepared how they will present the information, and follow the autocue when presenting.

In the second format, the Deaf T/Is present the news stories of a reporter on location or of some video footage and a voiceover. The Deaf T/Is have similarly had sight of the script and prepared their presentations using the information. The Deaf T/Is are introduced by the anchor (hearing only, if during a news headlines format; hearing and Deaf during a news-week review format) and will not be present other than to present the information in the news story.

In both formats the Deaf T/Is read an English script, prepare a BSL translation of that script, and then read the English autocue while presenting their BSL versions of the information. The situations differ, though, in the status of the Deaf T/Is: in the first situation they are co-presenting information with the newsreader (in the anchor position), and in the second situation they are re-presenting prerecorded news from a reporter. These formats are also used for Web translations.

When in the anchor position, the T/Is comment on the news stories. Time and the co-presentation of information allow for a more relevant translation to the audience. When the Deaf T/Is translate reports, the English voiceover is prerecorded, which imposes a fixed time within which the translation must occur.

The space created while being a "presenter" also allows for the anchor to introduce things, for instance, the names of protagonists and their ages, making it easier for the Deaf T/I translating the reports. The Deaf anchor always greets the audience, and the Deaf T/Is acting as translators also try to do this to build rapport with the audience. The anchor Deaf T/I, however, has a far greater presence.

The Deaf T/Is do not see the task of "anchor" and "signer" as different translation acts, but they are aware they are labeled differently. The Deaf T/Is know they are translating from the English, and since they are doing this within a mainstream news program, they see themselves as newsreaders for the Deaf community, their community. One of the highest accomplishments valued by the Deaf T/Is is that they produce a comprehensible TL for their target audience.

The translating from English into BSL is a task the Deaf T/Is working as anchors acknowledge as being different from their hearing newsreader counterparts. As part of their additional translation task, all of the Deaf T/Is interviewed mention how they often ask their hearing colleague what the script means. One of the Deaf T/Is states,

> They say, "I don't know," I think, "you don't know!," they are only responsible for reading the autocue, they don't have to understand the meaning, the content, the whole thing, I need to know what it means, I ask them "come on tell me," in BSL I can't sign it, I want more information, I need to know if something is related to something else, right, then I need to create the BSL and think how to do that, you can't just sign it, that's impossible . . . so what I've learned is that they only present what is there in clear spoken language, they don't think about what is being said, what it means, or of processing the meaning of that information at all. (Georgina)

This response not only shows that the hearing newsreaders are perceived to be concentrating solely on reading, but also that there is also a lack of understanding by the hearing newsreader of what the Deaf T/Is are trying to achieve. This confirms what we already know, that the Deaf T/Is reformulate the information from one language to another in a way that the newsreader does not. Some parallels exist in the language use of the Deaf T/Is.

> I am there to interpret for Deaf people, me for them, but I sign differently because of the screen, so I become like a newsreader, speaking the news, equal to English, so the Deaf community feels the same as the hearing community. (Kim)

The motivation for these changes stem from the intrinsic nature of BSL, a three-dimensional language, and how BSL appears on a two-dimensional screen when broadcast. Other examples of BSL news being broadcast on television can be found. News has been a part of both *See Hear* and *Sign On*. In these news programs, Deaf people were presenters and reporters, but they still read the autocue in English when presenting the news in BSL.

Toury (1978/1995) suggests one way in which translators can create the TL drawing upon a discourse norm for the genre they are translating. The Deaf T/Is could draw upon the BSL news genre already established by *See Hear* and *Sign On*. Despite the existence of this genre, one of the problems mentioned by one of the Deaf T/Is is that some Deaf T/Is are following the norms of hearing interpreters rather than creating or maintaining a Deaf norm.

> I think hearing interpreters [when interpreting] should copy Deaf people exactly, so they do the same as a Deaf person, but it seems to be happening the other way around. (Kat)

Although differences in translation and interpreting styles will be explored later (see chapter 6), the idea Kat expressed shows how some Deaf people are not following some of the established ways of working for Deaf T/Is. Tension arises between using a BSL discourse norm for presenting and using an interpreted (non-Deaf) discourse norm. When rendering, Deaf professionals could readily draw on some of the strategies used by their (non-Deaf) interpreter colleagues. Alternatively, Deaf T/Is may develop a Deaf, culturally-centered form of translation, consisting of their own perspectives on the job, information, language, and their agency for the community, a form seen as preferable by Deaf T/Is. This might create roles and translation acts that differ between Deaf and hearing T/Is.

Deaf professionals use translation as part of their jobs, irrespective of whether they are in the anchor position or in the "signer" position. Principally, if the hearing anchor or newsreader is reading the autocue, and the Deaf professional is doing the same, then, despite the additional task of needing to translate the English into BSL, they are doing essentially the same job. The Deaf newsreaders use the additional space negotiated with their hearing newsreader colleague to enable them to fulfill this role. When the Deaf professionals are unable to negotiate this space, then they act as on-screen translators.

A crucial point to explore concerned how Deaf T/Is defined the job and how they defined an interpreter. These differences can identify whether the Deaf T/Is undertake the same job, a different job, or define the role of a "Deaf" interpreter as different from that of a "hearing" interpreter.

All of the Deaf T/Is agree an interpreter works from one language to another. And an interpreter aims to achieve functional equivalence between the SL and the TL. Georgina explains that "an interpreter is someone who takes on board (digests) one language and then produces that digested meaning in a second language." However, the sign INTER-PRETER does not embody the type of rendering expected of a Deaf T/I. Kim explains, "just the term interpreting really, when I think about it, most people automatically imagine a hearing person."

While the Deaf T/Is work from one language to another, INTERPRETER appears to be too limiting to describe the work of Deaf T/Is. One of the main differences is the level of relevance to the constructed audience. As such, INTERPRETER tends to represent hearing interpreters and DEAF IN-VISION represents Deaf T/Is; the Deaf T/Is perceive the hearing interpreters as doing a slightly different job from themselves in both process and TL production. Kim describes how, "interpreting means from one language to another, 'online,' but this [TV work] is a prepared presentation which is different."

The Deaf T/Is are reading and practicing with the written text in the same way the newsreaders are, but with the added task of translating the English into BSL.

> The newsreader just reads the information and then speaks, while the interpreter can read and listen simultaneously, then processes the information, then continues with the interpreting, I don't do that, I have the same input as the newsreader, so I feel that I could be said to be interpreting based on translation, but really the task for me is translation. (Kim)

The translation is something worked on before the live broadcast, the Deaf T/Is rehearse the translation and use the autocue as a prompt when "presenting" the news to the constructed audience.

The Deaf T/Is see the hearing interpreters listening to the newsreader and interpret the information the newsreader presents rather than reading the autocue. This creates a difference and the lack of distance between the TL and SL is attributed to this. One of the informants (Georgina) described hearing interpreters that had worked on BBC 2 morning news in the mid-90s say, "interpreters had the information there, but it didn't connect with the audience, that was the difference, connecting through to the audience, or being slightly detached from the audience." Whereas the Deaf T/Is as "presenters" are more involved with the presentation of the information, the Deaf T/Is perceive that the hearing interpreters maintain an impartial role of information delivery, and this makes it difficult for the audience. This awareness will be explored in greater depth later.

## THE TRANSLATION ACT

The translation act, while occurring within the confines of the broadcast, aims to make the news relevant to the Deaf audience (as the Deaf T/Is construct it). The news aims to disseminate information about the world. As newsreaders and (ideally) as part of the news team, the Deaf T/Is are able to ensure the TL is appropriate for the audience to gain an understanding of this information. They achieve this goal by drawing upon native language intuitions and culturally rich understandings of how to present information in an accessible way for the Deaf audience.

The Deaf T/Is make the news relevant to the constructed audience of BSL users, irrespective of the presence of the subtitles. They aim to create a TL text that can stand-alone and deliver functional equivalence. The TL is not bound by the English SL, but constructed giving primacy to the Deaf T/Is' identities and membership in the Deaf community. The role of "interpreter" and "interpreting" is secondary in the translation act. The Deaf T/Is use the English script as an information guide to achieve functional equivalence. One of the informants, Clark, explains, "the in-vision interpreter should be really different [from the subtitles], they should be different but the information you understand for them should be the same."

This notion of functional equivalence is akin to Gutt's idea of "faithfulness." It suggests the TL is created as an interpretive language text, constructed for its relevance to the audience. As the Deaf T/Is envisage the audience as BSL users only (irrespective of their level of English) they,

> know how to connect with the Deaf audience because they think that way too, where as the hearing interpreter's concept/mental picture is different, I watch some interpreters and it's obvious that they are still fixed with English structure, and English ways of thinking, and they need to change to a Deaf way of thinking, that's what they need. (Georgina)

This "Deaf way of thinking" is explored in more detail later, but it can be understood that the TL needs to be unmarked BSL for a Deaf norm, one that does not look like a translation.

The initial norm (Toury 1978/1995) for the Deaf T/Is is of acceptability; the translation is TL driven. This contrasts with the notion the Deaf T/Is have of the hearing interpreters.

> I feel hearing interpreters should still relate things to me, to Deaf people, so Deaf people understand, Deaf T/Is sign that way, but hearing interpreters follow what is it? They [hearing interpreters] follow their interpreter role, theirs, so they sign, bring English to us, that is not interpreting. (Kim)

The hearing interpreters bring the worldview of the mainstream text to the audience, but Deaf T/Is want the TL to be maximally relevant to the Deaf audience.

> It's like you switch modes, like the Tardis,[1] if you want to go to Mars, you get in and get transported to Mars, British culture, Earth culture you have internalized, there you're interested in Mars, then you come back and explain what it's like there, from your perspective, but if a Mars alien came here, and explained Mars to Earth people, it would be different. (Kat)

This analogy was used to explain the difference between Deaf and hearing T/Is where one "comes from Earth" and the other "comes from Mars." Their different cultural backgrounds, for some, creates a situation whereby Deaf T/Is legitimize a Deaf cultural and community view while the hearing interpreters legitimize a hearing mainstream view. This can be compounded with the hearing interpreters being viewed as "cultural others." Any notion the hearing interpreters have of being allies to the Deaf community are still understood through the lens of difference and the impossibility of achieving neutrality when rendering one language to another.

> Hearing interpreters job is "interpreting," that is it, your job contract says interpreter, but we [Deaf people] relate to you [the interpreter], you

1. Acronym for Time and Relative Dimensions in Space, this is the spaceship used by Doctor Who, the main character in a BBC children's sci-fi television program.

sign and explain, we watch and understand, the information is impor-
tant/interesting, there is a rapport between the Deaf audience and the
interpreter. (Kim)

This strikes a chord with the discussions on neutrality (Inghilleri 2003;
Metzger 1999; Rudkin 1995) being unachievable, and undesirable in collective cultures.

At the moment that rapport doesn't happen, the word "interpreter"
dominates everything, "interpreter" is written all over them [hearing
interpreters], I feel keep that away, push it away, why? I feel there are
two different groups of interpreters, you're right it depends how they
[the hearing interpreters] sign, if they just relay the information that's
hearing values, the audience thinks yeah, yeah whatever. (Kim)

If an interpreter constructs the TL as a representation of English mainstream thinking, then this forms one group of interpreters that just relays
information. Interpreters who relate language to the audience and situate
themselves as understanding and presenting Deaf thinking, form another
group of interpreters. This second group of interpreters uses the "Deaf
translation norm," which requires cultural and linguistic competence
when constructing both the audience and their role within any situation.

## THE HISTORICAL ROOTS

The Deaf T/Is understand the role they undertake in television as a fur-
therance of the role bilingual Deaf people have undertaken for many
years. Since the inception of Deaf clubs, bilingual Deaf people have
supported the community by translating letters, newspapers, and other
information to semilingual and monolingual Deaf people (see chapter 2).
The rendering of broadcast news is the first time this role has emerged in
the mainstream public domain.

Using the script as a guide, the Deaf T/Is move toward considering
themselves as bilingual newsreaders, both when anchors and "signers."
They do not consider themselves knowers of the information, but deliverers of information.

If the text is clear then I can produce the information clearly, if the information is complex I don't repeat it complexly, as the audience would
not understand it, I need to make changes, what it means exactly, then I
ignore the script, change the delivery, so that I say exactly what the story

means, then add the details and build it up, so that it matches the meaning of the script. (Clark)

This action fulfils a role that historically proficient English readers would have had in the Deaf community and creates a covert translation.

Always have Deaf "interpreter" always . . . I don't mean for example, maybe hearing interpreters straight away sign to Deaf people, no, I mean what's going on in society, tell Deaf people that something is interesting, Deaf [people] say "oh wow, interesting," we've always had that, to me that's part of interpreting, like with newspapers, in the morning been read, or TV been read subtitles, then let people know, "oh that was really bad" you know, and explain that, Deaf people really interested, always been, or Deaf person has a letter, know someone [Deaf ] with excellent English, ask them to explain, that has always been in the community but not in the open and public. (Clark)

In the past, Deaf people who were proficient readers passed on information they considered community members would find interesting to less proficient readers in the Deaf club. This is considered part of one's responsibility to the community, an example of the reciprocal sharing of skills within the community's collectivist culture.

This historical role informs the translation style the Deaf T/Is use today; it is the precursor of the present-day Deaf translation norm. The translation act needs to be relevant to the constructed audience.

Hearing in-vision, I look between the subtitles and the in-vision interpreters and I think, yes, but I would call it hearing structure, you don't want that, the audience it will fly over their heads, the subtitles are enough, what is the in-vision interpreter there for? It's a waste them being there, I always say the subtitles and the in-vision interpreter should be really different, they should be different, but the information you understand for them should be the same, if they are very similar then what is the in-vision interpreter there for? (Clark)

The differences between the SL and TL interact with the information seen on the screen so the viewer experiences a parallel understanding of the information. These differences also ensure the information is maximally relevant to the audience.

I have to create a clear mental picture for the Deaf audience, which means I have to try to digest the information, and then think how I can sign output which gives them a clear mental picture, by creating a clear picture for myself, then think that's it, I want the Deaf audience to have the same mental picture as me, not sign it so Deaf people have to build their own picture, bit by bit. (Georgina)

One of the differences of the T/Is role within the broadcast news is that Deaf bilinguals have, in the past, chosen what they believe is relevant to their community. To some extent the Deaf bilinguals acted as gatekeepers to the information being passed on to their community; if they did not think the information was relevant then it was not passed onto the community. Within broadcasts, the Deaf community is not able to commission which news will be translated. Unlike when a member of the community takes their letter, or a newspaper article to be translated, the news being translated is chosen by hearing, non-Deaf, producers and journalists. This is noted, as described by one of the informants (Rebecca): "Some of the reports are really coming from hearing culture, but we have to deliver the information, we can't edit it or change it, but just deliver it." The new role differs because both the Deaf community and the Deaf T/Is have no choice in the news rendered for the Deaf community. And some of the topics chosen are not judged, by the Deaf T/Is, to be of interest (or relevant) to the Deaf audience.

## RELEVANCE TO THE AUDIENCE

The Deaf T/Is aim to use the autocue English interpretively (Gutt 1998); they are not creating a "faithful" TL but rather a TL optimally relevant to the Deaf audience. This involves including information that will have appeared either earlier during the week (for news-week review programs) or earlier in the broadcast (for news headlines). As information is the key to the news broadcast, it is given primacy over other parts of the message.

Clark questions the *skopos* (Hatim 2001, 73; Vermeer 2000) or goal of the translation and how the SL is to be used by the in-vision interpreter.

I know in training interpreters are told not to make additions to what someone says, if they are monotonous or boring then you need to match their style, not add things so the audience think it's great . . . that's a dilemma, should you match the style of the person, or just deliver the information, not give their style over, that's hard . . . there is no easy answer, if people specifically ask you to portray the character of the person, then you are clear, but I don't think it is specifically needed in this situation, what is important is information.

The information in the script is understood and re-presented in a way that is pragmatically understood by the audience. The information previously broadcast is used to incorporate enrichments and impoverishments into the TL to minimize the effort on the part of the constructed audience.

The implicatures constructed within the BSL text are different in some instances to those of English. The in-vision T/I needs to ensure the language points toward the same inferred meaning; the BSL needs to be presented as an ostensive utterance in an appropriate way. In this way, the TL interpretive utterance gains greater resemblance to the SL original (Gutt 1998).

The news headlines are short and give minimal time for a relevant BSL text to be rendered. Here the Deaf T/Is aim to draw upon the additional information already available to the Deaf audience from previous broadcast (via subtitles) to create the most relevant BSL text. In order to do this, the Deaf T/Is need more information than is contained in the English news summary, so they use the additional information to ensure the BSL is made maximally relevant to the constructed audience.

> There is background information on the news, the news from six to twenty five past has lots of information and I read that to find out what they are talking about, then look at my script, much reduced information, if I feel it can be delivered as is I do it, if there is one word that is difficult, I can take information from the larger script, add it, so that it has the same meaning, with that background information, I only started doing this recently and Clark is the same, it's good restructuring and adding background information, so that it is clear . . . really for a Deaf audience it's only thirty seconds, what I feel is appropriate information from the larger script, I can't tell the script writers that their summary is poor, so I add information, just one or two pieces so it's clear. (Rebecca)

Rebecca describes how the Deaf T/Is not only enrich the SL, but also act as journalists in that they appropriately edit larger stories for the BSL headlines summary. This rendering happens within the constraints of the time and visual information being shown on the screen, and it fulfils the agency they believe they should use to achieve the Deaf translation norm.

This role highlights the tension between the Deaf T/Is, perception of an interpreter and the role they have ensuring the information is relevant to their audience. This level of agency is seen to be a different, albeit an emerging, one, and the response to the historically informed role in a public sphere.

One of the news-review programs changed its format slightly during the course of the research. The program started to include a preview of television programs to be broadcast in the coming week. The new floor manager, who is the person in charge of the studio, the timings and the link between the control room and the presenters also changed with the new format. The previous floor manager had worked well with the Deaf T/Is, making them feel accepted as part of the team. The new floor manager saw the Deaf T/Is as outside of the team, and consequently the Deaf T/Is felt there was little acceptance of them as part of the newsreading team.

The Deaf T/Is felt that after filming a section in the new format, their agency was limited and changes could not be made. In the previous style, if the Deaf T/Is were dissatisfied with their work, there was an opportunity for the section to be re-filmed. The Deaf T/Is felt this lack of agency was compounded by the format of the new style. It comprised many clips and short pieces of information, combined with video footage. This style of programming gave the Deaf T/Is little chance to re-structure or re-order the news and program information. One of the Deaf T/Is, Kat, reported to me she felt like a HEARING INTERPRETER. When I raised this issue with the other informants, they agreed with Kat's sentiment.

This indicates that for the Deaf T/Is, this confined role is more indicative of hearing interpreters, and the Deaf T/Is want more agency. The hearing interpreter role, from the Deaf T/Is' perspective, accepts the lack of space for changing the TL with respect to the SL and results in less opportunity for cultural and linguistic adjustments and enrichments. Of the two groups of interpreters previously mentioned by Kim, the Deaf group would be more likely to make cultural and linguistic adjustments. It is not clear, however, whether all interpreters should be doing this, or whether all interpreters that work in television should be doing this.

The preliminary norm (Toury 1978/1995) is one where Deaf T/Is are not able to choose the news items translated. In spite of this, the Deaf T/Is feel that in some contexts they are given enough agency to create some ownership of the process and the information.

> On *Newsweek* or the headlines we are always talking about changing to match the audience . . . we have to find out what the background information is, the script may not be clear, and so we need the background information so that we can put those in and sign it so that it is understood by the audience, we need to put in cultural information. (Clark)

When this agency is denied, the Deaf T/Is feel used by the institution in perpetuating majority culture.

> Some of the reports are really coming from hearing culture, but we have to deliver the information, we can't edit it or change it but just deliver it, sometimes they are trying to be funny and I would question whether the Deaf audience gets it or not because it is a hearing thing, but I can't do anything about that, that's beyond my control. (Rebecca)

This conflicts with the Deaf T/Is' historical role that included selecting the information to be passed on to the Deaf community. Accordingly, the Deaf T/Is are unable to fulfill the skopos of the translation as they see it. The Deaf T/Is are not able to follow their Deaf translation norm, a norm not identified by or accommodated by the news broadcast institutions.

## Presence

As shown, the Deaf T/Is see themselves as being more "present" when delivering the news information in BSL than hearing interpreters. They believe this greater presence forms a core part of the Deaf translation norm; the Deaf T/Is are re-presenting the information. Georgina explains, "We look at the whole thing, take it on board, chew on it, conceptualize the whole thing, what it is, then take on board that conceptualization and present that in BSL." The information is not "just" translated or interpreted into BSL but presented to the audience. The presentation does not embody a notion of neutrality. This presence means the Deaf T/Is see themselves more as bilingual reporters/journalists than interpreters. They feel some ownership of the information and the way it is presented to the Deaf audience.

> Simultaneous interpreting just goes on and on and on, you focus on processing and editing and reformulating information, and as you said relay the information, so I feel for it to become Deaf you have to be in it, for it to become a full translation it has to be consecutive . . . it is more BSL when you sign the target language . . . you have the information in your head and sign it clearly to the Deaf person, that creates instant rapport, with simultaneous you are out of the information. (Kim)

By undertaking an offline rendering, the Deaf T/Is are able to have greater rapport with their constructed audience. And this is how the Deaf T/Is create presence in their renderings. This presence occurs more readily when the news stories are deemed relevant by the Deaf T/Is. When the news stories are viewed as inappropriate for a Deaf audience, the Deaf T/Is move into functioning in the way they perceive the hearing interpreters to work. The Deaf T/Is become more detached from the information and less present when delivering the news story.

One of the Deaf T/Is mentioned the difference between working on television and working from BSL to International Sign (IS).

> I feel I sometimes become like a hearing interpreter, I am forced away from BSL, I mean I take on board information, process its meaning and sign, when doing that I drift away from BSL and become like an interpreter . . . I feel like a hearing interpreter when it is simultaneous, as you said relaying information simultaneously, if a hearing person is signing English and I am watching and signing simultaneously that's not mine, if I wait and watch, then clearly understand, then sign it to the Deaf person, consecutively, that is Deaf. (Kim)

In the BSL to IS situation, the SL is live and the interpreter cannot fully prepare the translation beforehand. Interpreting decisions need to be made as the SL is presented and the target audience is in front of the interpreter. Here the only way presence could be created would be by using the consecutive interpreting mode. This highlights consideredness of translation as the core of the difference between Deaf T/Is and hearing interpreters: the act of translation being more considered than an interpretation, the Deaf T/Is want to approach the task as a translation to achieve their translation goals.

## Translation Performance

The translation of a written language into an unwritten language limits the extent to which the TL can be edited. The longer the news story, the less likely it is that the Deaf T/Is are able to construct a fully edited TL. And even with short news stories, once a live broadcast has started, any performance errors need to be corrected "online." This is also true, to a lesser extent, with prerecorded broadcasts where time is still limited; should the Deaf T/Is be seen as part of the team they may be allowed to re-record stories, otherwise it is "as live."

Both the newsreader and the T/I use the autocue. The reformulation is undertaken by the Deaf T/Is beforehand, but if this cannot be remembered due to the live nature of the translation, then the English autocue will still interfere with the TL production when being broadcast.

If you do not remember the translation, the problem is the autocue is unchangeable . . . that's difficult, sometimes I remember, I can sign sometimes and not follow the autocue, it interferes and influences our structure. (Georgina)

The lack of control the Deaf T/Is have in a live broadcast compounds these difficulties since the broadcast cannot be stopped for clarifications. In a prerecorded program more control can be exerted. Kat explains, "Lots of interpreters I feel play safe, stick to English order, because it's live, if it were prerecorded it's better, you have more control."

Some idea of translation performance is useful for unwritten languages, analogous to language competence and performance (Akmajian 1995), where internal language competence cannot be judged by performance errors. The translators can construct an internal "mental" translation using their translation competence and judge the grammaticality of another translation; errors can still occur in the translations they produce themselves.

Clark is really skilled at presenting, sometimes you can tell if the script was given to him last minute, but most of the time it doesn't bother him and he signs naturally, Clark is good and one of the few compared to others, we know he can read and understand and memorize the information, you know he is skilled at translating, he doesn't allow the order to influence him at all, he just delivers the information, sometimes he is reading but that doesn't affect his output, but sometimes you catch him hesitating and you know that it is last-minute information, that he hasn't had a chance to fully digest it, but when he does have time he is great. (Kim)

Interestingly, when a story is repeated and the Deaf T/Is become more familiar with the information, they are better able to act as information deliverers.

Sometimes me not mentally processing, nothing sometimes, I read the script, translate it but I already know the information, I don't need to think, if it is a repeated news story, like Soham the small girls murdered, that was repeated so I did not need to process. (Kim)

This could also be a case of recalling "old" information rather than retrieving "new" information. In processing terms, a previously formed schema is being applied rather than forming a new schema (Halverson 2003). The less familiar the information is to the Deaf T/Is, the more likely they are to perform in a way that is perceived to be like a hearing interpreter (as quoted earlier).

> I feel I behave more like an interpreter when doing International Sign simultaneous interpreting, watching the SL and signing International Sign the output is not mine, if I wait until I understand it and then tell the Deaf person what I understand that's it consecutive, that's Deaf, simultaneous is just passing on information. (Kim)

Here the information is unscripted and therefore less familiar to the Deaf T/I. Even though an interpreter will rely on prediction skills and will prepare for a job, there still remains a difference between a fully scripted, well-prepared and spontaneous SL.

There have always been information sharers, and their responsibility within the Deaf community is to ensure that community members understand the information. In giving space for the covert translation to be made, with a consequent connection to the audience, the Deaf T/Is maintain the Deaf translation norm. Clearly, simultaneous interpreting is not conducive to a Deaf translation style. Kat notes, "I feel that it is hearing their rules, following this, that and the other, theirs hearing, if Deaf it would not be like that, Deaf rules are different." Hearing interpreters are deemed to follow their professional rules, which are seen as being led by the mainstream and not sensitive to Deaf culture, rather than becoming involved in the information and involved in ensuring that the message is understood.

> Theirs, I feel interpreting hearing theirs, I feel the rules, how to behave, stiff, how to sign, all these rules, they are trained, like that, I feel that is there. (Kat)

> The information is signed outside of the interpreter. (Georgina)

Rather than being involved in a scene and using either constructed dialogue or constructed action (Quinto-Pozos 2005), the hearing interpreters use other devices. This lack of involvement, described as empathetic and participatory by Ong (1982), compounds the lack of language adjustment on the part of the hearing interpreters.

It is important to note that this understanding doesn't describe all hearing interpreters or the needs of all of the Deaf community. Kat explains that, "the point is interpreters can hear the information and relay it, Deaf can relay the information too, but in a Deaf way, the Deaf [audience] can follow, suits Deaf way but if they don't that becomes like hearing interpreting." The comments of the Deaf T/Is are couched within the notion of the differences between Deaf T/Is and hearing interpreters where those differences could be seen as problematic. There are hearing interpreters who are able to take control of communicative situations (and, conversely, Deaf interpreters who are not). Some people in the community are less empowered because of their language usage and need greater action on the part of the interpreter to ensure the message is understood. In these situations, the Deaf T/Is describe the need for Deaf T/Is to be brought in since they are pragmatically competent. The Deaf T/Is aim to achieve within the broadcast media this additional action of ensuring the message is understood.

> Again lots of the time we all think we are aiming for people like us, and those we mix with, often we forget grassroots Deaf people, and it's worse for grassroots Deaf people because the newspaper isn't accessible because it's in English, the TV subtitles don't provide access, so really the program is for them, not to others who have access, they have it already. (Kat)

Kat gives voice to the reality that the Deaf translation norm is not just about doing a "good" translation but about creating a TL that is understood.

## TELEVISION STANDARDS

Deaf T/Is are aware that language within the television medium needs to be different from BSL in face-to-face interaction. Kim notes, "My language alters because there is a camera there, TV is different from real life." There needs to be a wider debate to create television guidelines or standards.

T/Is are also concerned about the lack of consensus of language modification for television and how the language might naturally interact with the images that appear on the screen.

> Right, wrong, I don't know, there has not been a discussion yet. (Rebecca)

> There's no standard if you are on TV, there is no compulsory conditions, because who would set them? We have a set of rules for interpreting in general and should have something specifically for TV. (Kim)

> I feel there should be guidelines they'd be welcomed like . . . same as myself, I know why bring in an interpreter, if the subtitles are good enough, why? Still, I know Deaf people read the subtitles and then the in-vision interpreters makes it a little better to understand, still it's English structure what for? . . . I need to challenge myself, what's the aim of the in-vision and adjust to that. . . . Secondly, guidelines related to the sign vocabulary, regional, or national vocabulary, we need to reflect on that. Thirdly, we should think more on what we mean by BSL, what is easily understood by an audience in BSL, like facial expression being

important, placement, and other features, it should be that the audience can just take on board what is signed, that's what's important, those features, and then that reminds you when signing, so with guidelines established in these areas there can be more parity, now it's individualistic. (Clark)

As the television program is in English, this language drives content creation. The translated BSL has to fit into the program; there is no mutual adjustment. This normally results in insufficient time to present the information in BSL in an appropriate way for a Deaf audience. Simplifying the information provides one way to overcome this obstacle, but the danger becomes this could patronize the audience.

It's like, well, I feel that it's because of the TV controlling the situation, I can tell how the TV situation has controlled the situation, it flows but the language level drops, it's not natural, I feel the language level is too low because it's slow it lowers, I saw one of the [late night interpreted] programs about the turn of the century, the information was interesting, but I feel that it really patronized Deaf people, so that means how has the program been directed and how does that affect the language? (Kim)

The danger also exists that hearing interpreters fall into this trap, due to a variety of factors (the complexity of the SL, lack of skills in TL production, lack of mastery of BSL register, or overreliance on certain structures that are thought to be culturally Deaf, but whose overuse identify the interpreter as an L2 BSL user). "She tries to sign like she is Deaf," Kat explains. "She signs, feels patronizing, brief, brief information, I feel 'ooh, broken BSL.'"

These examples show the joint desire for some standards in public broadcast translation, and highlight the need for skills to be passed on, be that in mainstream institutional training or in more traditional ways within the Deaf community, in order to develop greater consistency by the professionals involved.

## DEAF IDENTITY

The Deaf T/Is are well aware of their core membership in the community, and they still socialize with the Deaf community. This reinforces the Deaf T/Is' identities and adeptness at modifying their language so as to be understood by other members of their community. The Deaf interpreters make decisions in relation to their translations according to their construction of themselves as core community members who regularly interact with the their community. Clark explains how this works, "Deaf people identify those language factors without thinking about it and adjust their language without training, they just adjust their language because this the community they mix in, so they just know how to adjust their language."

When the Deaf T/Is categorize "hearing" (non-Deaf) interpreters as nonmembers of the Deaf community, it follows that they do not want to license these non-Deaf interpreters to make similar decisions.

> Hearing interpreters dip in and out of the Deaf community, if a hearing interpreter was deeply involved in the community all the time then maybe they could take on board all of these factors perhaps, but most interpreters nowadays dip in and out, that's it, they work in the community and then leave, it's rare that interpreters nowadays are like those in the past, that was different, they were part of the community and socialized within it, it's different now. (Clark)

> As I read down the text I pick out what my mental picture is, which is automatically the same as Deaf people, but those interpreting read the information and try to change the order, but the picture they have isn't right. (Kim)

The aim of the Deaf translation norm is to remove traces of the SL so the TL audience perceives the text as their own.

> Hearing people are different, I don't know how hearing interpreters create their mental pictures, I can talk about Deaf interpreters as one of them, or how I understand/receive information from hearing interpreters, so what I normally do is read the piece of text and try to think of the Deaf audience, I have to create a clear mental picture for them, which means that I have to try to digest the information and then think how I can sign output which gives them a clear mental picture by creating a clear picture for myself, then think "that's it," I want the Deaf audience to have the same mental picture as me, not sign it so that the Deaf people have to build their own picture, bit by bit. (Georgina)

In this way the Deaf T/Is use this space on televised news broadcasts to create a Deaf space.

> Maybe Deaf [T/Is] read the script, have understanding of it, they have their experience, their background, their own, this they relate to the script, and add cultural knowledge, maybe hearing interpreters read the English autocue or hear it, they think, "oh yes, I know I've done that before," relate as hearing people to autocue, I feel hearing maybe have

limit, through have to be Deaf to empathize, same Deaf [T/Is] have limits too through English script. (Kat)

Similarly, it is reported by the Deaf T/I informants that some Deaf T/Is use hearing interpreters as role models. Kat commented, "Hearing interpreters should copy Deaf interpreters, but it's happening the other way around, Deaf interpreters are copying hearing interpreters, why is that?" This implies that the Deaf interpreters are not following the Deaf translation norm, but following models used by hearing interpreters. This may be because hearing interpreters are the norm in most situations other than television. The hearing interpreters can interact with the mainstream majority, and theirs is clearly the dominant discourse within the sign language interpreting profession.

Since the Deaf translation norm has evolved and developed within the Deaf community, it is this community-grown quality that is important in creating a Deaf space on television. A covert translation that the Deaf-constructed audience can identify with.

Although there are some Deaf in-vision here [region location of T/I] and elsewhere [in the UK], the other [Deaf T/Is] are not suitable, they are not native users of BSL, sign with bad articulation, fingerspelling, not clear, shame that group are not better, more groups then can compare. At the moment, too many learn BSL late, become in-vision, it's a mess, some hearing interpreters better than them, yes. (Rebecca)

Not criticism but, hearing interpreters good but not have some specific skills, like really hearing will never have those skills, same as [some] Deaf people will never have some skills that hearing have, never. I think it's impossible for us, impossible for them, through influence from sound, impossible, hearing way of thinking, impossible, do your best fine, but Deaf natural, grow up natural, comma full-stop from head, you tell me I've been doing that, I don't know why, not taught in school, how to move head nothing, just using language naturally, have head movement there naturally. (Rebecca)

As indicated, notions of naturalness are an important part of the Deaf translation norm, and this comes from growing up in the community and being natively fluent in the language. Similarly, it would appear these skills are difficult or impossible for hearing or nonnative Deaf interpreters to achieve, although some aspects of the Deaf translation norm are achievable. Even if interpreters are Deaf (hearing), they have grown up in the community and potentially have a high degree of fluency, but cannot reduce the influence hearing sound has on their way of thinking.

In striving to achieve a TL product understood with minimal additional processing effort by the audience, the Deaf T/Is still have to work within the limits of the organization for which they are working. In this study, the television news company chooses the headlines and news stories to be translated for the Deaf community. From the Deaf T/Is' perspective, no thought is given to the types of stories that might be appropriate; the Deaf T/Is are not consulted on what stories are more appropriate and how they can be structured in a more appropriate way for the Deaf audience.

> I'm in their hearing news, me in hearing their news, I do not make big changes to Deaf-cultural their way, I don't, at first when learning I struggled, now I do not always sign in a strong Deaf way, really should do, and I can drift between strong Deaf and less strong, I do not sign so strong Deaf, I have thought, why? Of course it is because it is hearing news, their structure, that means how can I radically change it to Deaf news structure if it is based on English, based on hearing structure, it would have to be the other way round with me sitting at the desk presenting the SL news in BSL and the hearing person standing at the side presenting the TL news in English, that would be Deaf. (Kim)

There are limits to the agency the Deaf T/Is have within the news team. If the team accepts the Deaf people as part of the team, then changes can be made so the BSL is audience appropriate; if they do not, there is a conflict between how the Deaf T/I wants to present the news and the demands for fidelity in the translation when it is clear the news team wants a token-for-token translation rather than a functional one.

> I know that the news team try to give me time, lengthen the time per story, often, it depends on the producer, if they know when to slow down or give me longer, for some stories it's short and that's that it can't be changed, this can happen but it's rare. (Kim)

With the news broadcast, especially the news review-style programs, the Deaf T/Is express a desire to reorder the language of the broadcast. The brevity of the summary headlines and that they are recapitulations mean the Deaf T/Is feel less need for a reordering. Kim explains that, "the summary headlines are really short, the context has already been established by the Deaf audience by reading the news subtitles throughout the lunchtime news, meaning that there is no need to reorder the headlines."

If the headlines are reordered, then they must be short enough for the Deaf T/Is to remember, allowing them to be less reliant on the autocue. With the longer news-review stories, the Deaf T/Is often want to restructure the news stories. The television studio hampers this restructuring because the autocue provided for the Deaf T/Is is identical to the one provided for the newsreader. The autocue follows the pace of the hearing newsreader catering for the hearing audience; the Deaf audience relies solely on the ability of the Deaf T/Is to provide access to the hearing news, without any support during the broadcast from the hearing institution.

> This is hearing news, it is only to give Deaf access to information. I give information, as much as possible for the audience to understand, more in the language that they understand but not 100 percent, no. I know because of the structure the brevity the time, that's not our rules. (Rebecca)

One of the factors all the Deaf T/Is rate as supremely important in their construction of a TL is an individual T/I's memory. The longer the story, the more the Deaf T/Is must remember their TL, and this can lead to translation performance errors.

> Sometimes you finish feeling great because you have remembered the story and been able to reorder the information. Other times you are wanting the autocue to speed up so that you can be reminded of the next part of the story because you have forgotten what comes next, or what more needs to be said. (Georgina)

This also indicates the amount of agency the Deaf T/Is have within the institution. The autocue is the feed for the hearing newsreader, and an additional camera with autocue could easily be set up for the Deaf T/Is. This is not necessarily the preferred way of working for the Deaf T/Is, but it is the minimum the television studio could do to accommodate Deaf T/Is and assist them in their performance of a live translation of the news.


## POLITICAL IDEOLOGY

The Deaf space is created not only by the fact the Deaf T/Is judge they are going into their first language and their first culture; they also use English information and videotape information so that accurate contextual assumptions can be extracted from the SL and then replaced by appropriate implicature and explicature within the TL. The Deaf interpreters hold the view that that the non-Deaf T/Is are neither linguistically nor culturally competent enough to make the same judgments. "The hearing person can sign, why hearing interpreters, what-for, get them off, Deaf are better, BSL our language, bring in a hearing interpreter what-for?" Rebecca explains.

No differentiation occurs for Deaf (hearing) interpreters either. It appears this is an attitudinal factor. It expresses notions of language ownership, at least in terms of who "should" be role-modeling BSL within this public sphere—these should be Deaf native BSL-users.

## The Deaf Audience

Constructing this Deaf space also requires the Deaf T/Is to construct an audience. The constructed audience will necessarily alter the type of language produced by the interpreters (Ruuskanen 1996) as well as the type of information assumed to be known by the audience (Gutt 1991) (see chapter 5).

> I always read the script, "do I understand it?," then try to sign it to myself, "does it make sense?" I try to think of them [the audience], people who are Deaf, them, or Deaf club, possibly I focus on older people, or those I know don't read English subtitles, no, I don't mean no English, more strong BSL, I never think of my sister I know she has good English, I conceptualize my mother, my friends . . . I conceptualize them, sign thinking is this information clear enough for them? (Georgina)

These audience members are constructed as equals, albeit Deaf people who do not read the English subtitles or have English as a weak second language. Then the T/I creates a mental picture to ensure the Deaf audience has access to the information. No information is given regarding Deaf (hearing) interpreters; it is possible that they envision their parents (and Arthur says this during the TAPs). This can come across as patronizing and suggests that while Deaf T/Is envision their Deaf audience as equals (or even an audience with seniority) to demonstrate a strong, Deaf cultural value, Deaf (hearing) hearing interpreters do not always construct an audience of equals.

## It's a Deaf T/I Job

A question of the double oppression of the Deaf community arises, in terms of denying Deaf people interpreters in the community and taking the jobs of Deaf T/Is in the television studios.

Hearing interpreters are needed for conferences, real life without autocue, one-to-one interpreting, go and do that. Deaf can do the job on television, so we work together for the community, but I feel hearing are taking over. Deaf are wanting to examine where we can share, now I have been doing this interpreting I know I can share with a hearing interpreter like "supporting" for them to do a better job, if they oppress us there are no jobs for us in the end, there is plenty of work for hearing interpreters, some just want to be seen on television. If someone really is as fluent as a Deaf person fine go ahead but it's a Deaf job, hearing people cannot be bothered to employ a Deaf person so hearing interpreters make it worse. I like to see more hearing interpreters in the community at conferences and in one-to-one meetings where they work in both directions. (Rebecca)

Hearing interpreters (and perhaps by implication Deaf (hearing) interpreters) are required to be at least as fluent as Deaf native BSL users (if that's possible) to fulfill a Deaf translation style, but in doing so should also be sensitive to notions of reciprocity in the Deaf community.

Political why through historically oppressed, self-oppressed, elbow [reject] that firstly. Secondly, I think Deaf now interested, roll up sleeves, for media, in-vision, filming, lots of things, looking around for job opportunities and they are not there, become annoyed, hearing stay out. (Kat)

Hearing interpreters need to act as supporters of Deaf T/Is and as allies, and they should support their Deaf colleagues if they find themselves in the position to do so. The Deaf T/Is feel there exists a bias within institutions for hearing interpreters and that the hearing interpreters should not be gatekeeping these jobs. Kat notes, "TV will automatically bring in a hearing person who can sign." This is not a surprise as it is easier to interact with someone who speaks one's language and behaves in the same cultural way. But these judgments are based on ease of interaction and integration into the institution rather than on creating a TL product that best serves the audience.

Hearing interpreters in positions of power by virtue of their mainstream status introduce a level of tension. They are often brought in to interpret for meetings between Deaf T/Is and studios when wishing to establish in-vision news. Since the hearing interpreters are trained and qualified, the institutions can see them as sufficiently fulfilling statutory obligations. These qualifications are not seen as being enough to meet the needs of the Deaf community by Deaf T/Is or enough to create a Deaf space within the news for a Deaf audience to gain a clear mental picture of the news.

More importantly in terms of employment, jobs in the news and television in general are jobs Deaf T/Is are able to do, and as such are seen as "Deaf jobs." The dearth of interpreters in the UK means hearing interpreters are always in high demand in the community where Deaf T/Is are not able to work. By ensuring television work is given to Deaf T/Is, hearing interpreters are also able to ensure that the Deaf community plays a core role in publicly showing its language to the mainstream community.

Having addressed cultural issues and the role of the T/Is, the next chapter will examine the language features seen in the TL. While this will involve some comparison of Deaf and hearing T/Is, the focus will be on teasing out which language features contribute to a Deaf translation style.

## Chapter 5

# Interpreted/Translated Language Features

This chapter examines the BSL TL produced by the T/Is as a stand-alone linguistic text and explores the construction of the pragmatic other by Deaf T/Is and the influence it has on the TL. Prosodic or intonation features of the BSL TL are analyzed, specifically, the blinking features compared with the blinking behavior expected in prepared and spontaneous texts. The head movements prosodically segmenting the BSL TL are then examined, demonstrating differences between the Deaf, Deaf (hearing), and hearing T/Is in phrasal and discourse prosodic head movement segmentation. This analysis highlights some of the differences between Deaf and hearing T/Is and contributes toward a greater understanding of a Deaf translation norm.

## LANGUAGE CONSTRUCTION

The Deaf T/Is have a sense of how they wish to construct an unmarked BSL (covert) TL in order for it to be well received by their Deaf constructed audience.

> For some Deaf people, the in-vision interpreter can help them understand a little bit better but why does the interpreter follow English structure, the interpreter needs to meet the challenge, the purpose of the in-vision interpreter is to change the language. (Clark)

This is achieved when Deaf T/Is draw upon their experiences growing up within the community as bilingual Deaf people and by experiencing other Deaf bilingual role models (as described previously).

The construction of a target audience does not essentialize the audience as one particular subset of the Deaf community. Rather, it shows how Deaf T/Is acknowledge the heterogeneity of the Deaf community, or at least the diversity of Deaf people who have historically attended, and still attend, Deaf clubs. The audience is seen to be one of Deaf BSL users; the Deaf T/Is do not aim to construct a contact form of the language.

## Considering the Audience

This Deaf club not only informs the Deaf T/Is' construction of the audience but also acts as a linguistic resource to draw upon. Deaf T/Is recall how Deaf enthusiasts sign about specific subjects using that vocabulary as their first approximation of the TL.

> If the topic is planes then I know who will be interested in the airplanes, and so I think of how they [the person interested in airplanes] sign it first, then when ready to broadcast, I change the language so that it is suitable for a wider audience. (Kim)

This approach not only encourages appropriate language choice but also provides linguistic resources for jargon and other language elements and can function as a glossary. This follows a similar process to that used by professional translators (Ruuskanen 1996) as well as for trained sign language interpreters (Leeson 2005b; Leeson and Foley-Cave 2004) who use their knowledge of the audience to construct the TL. The linguistic (BSL) and (Deaf) cultural resources native Deaf T/Is are exposed to come into play.

Under time pressure, the Deaf T/Is make split-second decisions about the information contained in the script and how best to represent this in BSL. The Deaf T/Is are mindful of the comprehension of BSL on a two-dimensional television screen when BSL is a three-dimensional language. Fingerspelling provides one feature for consideration.

> If the newsreader is speaking fast I can tell that they are speaking fast, that means I think if I fingerspell really fast it will go over Deaf peoples' heads, so I look at the script, and like the name of an army regiment, royal whatever, that can be reduced too, "from Wiltshire army group going to Iraq, training ready for the war." (Rebecca)

Rebecca's example shows the types of decisions hearing interpreters are trained to consider. The Deaf T/Is are able to do this is not only because of their native fluency, but also because they regularly access BSL information from television, watching programs such as *See Hear*, etc. The Deaf T/Is also draw upon their personal experience of watching BSL, be it as stand-alone text or a text rendered from English, to inform their discourse style.

## Referencing

The visual information on the screen is easier to reference than finger-spelling, which (anecdotally) is harder to comprehend from the screen than in face-to-face communication.

> For the name of a person, Deaf [T/Is] do more indexing, referencing. Hearing interpreters will fingerspell Sharon Tony. Deaf people have started to copy them, is that right? I'm not sure, the Deaf audience often say what-for? I'd rather you pointed, I know it is related to the visual information, to the people on screen, I know and identify with the Deaf audience, I know hearing interpreters will drop some things and Deaf interpreters will drop some things, but will they drop the same things? I don't know. (Kat)

Here the "power" of the institution and the hearing interpreters place within it, appears to disempower the Deaf T/Is who do not use their own translation norm. Manifesting not only by referencing in a cultur-ally inappropriate way, but also by forcing different "in" and "out" (Vuorinen 1995) decisions made by the T/Is. The Deaf T/Is and hearing T/Is potentially identify different things as relevant to the audience, but its manifestation in the TL is mediated by the institutional limits placed on the Deaf T/Is. The Deaf T/Is can feel constrained by the broadcasting companies themselves and the role models of interpreting the Deaf T/Is feel they should adopt, and they may not adhere to the translation model developed within the community.

## NMF (Nonmanual Features)

Limits apply to the language restructuring feasible in a live broadcast. As discussed previously, the issue of translation performance affects the BSL text produced, but some specific language features need to be retained.

> NMF is less so grammar is lost right, but if less NMF and still BSL in English order it means information is lost, everything reduced, like a question, everyone knows eyebrow raise and it's a question, you need to know linguistics to make a good translation. (Kat)

> Deaf interpreters are more fluid, fluent, reflect about it [the rendering] . . . sign with more fluency and facial expression, whereas the hearing interpreters are more like "I've been trained." (Rebecca)

Lack of fluency is one of the reasons less facial expression occurs in BSL, and the training of hearing T/Is induces formulaic interpreting. Training is blamed for specific "crutches" being used by the hearing T/Is that result in a loss of flexibility. Deaf T/Is are perceived to be less formulaic, and they include more nonmanual information as part of their domesticated translation rather than focusing on a solely manual lexical rendering.

## Levels of Required Bilingualism

Some meta-awareness of the language and the process are needed. Kat, for example, still feels the T/Is need to know about linguistics. These are not the only skills necessary; however, she lists other skills too.

> The Deaf person has to firstly be bilingual, secondly have translation skills, I know the skills can work together, but, there are some Deaf people that try really hard, are to be praised for that, but their English is limited, which means they are not suitable for the news, but they are adamant they can do it and haven't yet taken the time to look at themselves, so how can we work together with them? I have to tell them straight, you're not suitable for this work. But they believe they can do it, but the most important thing is English proficiency being bilingual and having signing as well, both languages, some people have great English but poor signing, some have excellent signing skills but no English. There needs to be balance, there are only a few Deaf people who have both, it's the same with hearing interpreters, there are those with really hot English skills and lousy signing, or they have really hot signing but poor English, you need both. (Kat)

Kat gives some indication of the emergent status of the Deaf T/I profession. The industry could be regulated by gateway qualifications ensuring requisite skills were developed before working in the field. The people working this field at the moment are self-selecting (much like the non-Deaf interpreting profession), unless translations are commissioned by the Deaf community (for Web sites, DVDs, etc.).

## Participatory Perspective

Deaf T/Is construct the TL from a participatory perspective, either by using the first person to represent non-first person reported speech or action. Georgina describes how, "Deaf [T/Is] are more in the situation, hearing interpreters sign the information without being in it, without involving themselves." This is a feature common in unwritten languages (Ong 1982); the Deaf T/Is construct the action or dialogue as if involved in the scene rather than external to it. This participation forms part of a domesticated TL and therefore contributes to the Deaf translation norm. The Deaf T/Is do not use classifier constructions from an observer perspective, rather they construct a TL from a participant perspective in the action, or speech.

> English: a man from Bristol's recovering from a fractured skull eye socket and broken rib
>
> BSL: HELLO MAN FROM BRISTOL BAD-AWFUL INJURY HEAD EYE BREAK RIB
>
> (Kat headlines)

As shown in the example above, the Deaf T/Is give both a personal introduction and comment on the information. By foregrounding (Talmy 2000a, 2000b) the TL discourse with information such as BAD, the Deaf T/Is create rapport with the audience without subjectively commenting on the information.

> Yes, involved in the scene, but not commenting about the information, still impartial, if commenting the facial expression would be different, the body would lean forward. (Kim)

> Recently there was a lovely example of a news story, there was a farmer who went bankrupt because of foot and mouth, he had ten puppies, they were really sweet, really cute dogs. Well I saw it on one of the clips of video footage, so I was signing it and it was a sad story, but in the end it made you go "aah," so for the dog story I had to carefully balance the facial expression I used, I don't want to add my view onto the story line, I was there to interpret the TV news, so my views and opinions as Kat have to be removed. (Kat)

The Deaf T/Is use the empathetic and participatory language they consider appropriate for this genre.

## INTERPRETER PREFERENCES

The Deaf T/Is also work with hearing interpreters as service users to gain access to mainstream environments where BSL is not the language used for communication. In light of this, the interpreter preferences of the Deaf T/Is were explored and related to T/Is on the television. All of the

Deaf T/Is expressed ideas about their preferences, and each Deaf T/I mentioned different interpreters she prefers watching on television. Whether the interpreter is known to the Deaf T/Is and liked by them for their skills plays a major role in determining who they watch.

> Individuals have different styles, and I prefer different interpreters because of their individual styles. . . . If it is an interpreter I like then I will watch the interpreter, but otherwise I prefer to view the subtitles. (Kim)

These views are not much different from those expressed by service users of minority spoken language interpreters in the UK (Alexander et al. 2004). Some of the informants mention explicitly what it is they like or do not like.

> Hearing interpreters produce the information in their second language, so often you see a heavy influence carried over from their first language, as they convey the message from one language to the other, so the second language is damaged and influenced by the first language. Their [hearing interpreters] signing can have English structure, secondly maybe there are contextual errors because they listen to the [SL] information and panic, watching you think, "that's not right," and thirdly you watch their output/signing, have to concentrate on what they mean by using that grammatical structure, and it can be incomprehensible, the order can be confused, which isn't good. With some interpreters, they are confident and use lots of placement, whilst others don't use it at all. . . . Also some interpreters heavily use regional signs and I think that they need to be careful of that. (Clark)

From the informants, I discovered that a preferred interpreter creates a TL free from "translationeze," and this differs from interpreters who make deliberate decisions to represent the SL with marked language in order to bring mainstream concepts to the Deaf audience. The Deaf T/Is do not desire marked language, preferring instead metanotative features or individual style. However, the Deaf T/Is like some features of hearing interpreters' TL.

> I like him because he's daft with all of his facial expressions, I think it is amusing, but at the same time I can relax, he tries to change the structure with placement and facial expressions, and that's good, with his structure and dropping [omitting] things, he needs to be a little careful but I can take on board the information, so he's good it's clever how he changes it. (Clark)

Clark reinforces how individualistic styles contribute to interpreting preferences, although these interpreters need to ensure their language production is grammatical and follows some of the features of a Deaf translation style.

> Well, there are a few things, he uses BSL features, lots of facial expressions, he has a fluid style, it's very relaxed, easy to watch, it's not proper and formal but more relaxed and fluid, he uses a lot of placement, he uses a lot of possible BSL features for example, mm, maybe what would be called metaphors, and other areas that other interpreters don't use much he incorporates, a lot that's the differences that I recognise in him. (Clark)

> I think point one their [hearing interpreters] NMF facial expressions, which is related to the language [fluency]. (Kim)

The Deaf T/Is suggest that hearing interpreters need to move away from the translation or interpreting templates that were useful to them during training and as novice interpreters. These preferred changes depend on the amount of time the T/Is take to ensure they are able to restructure and change the information from the SL to create an appropriate TL.

> She can do more, but recently I have seen her just relaying the information, I realized that she has to do too much, so she just relays the information, but she should be more determined to change her output, but she is too exhausted [by doing too much]. (Clark)

Just "relaying" information is not enough to achieve a desired TL text. If the TL is manually no different from the English subtitles, then the subtitles are preferred by the Deaf T/Is.

Preference is also informed by the level of re-processing of the TL, presented by the hearing interpreters, that the Deaf T/Is have to undertake. The closer the hearing interpreters are to a translationeze contact variety of BSL, the more processing the Deaf T/Is have to do (Cokely 1992). For this processing to be successful, the Deaf T/Is rely on their level of English knowledge.

> I have two languages . . . means I can watch hearing interpreters with English [influenced BSL], their [way of thinking] in quotes . . . watch it, take it in board . . . it's hard . . . I have to think, grow a mental picture, concept . . . there's nothing, picture nothing . . . Deaf [T/Is] can picture the concept but that hearing [interpreter language gives] nothing. (Georgina)

> If you follow the order of the English on TV it means that you need to process the information twice before you understand the person, and

that's hard work doing that mental processing because it's not the language you are used to, so it's the same as in Britain we use a spoon and a knife and fork, if you go to Japanese or Chinese restaurant they use chopsticks and you need time to get used to them because you don't use them that often. It's the same with the order of the paragraphs, if you follow it exactly then it can be confusing, you have to use the audience's style. (Kat)

The information is streamed steadily and has a good flow so that it can be digested easily. Without that then you need to mentally interpret it because you cannot understand it as easily. (Clark)

Just relaying information puts the onus on the audience to understand and reprocess the information as fully as possible. Part of the problem may lie in how the T/Is conceptualize the information (explored in more detail later). Interpreters have to be trained, and they need to interact with the Deaf community to be able to produce a TL that presents information in the most relevant way.

## PRESENTING LIKE DEAF PEOPLE

The Deaf T/Is also perceive that of some hearing interpreters try too hard to produce language like a Deaf person and become over idiomatic.

Some of the hearing interpreters on television, they try too hard to be like Deaf people signing, but they shouldn't, they aren't, which makes it worse. I can't forget that they are interpreters, I want to forget that they are interpreters, but I feel that because they try so hard it becomes stilted/jerky/bitty, like chunk by chunk, and Deaf people don't want all those pauses, Deaf people need it to flow/to be smooth. (Kim)

In trying to be like Deaf people, the hearing T/Is overcompensate and mark their TL as something produced by a hearing T/I. The "jerkiness" reported by Kat suggests problems using appropriate prosodic features, and this will be examined in more detail later. One of the reasons that this overcompensation becomes a problem is that it is distracting and inhibits comprehension.

I think that hearing people shouldn't try to sign the same as Deaf people. No it's a fact, and it only takes one look to know that they are hearing, that's it, seriously, that's one point, but that doesn't mean that they can't be interpreters. If they sign well so that the information is beautiful and clear I can forget that they are interpreting because the information is clear, it means that I can make a connection [with the information], and it doesn't matter whether the interpreter is Deaf or hearing, I forget that they are interpreting and that's important. (Kim)

When the audience can focus on the information rather than the interpreter, then presence is achieved. This may seem to contradict the notion of presence being required according to the Deaf translation norm, but this presence is about being aware of one's part in presenting information. When constructing the TL one resists the idea of merely "relaying the information," but knows the public role being fulfilled (including the acknowledgement of one's own hearing status).

The Deaf T/Is do not have complete consensus regarding whether or not hearing interpreters should avoid emulating Deaf people. Some of the Deaf T/Is feel that hearing interpreters should strive to be like Deaf T/Is.

I think hearing interpreters should copy Deaf people exactly so they are the same as a Deaf person but it seems to be happening the other way round. Deaf people are copying interpreters. Why is that it should be the other way round and they should copy us? (Kat)

Kat does not, however, contradict the quote earlier from Kim suggesting that in trying too hard to be like Deaf people, the hearing T/Is caricature Deaf T/Is. Kat argues within the television medium, and perhaps more generally, that the hearing T/Is translation norm is dominant. If television is truly a domain where Deaf T/Is can work freely, and a Deaf translation norm exists that fulfils the needs of the community, then this is the model that should be emulated.

The Deaf translation norm places the greatest importance on the Deaf consumer understanding the TL information.

As a Deaf person I see a Deaf interpreter, and I just feel that I can make a connection with the information, and it can become like, "oh they are hearing, wow" [if you thought they were Deaf], lots of interpreters try to gradually adjust to be like Deaf people, that makes it worse, the audience can be puzzled and not understand, they try to be something and they shouldn't, it's important that they understand what the source language means and sign it clearly, to deliver the information so that the audience can engage with the information, and that means eventually the audience will forget the interpreter, and the audience will react that they thought the interpreter is Deaf and be pleasantly surprised that they are a hearing interpreter, "oh that's good, I didn't think that," but if they try to sign like a Deaf person it's like, you look them up and down, "what are you doing? I think that it's difficult, yeah, because trying to sign like a Deaf person is like a performance or acting. (Kim)

Kim gives voice to the idea that if the interpreter is understood and the TL is clear, this leads to acceptance of the interpreter. This acceptance involves some conferring of community membership because it is assumed the interpreter socializes enough within the community to achieve the associated degree of fluency. Instead of "dipping in and out," the interpreter shows commitment to the community by socializing, etc. These interpreters do not need to "try" to sign like a Deaf person but use their own "voice" in BSL or create enough presence to deliver the message clearly.

The Deaf T/Is who express a desire for hearing T/Is to present information like Deaf people relate this to the goal of the Deaf T/Is—to create a covert translation so the TL is unmarked; the TL appears as if it were an original text rather than a translation or interpretation. This is in accordance with preserving the difference of the minority language values against the mainstream (see chapter 2).

Yet it is not enough for the prosody of the language of the hearing T/I to be native looking. This is not enough to create a TL that presents information like the Deaf T/Is do. The hearing T/Is also have to have conceptualization competency.

> Some interpreters have same understanding as Deaf signing but still not with the development of a mental picture concept, they need to think what is target, create the mental picture concept . . . where is that? . . . the meaning, perhaps the meaning is translated . . . the structure good, but they use the wrong order, where is the development of a mental picture concept? (Georgina)

A different use of the prosody of the language also compounds conceptualization. A discussion in chapter 5 explores this conceptualization in greater depth.

Prosody provides a way of creating cohesion in signed languages (Jouison 1989; Metzger and Bahan 2001; Sandler 1999b), and this level of cohesion is raised by the informants.

> Well I think that we grew up signing and we have all the deep rules about facial expressions automatically, the hearing interpreters need to internalize them more, facial expressions, more and a lot deeper to give them more clearly, and by that I don't mean over-do it. It can be quite subtle, especially Clark if you look at him, there is lots of information,

and I know that because he uses his facial expression subtly, maybe one eye brow movement which means you know he is talking about the past, a completed action. I might not use a manual marker just an eyebrow movement, hearing interpreters aren't able to do that, they will sign "oh been talk about this in the past," so they add a manual component and add extra things, when Clark just does it with one eye brow movement, he has rich layers of information, it's really fantastic. (Georgina)

The Deaf T/Is feel this creates a better cohesion than hearing T/Is are able to produce, or at least creates cohesion in an efficient way within a time-constrained translation. This native fluency appears to be one of the features of a Deaf translation norm too.

The visual information from the accompanying video footage needs to be used in a relevant way to ensure the Deaf audience relates to the information.

It is better to add extra information, it is worth thinking about, if you are index a picture you can then say, "they are talking about a car and how a crash between two cars happened," or whatever, then look at the picture again, or do something like that. (Georgina)

The visual information forms part of the multimedia environment and can be used to construct language in a maximally relevant way, drawing upon the shared cognitive environment.

## Use of Eye Gaze

When referencing visual information broadcast simultaneously on the television screen, eye gaze can be used (Engberg-Pedersen 1993) so the audience looks at the information or maintains eye contact with the T/I. Looking at the screen can cause problems for the Deaf T/Is, depending on their confidence and memory skills.

Deaf T/I Clark is very confident when indexing the images on the screen and looking away, he is able to do this because he has such a good memory and as such does not need to rely on the autocue, whereas I rely on the autocue. Maybe I need to be more confident, but in this program Clark might save it [enable it to still be perceived] as a Deaf program because of the way that he uses all of the indexing. (Kat)

Kat not only describes how the referencing is useful, but also how this creates a more relevant TL. The referencing by indexing also creates a well-determined reference in contrast to the underdetermined reference of the English SL. Whereas the BSL specifies the reference by indexing the specific reference, the English relies on the audience to infer that the underspecified reference is the image being shown on the screen. The BSL reduces the cognitive effort of the constructed Deaf audience as it relies on the most relevant interaction between the linguistic message and the shared cognitive environment.

The T/Is need to be able to establish an appropriate eye gaze in the first place in order to use referencing in general and to interact with the multimedia environment.

> Sometimes when the interpreter is starting I feel hold on, and they just sign as fast as possible, what is better is when their gaze meets mine, and then moves away, and around, and then back to meet my gaze, etc., that feels comfortable to me, like when I'm chatting to you [the researcher], I don't stare at you, my gaze drifts around and that holds your gaze to pay attention to what I am saying, so the signer knows that they are allowed to look away from the addressee, that, that's okay, if that is done then that is great. Weaker people or those I don't like are those that just stare, because that is not natural, similarly with those that stare up off center, that's like, "oh dear, I'm over here, look at me," that spoils it, if you look at Deaf in-vision interpreters it's the eyes and eye gaze that are different. (Clark)

Part of conversation is the continual engagement of eye gaze with a conversational partner when eye gaze is not being used grammatically (Coates and Sutton-Spence 2001; Stone 2001; Sze 2004). The inappropriate use of eye gaze can act to distance the audience from the presenter or T/I. This lack of presence reduces the relevance of the TL and moves it away from a Deaf translation norm.

## Other Language Differences between Deaf and Hearing T/Is

As stated earlier, the Deaf T/Is believe one of the differences between their language construction and that of hearing T/Is is the use of non-manual features.

> I think possible extra difference what NMF . . . Deaf have many different facial expressions, can do subtle facial expressions, information is added by that . . . hearing interpreters sometimes sign but with no facial expres-sions, sign with blank faces, they forgot information there on the face can add information. (Georgina)

This behavior is attributed to two causes: first, the Deaf T/Is use prosody naturally as native users of BSL having acquired this naturally.

NMF, facial expressions, which are related to the language, they are making connections [cohesion], but I think it is to do with timing, no not timing, maybe it's because when I was growing up I acquired the physical body part of the language, I didn't hear anything at all, which means that my language was already eyes, based on my eyes seeing, and connected with my thought processes, which were connected to my physical body, my body moving when I sign naturally, without conscious thought, nothing, just signing and moving, in the same way when you drive, using the gear stick and steering, you do without thinking, yeah like that, which means that signing is the same as that okay. (Kim)

Second, the hearing T/Is are listening to the spoken English of the newsreader, rather than reading the autocue, and this influences their TL.

But with hearing interpreters they have to listen, then think, and process, and change the information, and try to make that connection, which is odd, and they don't look natural, maybe because sound is interfering, so that when they process the information that affects them. (Kim)

These nonmanual features of BSL can be affective, adverbial, adjectival, or prosodic. The Deaf T/Is do not need to think of specific prosodic features when translating, whereas this area is identified as more conscious for hearing T/Is. Here the additional factor of listening to the newsreader and then interpreting, rather than using the autocue as a guide and delivering something practised as a translation previously, comes into play.

From the data it appears the hearing T/Is have a well-prepared interpretation driven by the spoken message rather than a practiced translation using the autocue as a memory aid. It is worth highlighting the different processing tasks the Deaf and hearing T/Is undertake with prescripted rendering (explored in greater depth in chapter 6). The Deaf T/Is read the English script, relating it to the video footage, and then render the information in BSL. The hearing interpreters listen to the English news reports as preparation, watching the footage with the accompanying voice-over, and then render the spoken English into BSL.

Other areas of poor use of prosody by the hearing interpreters are affirmation and negation.

The first one of nodding to affirm, or secondly of headshakes to negate are contrastive, make it easy to spot, lack of NMF, if they [hearing interpreters] use less NMF then you are not sure if something is or is not true, double negatives are also confusing, we [Deaf T/Is] change them because we know this, those are two of the main differences. (Clark)

Again, this could be attributed to BSL being the hearing T/Is' weaker language and because the TL is prepared differently. By listening to the spoken English, even if just to remind them of the script, the hearing T/Is undergo a different process. The hearing T/Is listen to a piece of language with prosody, whereas the Deaf T/Is are reading from an autocue with no prosody. In spoken language interpreting the SL can influence the prosody of the TL (Shlesinger 1994). Reading the English written script allows the Deaf T/Is to prosodically segment the information appropriately in BSL without any prosodic influence from English.

If the hearing T/Is use the newsreader as the main SL and the script as preparation material only, this implies they are interpreting "live." They are processing online unlike the Deaf T/Is who do not necessarily do much processing online. This online processing reduces the T/I's ability to include some of the prosodic features prepared in a translation. These features (prosody and intonation) are discussed in greater depth in the next section.

## Prosody and Intonation

In light of the reported differences in the use of NMF by Deaf and hearing T/Is, the use of blinking and the use of head movements have been examined when these actions mark the beginning and ending of phrases, and where phrasal units were nested within larger phrasal or discourse units.

Two different types of interpreted BSL data were analyzed: broadcast news and TAPs. The news allowed for an "ecologically" valid analysis of nonexperimental data, and the TAPs allowed a greater analysis of the process related to the output; the TAPs also allow for direct comparison of all the T/Is.

## The Degree of Language Preparedness

As noted by Sze (2004), spontaneous language uses blinks differently from prepared language. The presence of different types of blinks, specifically hesitations and false starts (type five blinks), gives us insight into the nature of the TL itself. This is supported by the comments of the informants and the researcher coding for intersubjective reliability; the Deaf native BSL-users likened the blinking and head movements to commas and full-stops.

## Types of Blinking Activity

Sze (2004) found additional blink categories to Wilbur (1994), indicating a difference between prepared and spontaneous language. Examining the types of blinking activity helps analyze whether the TL has features associated with prepared or spontaneous signed language texts. This indicates the apparent level of preparedness within a Deaf translation norm and differentiates between translation and interpretation. It might also indicate differing levels of fluency or the influence of the prosody of the SL.

The two types of data, live television data and TAP data, can be further divided: within the television data, into either final headlines or weekly news reviews, and within the TAP data, into shorter stories and one long story. About 6 minutes (347 seconds) of four Deaf T/Is rendering English headline news data into BSL was analyzed. Within that time, the Deaf T/Is blink 100 times giving an average blink rate of 0.29 blinks per second. Table 5.1 shows the different types of blinks noted in the data.

TABLE 5.1. *Deaf Headlines Blinking Categories*

| Blink Type | No. (and %) |
| --- | --- |
| Physiological | 3 |
| Boundary sensitive | 89 |
| Co-occurring with head/eye movement | 0 |
| Voluntary | 8 |
| Hesitations and false starts | 0 |
| Total | 100 |

Figure 5.1 provides an example of a physiological blink, where the "v" represents the blink, the "single" represents the head movement, and the capitalized gloss represents the manual component of BSL.

The blink does not occur at a boundary, and is neither lexically nor semantically motivated. It co-occurs with the downward movement of the forearm and involves the elbow joint (Sze 2004). Figure 5.2 provides an example of boundary sensitive blinks.

The blinks in this example occur before each noun phrase, British Airways and Air France, and at a boundary. As can be seen, the blink occurs over less than half of the manual sign and so this is taken to be a boundary sensitive blink.

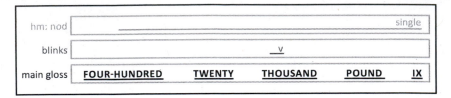

| hm: nod | | | | | single |
|---|---|---|---|---|---|
| blinks | | | v | | |
| main gloss | **FOUR-HUNDRED** | **TWENTY** | **THOUSAND** | **POUND** | **IX** |

FIGURE 5.1. *Kat headlines physiological blink*

Translation of a sentence meaning, "the four hundred and twenty thousand pounds"

| hm: nod | single | single | single | single |
|---|---|---|---|---|
| blinks | v | | v | |
| main gloss | **FLY** | **BRITISH** | **AIRWAYS** | **AIR** **FRANCE** |

FIGURE 5.2. *Rebecca headlines boundary sensitive blinks*

Translation of a sentence meaning, "flight with British Airways and Air France"

Figure 5.3 provides an example of a voluntary blink.

| hm: nod | | single | single | single |
|---|---|---|---|---|
| blinks | | v | | |
| main gloss | **E** **PERSON** | **SHOCK** | **RETIRE** | **THROUGH** |

FIGURE 5.3. *Kim headlines voluntary blink*

Translation of sentence meaning, ". . . in him. A shock retirement because"

The voluntary blink occurs during the sign SHOCK and is semantically motivated, adding the additional information of surprise.

In the headlines, the blinks are predominantly boundary sensitive, with some voluntary blinks (semantically or lexically driven), and a few physiological blinks. This suggests a high level of preparedness. In one example of a hearing T/I rendering final headline news from English into BSL, a total of 71 seconds contains 66 blinks, giving is a blink rate of 0.93 blinks per second (much higher than the 0.29 blinks per second for the Deaf T/Is). We can see the examples of his blink categories in figures 5.4 and 5.5.

| hm: nod |  |  |  | single |  | single |
|---|---|---|---|---|---|---|
| blinks | v | v | v | v | v | v |
| main gloss | GIRL |  | BACK | HOME | SAFE | IX |

FIGURE 5.4. *Sole hearing headlines physiological blink and boundary sensitive blink*

Translation of sentence meaning, "girls back home safe here"

The blink in the middle of the sign GIRL is motivated by the movement of the hand to the face, neither adding semantic meaning nor being lexically driven. As this blink occurs in the middle of the sign, it is a physiological blink (category I from Sze 2004). This blink is followed by a blink marking a boundary, hence a boundary sensitive blink.

| hm: nod |  | single |  | single |
|---|---|---|---|---|
| blinks | v | v | v | v |
| main gloss | IX | SEEM | HAVE | GUN-FIRE++ |

FIGURE 5.5. *Sole Hearing headlines voluntary blink*

Translation of sentence meaning, "there it seems there was gunfire"

The voluntary blink co-occurs with the shooting of the gun and is lexically motivated. The numbers of blinks per category are shown in table 5.2.

TABLE 5.2. *Sole Hearing Headlines Blinks Categories with Deaf Blinks from Table 5.1*

| Blink Type | No. | % | Deaf % |
|---|---|---|---|
| Physiological | 8 | 12 | 3 |
| Boundary sensitive | 45 | 68 | 89 |
| Voluntary | 13 | 20 | 8 |
| Hesitations and false starts | 0 | 0 | 0 |
| Total | 66 | 100 | 100 |

Two features are immediately clear: the blink rate is much higher for the hearing T/I, but the categories are ranked in the same order of occurrence, that is, boundary sensitive blinks occur the most, then voluntary blinks, and finally physiological blinks. Although the hearing T/I has a relatively similar distribution of blinks, there is greater emphasis from voluntary blinks and less segmentation of the boundaries. The TL text of the hearing T/I is marked differently from the Deaf T/Is' TL text: the Deaf T/Is demonstrate better preparedness than the hearing T/I. This difference can partially be attributed to a different process and to the interference of SL intonation.

We know from Sze (2004) that with higher rate of blinks more blinks occur at nonintonational phrase boundaries, and with lower blink rates a larger proportion of blinks occur at intonational phrases. Sze attributes this lower blink rate to higher visual attention demand, and finds higher blink rates in monologues and lower blink rates in conversation. In interviews the Deaf T/Is identified their translation process (in comparison with the interpreting and listening process of hearing T/Is) and its effect on the TL. Even though the news is a monologue, the greater attentional demand for Deaf T/Is (of reading the autocue) influences the creation of a TL text. The TL is more like a conversational piece, because of a lower blinking rate when compared with hearing T/Is, which creates a greater connection with the audience. This factor may contribute to both the presence and the prosody of the Deaf T/Is' TL.

Blink analysis alone cannot identify whether this difference is solely a consequence of reading the autocue, or also motivated by Deaf T/Is wanting to create a greater rapport with the audience. The interview accounts and other anecdotal reports do, however, comment on the connection felt when watching the Deaf T/Is. As such, one can read this as a purposeful combination of factors, even if the connection is made because the audience is subconsciously aware that Deaf T/Is are reading the autocue as demonstrated by their blinking activity.

## News Review

The analysis includes almost 9 minutes (519 seconds) of three Deaf T/Is rendering English into BSL. This includes ninety-nine seconds of a Deaf T/I as an anchor and 420 seconds (7 minutes) of two Deaf T/Is as reporters. The average blink rate is 0.45 blinks per second, higher than that of the headlines, suggesting either higher visual attention demand during the headlines, or (due to longer stories and greater preparation time) less prosodically marked text. As the Deaf T/Is have stated in the interviews, the autocue is used as a memory aid and gaze is more appropriate from Deaf T/Is than hearing T/Is. This would support the construction of a prosodically unmarked monologue.

In figures 5.6, 5.7, and 5.8 we can see examples of the news-review blinks. Figure 5.6 shows an example of a physiological blink.

| hm: nod | le | single | single | s |
|---|---|---|---|---|
| blinks | | v  v | | |
| main gloss | HOW | HITH | FINGERPRINTS | CHECKING |

FIGURE 5.6. *Georgina uses physiological blinking during the weekly news review.*

The double blink, in the middle of a sign, is neither lexically nor semantically motivated and does not occur at a boundary. The hands move up toward the face and motivating startle reflex blinking, or the eyes needs moisture. Figure 5.7 shows two examples of boundary sensitive blinks.

As seen in figure 5.7, the blinks occur at the end of one sentence and at the end of a subject preceding a predicate. In figure 5.8, a voluntary blink occurs during the manual sign DARK and is lexically motivated.

The sign DARK is intensified with the semantically related blink acting as an adverbial.

| hm: nod | single | | | single | single | |
|---|---|---|---|---|---|---|
| blinks | | v | | | v | |
| main gloss | **BOTH** | **WHY** | **BOTH** | | **LINK** | **WHAT** |

FIGURE 5.7. *Kat uses sensitive blinks during the weekly news review.*

Translation of sentence meaning, "both of them, both of them the relationship between them being . . ."

| hm: nod | | | | | single |
|---|---|---|---|---|---|
| blinks | | | | v | |
| main gloss | **BLACK** | **OVERHEAD** | **EYE-HOLE** | **DARK** | **CLOTHES** |

FIGURE 5.8. *Georgina shows a voluntary blink during the news week show.*

Translation of the sentence meaning, "a black balaclava and dark clothes"

The distribution of blinking types can be seen in table 5.3, with the number and percentage of blinking activity shown, along with the percentages from the headlines to provide comparison.

About 8 minutes (468 seconds) of weekly news-review data for four hearing T/Is was analyzed, with an average of 0.50 blinks per second, only 0.05 higher than the Deaf T/Is. The distribution of blinking is different as seen when comparing the number and percentage of blinking activity as shown in table 5.4.

TABLE 5.3. *Deaf Blinking Activity in Weekly News Reviews Compared with Headlines Blinking*

| Blink Type | No. | % | Headlines No & % |
|---|---|---|---|
| Physiological | 8 | 3 | 3 |
| Boundary sensitive | 199 | 86 | 89 |
| Co-occurring with head/eye movement | 1 ~ | 0 | 0 |
| Voluntary | 24 | 10 | 8 |
| Hesitations and false starts | 0 | 0 | 0 |
| Total | 232 | ~100 | 100 |

TABLE 5.4. *Hearing Blinking Activity in Weekly News Reviews Compared with the Blinking Activity of Deaf and Hearing Headlines*

| Blink Type | No. | % | Hearing Headlines % | Deaf Headlines No & % |
|---|---|---|---|---|
| Physiological | 36 | 8 | 12 | 3 |
| Boundary sensitive | 165 | 35 | 68 | 89 |
| Co-occurring with head/eye movement | 0 | 0 | 0 | 0 |
| Voluntary | 272 | 57 | 20 | 8 |
| Hesitations and false starts | 1 | ~ 0 | 0 | 0 |
| Total | 232 | 100 | 100 | 100 |

In the news headlines, the hearing T/Is maintain the same ranking as the Deaf T/Is, albeit with a higher blinking frequency. However, this relationship changes in the weekly news review. The Deaf and hearing T/Is have a similar blinking frequency, but a different ranking of blinking type. The hearing T/Is predominantly use voluntary blinks, while the Deaf T/Is still predominantly use boundary sensitive blinks. This overuse of voluntary blinking indicates lack of fluency in the hearing T/Is.

Any blinking occurring over more than half of a sign constitutes a voluntary blink (Wilbur 1994, Sze 2004). As shown in figure 5.9, however, the hearing T/Is use some periodic blinking over signs neither lexically nor semantically driven. This could either indicate an over generalisation of a prosodic rule, language processing activity (and hence an interpretation not a translation), or some stimulus in the environment inducing eye wetting (a physiological blink).

| hm: nod | | | | | | single | single | |
|---------|---|---|---|---|---|--------|--------|---|
| blinks | v | v v v v | v | v v | | | v v |
| main gloss | COACH | DRIVER | | TOLD | GUILTY | | | |

FIGURE 5.9. *Hearing blinking during weekly news review*

Translation of sentence meaning, "a coach driver was told they were guilty"

The distribution of blinking activity for the hearing T/Is rendering the weekly news review is different from that of the Deaf T/Is and from the hearing T/Is' headline blinking activity. The hearing headlines T/I had previously spoken with me and had knowledge of this research. He prepared the rendering of the SL into BSL using manual rehearsal in light of my preliminary findings and this could be a contributing factor to the increased level of preparedness seen in the TL text.

One of the hearing T/Is reports she read the autocue rather than listening to the English in the weekly news review. Although their data have been included in the tables above, it is presented in isolation (see table 5.5).

Although not enough data for statistical analysis is available, a trend seems to emerge. This trend is much closer to the distribution of blinks seen for the Deaf T/Is when doing the news weekly review, suggesting a greater level of preparedness. However, the process with which the T/Is approach the rendering of the SL clearly seems to influence the TL text.

**TAPS**

Next the types of blinking activity for the Deaf and hearing T/Is in the TAPs are examined. The Deaf and hearing T/Is rendered the same script

TABLE 5.5. *H01 Blinking Activity for Weekly News Review*

| Blink Type | No. 01 | % | Deaf Headlines No & % |
|---|---|---|---|
| Physiological | 0 | 0 | 3 |
| Boundary sensitive | 26 | 81 | 89 |
| Co-occurring with head/ eye movement | 0 | 0 | 0 |
| Voluntary | 5 | 16 | 8 |
| Hesitations and false starts | 1 | 3 | 0 |
| Total | 32 | 100 | 100 |

into BSL, which allowed a comparison of the numbers and frequencies of blinking, with the T/Is being free to approach the texts in the same way, under the same conditions. The TAP data contains 692 seconds (about 11 minutes) of three Deaf T/Is: Kim, 200 seconds; Georgina, 245 seconds; and Rebecca, 247 seconds. It also contains about 4 minutes (239 seconds) of one Deaf (hearing) T/I and 210 seconds (almost 4 minutes) of one hearing T/I.

The data in table 5.6 show no differences between the distributions of blink types for the Deaf and hearing T/Is. The Deaf T/Is have two instances of type five, occurring when there were problems with the speed of the autocue. Other than that, the T/Is exclusively have blink types two and four, suggesting a prepared piece of BSL.

The blink rate range for the Deaf T/Is is 0.24–0.30 s$^{-1}$ (blinks per second), for the Deaf (hearing) T/I 0.5 s$^{-1}$, and for the hearing T/I 0.53 s$^{-1}$. Considering the higher incidence of type two, the hearing T/Is have shorter chunks than the Deaf T/Is. Once again, this difference could be mediated by reading the autocue versus listening to spoken English. Either way, lower blink rates give longer segments than higher blink rates. The shorter segments of the hearing T/Is are indicative of interpreted language (Shlesinger 1995), the longer segments of the Deaf T/Is are more indicative of a translation.

In table 5.7, the Deaf (hearing) T/I and the hearing T/I from the TAPs are separated to identify any differences and any interaction between the L1 or L2 status. While the Deaf (hearing) T/I has BSL as L1 and English as L2, he listens to the English for the prompt, following the same process as the hearing T/I, rather than reading the English as the Deaf T/Is do.

Table 5.7 shows a higher percentage of boundary blinking for both of the (audiologically) hearing T/Is. The blink rates for the shorter stories are

TABLE 5.6. *Deaf, Deaf (Hearing), and Hearing T/Is Blinking Activity in TAPs*

| Blink type | Kim (D) | | Georgina (D) | | Rebecca (D) | | Arthur (Dh) | | David (h) | |
|---|---|---|---|---|---|---|---|---|---|---|
| | No. | % | No. | % | No. | % | No. | % | No. | % |
| Physiological | 0 | 0 | 0 | 0 | 0 | 0 | 0 | 0 | 0 | 0 |
| Boundary sensitive | 48 | 100 | 74 | 93 | 65 | 94 | 109 | 91 | 104 | 94 |
| Co-occurring with head/eye movement | 0 | 0 | 0 | 0 | 0 | 0 | 0 | 0 | 0 | 0 |
| Voluntary | 0 | 0 | 4 | 5 | 4 | 6 | 11 | 9 | 7 | 6 |
| Hesitations and false starts | 0 | 0 | 2 | 2 | 0 | 0 | 0 | 0 | 0 | 0 |
| Total | 48 | 100 | 80 | 100 | 69 | 100 | 120 | 100 | 111 | 100 |

**TABLE 5.7.** *Dh and H Blinking Activity Separated for TAPs*

| Blink Type | Dh | | H | |
|---|---|---|---|---|
| | No. | % | No. | % |
| Boundary sensitive | 109 | 91 | 104 | 94 |
| Voluntary | 11 | 9 | 7 | 6 |
| Total | 120 | 100 | 111 | 100 |

0.74 per second for the Deaf (hearing) T/I and 0.76 for the hearing T/I. For the longer stories, the blink rate is 0.41 for both of the T/Is. The high level of boundary sensitive blinks suggests a high level of preparation, uninhibited by listening to the English SL rather than reading the autocue.

Both of the blink rates for the Deaf T/Is fall within the same range for dialogue in Sze's (2004) study and the hearing T/Is blink rate varies —rating as monologue blinking (0.79–0.52) for the shorter stories and dialogue blinking (0.60–0.47) for the longer stories. While a greater difference exists for shorter stories, the blink rates converge for longer stories. This finding suggests that it may be easier to create a prosodically unmarked monologue TL text when the stories are longer and there is less time constraint on the production of the TL.

The Deaf T/Is and hearing T/Is exhibit different types of blinking activity in all of the data. There are several possible contributory factors. One is the differences mentioned previously,

the act of reading = higher visual attention demand = lower blink rate

the act of listening = lower visual attention demand = higher blink rate

Interference from spoken English may be another factor: the spoken English has prosody that the hearing T/Is hear and that may well influence the production of the TL.

## Types of Head Movement Activity

The head movement activity includes head nods and other head movements occurring at a lexical, phrasal, and discourse level and demonstrates the level of cohesion the T/Is create in the TL. Head movements, both at a phrasal and discourse level, show the level of interrelationship of the ideas in the TL and highlight the differing levels of control of the TL on the part of the T/Is.

| hm: nod | single | | | single |
|---|---|---|---|---|
| blinks | | | | v |
| main gloss | ASK++ | RESEARCH | OVER | SAFE |

FIGURE 5.10. *Example of verb phrase head movements from Rebecca's headlines*

Translation of sentence meaning, "an enquiry regarding the safety"

The other head movements can be split into two different categories: either boundary sensitive head movements or lexical head movements. The boundary sensitive head movements overarch and interrelate a variety of different constituent boundaries, including subject-predicate, predicate-predicate, verb phrase (see fig. 5.10), noun phrase, connectives (see fig. 5.11), and pronouns.

| hm: nod | single | single | |
|---|---|---|---|
| blinks | | | v |
| main gloss | BYPASS | THROUGH | BAD |

FIGURE 5.11. *Example of lexical and connective head movement from Rebecca's headline*

Translation of sentence meaning, ". . . bypass because it's bad . . ."

Head movements are also used with semantic and lexical motivations, including positive affirmation, negative affirmation, temporal information, and movement information. Some of the head movements occur above at a lexical level and combinations of lexical and phrasal head movements also exist.

In figure 5.12, Kim tilts her head to the right while signing WEST and staying to the right to sign SCOTLAND before returning to a neutral space. So we have a lexical movement initially to the right and then staying right to contain the noun phrase. The noun is overarched by a head nod separating the noun from the adjective.

| hp: tilt side | | | | right |
|---|---|---|---|---|
| hm: nod | | | | single |
| blinks | | | | |
| main gloss | SEAWEED | IX | WEST | SCOTLAND |

FIGURE 5.12. *Example from Kim's TAP of a lexical and phrasal head movement*

Translation of sentence meaning, "the seaweed there in the West of Scotland"

Similarly, in figure 5.13, Rebecca has two lexical head movements that are both examples of echo phonology. The signs FOCUS and ENVIRONMENT have head movements echoing the movement pathway of the manual sign. These head movements happen within a larger unit that is over-arched by the right side tilt of the head to prosodically mark the phrase.

| hp: tilt side | | | | right |
|---|---|---|---|---|
| hm: nod | | | single | single |
| blinks | v | | | |
| main gloss | PERSON-CL | WHO | FOCUS | ENVIRONMENT |

FIGURE 5.13. *Example from Rebecca's TAP of lexical and phrasal head movement*

Translation of sentence meaning, "person who specializes in the environment"

Both of these examples move us toward understanding how the TL is constructed on a prosodic level. If the Deaf T/Is mark the information differently, not only in their blinking frequencies and distribution, but also in the way information is prosodically marked in phrase and discourse units, then this informs us of the operational norms (Toury 1978/1995) of a Deaf translation norm.

Some examples show different directions of phrasal head movements nested within each other (see fig. 5.14). This creates something analogous to a relative clause (Wilbur, 1994, Wilbur and Patschke, 1999). Here we see an upward movement of the head, torso back, in the initial prosodic move, the torso remains back and the head moves to down and right relating the next information to OTHER. It then goes through a cycle in this down position, moves up again after FISH, and then the body moves forward after THING+++.

| hp: tilt fr/bk | | | | | | | | back |
| --- | --- | --- | --- | --- | --- | --- | --- | --- |
| hm: nod | | | | | | single | | |
| blinks | | | | v | | | | |
| main gloss | NOW | MEANS | IXe | OTHER | OUR | GROWING-PLANTS | FISH | THINGS++ |

FIGURE 5.14. *Example from Georgina's TAP of nested head movements*

Translation of sentence meaning, "now this means here the other things, our plants and fish, various things like that"

These nested head movements are also found in the television data as seen in figure 5.15.

| hp: tilt fr/bk | | | | | | front |
| --- | --- | --- | --- | --- | --- | --- |
| hp: tilt side | | | | right | | |
| hm: nod | | | | | single | |
| blinks | | | | | | |
| main gloss | BEEN | PUT-UNDER-HIDDEN | OVER | SIX | MILLION CIGARETTES | IX |

FIGURE 5.15. *Example from Kat's headlines of a nested structure*

Translation of sentence meaning, "stashed away over six million cigarettes there"

In figure 5.15, the head tilt forward creates a discourse segment of the whole sentence. The side movement to the right interrelates OVER SIX MILLION, and the head nod moves back and up before finishing both the head nod and the front head tilt.

These nested structures only occur with the Deaf T/Is; neither the Deaf (hearing) T/I nor the hearing T/Is in either the television data or the TAPs exhibit them. For the TAPs, with the script and footage being the same for all the T/Is, this demonstrates a clear difference between Deaf and (audiologically) hearing T/Is. Examples of prosodic marking of negation also occur within a larger nested unit marked by the head position as in figure 5.16. The head moves back and down with the first sign SEE and then performs a single lexically motivated backward nod during the sign RECENT. The head then tilts right during the sign SEE and maintains that position.

| | | | | | | | | |
|---|---|---|---|---|---|---|---|---|
| hp: tilt fr/bk | | | | | | | | front |
| hp: tilt side | | | | | | | | right |
| hm: nod | | single | | | | | | |
| blinks | v | | | v | | | | v |
| neg | | | | | | | | neg |
| main gloss | IRELAND | SEE | RECENTLY | SEE | CAN | STAY | WILL-NOT | DISAPPEAR |

FIGURE 5.16. *Example from Kim's TAP of negation within nested head movements*

Translation of sentence meaning, "in Ireland, as seen recently, we saw can take hold and not be got rid of"

In figure 5.16, the prosodic negation headshake *neg* happens in the lower position after which the head returns to a neutral position. We also see the interaction between the head movements and blinking activity at boundaries, constructing a superarticulatory array. The blink after the second SEE is boundary sensitive, occurring at subject predicate boundary. The next blink occurs at the end of the predicate, where all of the overarching head movements then also stop. With the Deaf (hearing) and hearing T/Is, this type of interaction between head movements and blinking, where larger structures are divided into smaller units, can be seen in figure 5.17. We do not, however, see the nested structures that the Deaf T/Is perform.

Figure 5.17 shows echo phonology head movement for the first two signs (NOW and PERSON-CL), followed by a lexical head movement on the sign SOLDIER, a predicate, then a boundary blink between BEFORE and BEEN (both temporal markers).

| hp: tilt fr/bk | | | | | front |
|---|---|---|---|---|---|
| hm: nod | | single | single | single | |
| blinks | | | | | ∨ |
| main gloss | NOW (DM) | PERSON-CL | SOLDIER | BEFORE | BEEN |

FIGURE 5.17. *Example from Arthur's TAP showing head movements and blinks*

Translation of sentence meaning, "now, a person, a soldier previously has . . ."

All of these signs are overarched by a forward head tilt marking a larger unit. Some interaction occurs between the different prosodic parts, but no nested structures, such as a forward or backward tilt combined with a left or right tilt to create larger discourse units, are made by the hearing T/Is. The Deaf T/Is create a higher amount of cohesion at a discourse level using spatial prosody.

## Frequency of Head Movements

As shown earlier, and as with blinking, head movement activity can be separated into different categories. These categories are lexical head movements accounted for by echo phonology, phrasal head movements, and discourse movements. Counting the largest overarching head movements, and not counting those nested inside the largest overarching head movements, we see how this prosodic feature is used to create text cohesion. Fewer overarching head movements per second indicate marked segments (noun phrase, verb phrase, sentence, etc.) are longer and constitute larger phrasal or discoursal units (Boyes-Braem 1999). This implies that these head movements act as boundary markers for larger discourse units, with phrase units contained within them. If these overarching head movements are not present, then the longest head movement will mark a smaller phrasal unit rather than a discourse unit. If there are a high number of phrasal units being marked, this indicates no overarching discourse head movements are being produced and discourse units are being omitted.

Table 5.8 shows the difference between Deaf and hearing T/Is for the television data and the TAPs data.

TABLE 5.8. *Deaf and Hearing T/Is' Overarching Head Movements*

| Data Type | D | | Dh | | H | |
|---|---|---|---|---|---|---|
| | No. | No. S | No. | No. S | No. | No. S |
| Headlines | 283 | 0.82 | | | 87 | 1.23 |
| Weekly news review | 246 | 0.71 | | | 440 | 0.94 |
| TAPs short stories | 195 | 0.95 | 82 | 1.14 | 80 | 1.07 |
| TAPs longer stories | 357 | 0.79 | 103 | 0.62 | 134 | 0.99 |

The general trend for the Deaf T/Is to have a ratio of less than one head movement per second with these head movements containing small, head-movement units within them (as seen in figures 5.14, 5.15, and 5.16) can be seen in table 5.8. Hearing T/Is are less able to create these longer discourse units in headlines or shorter stories. Once again, it seems the main difference between the Deaf and hearing T/Is is the control exercised over their prosodic marking of the BSL TL.

Although hearing T/Is can use lexical and phrasal head movements in the TL, they are not using overarching head movements to join these together in larger discourse units. This could simply indicate non-native usage and an L2 learner "accent," or it could be a consequence of the influence of the prosody of the SL on the TL text. This supports the intuitions of Deaf T/Is in the interview data. The lack of coherence in the way concepts are co-joined prosodically creates the disjointedness, which is discussed in greater depth in more detail later. Kim explains, "with interpreters it's like seeing isolated [jigsaw] pieces of the picture."

Ultimately, while the hearing T/Is use some of the prosodic features of BSL, they do not use them in the same way as Deaf T/Is. For a Deaf translation norm to be successfully achieved, the T/I must render the information using the appropriate discoursal prosody. This prosody ensures the relationship between the ideas in the text is made explicit and therefore reduces the cognitive effort of the constructed audience.

The next chapter looks closer at the process of the T/Is and the conceptualization of the TL in relation to the constructed audience. The T/Is' approach to the rendering of the SL into the TL in the TAPs will be examined, and the different types of enrichment and impoverishment (measuring differences in conceptualizing the TL) will be identified.

## Chapter 6

# The Translation and Interpretation Process

Differences occur in the translation and interpretation that lead to similarities and differences in the construction of the TL by the T/Is. As seen in chapter 3, translations and interpretations can be judged against the SL, the TL or, by using relevance theory (Hatim 2001) according to different linguistic and cultural needs for implicitness and explicitness. The final judgment should include whom the T/Is construct as the pragmatic other (Ruuskanen 1996) and the ways the Deaf and hearing T/Is conceptualize the information. It should also include translation shifts and the inferential processes that occur because of grammatical need (Sequeiros 1998, 2002) and because of the visual information present in the cognitive environment found in the screened video footage of the news.

## THE TARGET AUDIENCE

All of the Deaf T/Is are from Deaf families of at least two generations and draw upon this cultural resource in the construction of their target audience. As discussed previously, these T/Is show no desire to construct the TL constrained by the subtitles, by order, or by formal equivalence. The Deaf T/Is use their experience of re-telling information to relatives at home and Deaf friends at the Deaf club to inform the construction of their TL. They ensure the language used is broadly communicative and caters to a wide variety of Deaf people, addressing different language competence and educational backgrounds.

In the interviews of hearing T/Is, a theme emerged. They do not adjust their register or level of language for different audiences. This is also discussed in terms of socializing, or "dipping in and out of the Deaf community," as Clark notes. The Deaf T/Is perceive this difference as a lack of engagement with the Deaf community and a lack of exposure to a broad spectrum of Deaf sign language users, which compounds the linguistic inflexibility of the hearing interpreters. The hearing T/Is are unable to domesticate the TL to the same degree as Deaf T/Is and cannot draw from the personal experience of modifying their language for different parts of the Deaf community.

The informants also commented on the different target audiences that Deaf and hearing interpreters construct when interpreting to the camera. This is similar to Ruuskanen's (1996) idea of equivalence (mentioned earlier). She suggests there is no single meaning of equivalence, and equivalence has to be influenced by whom the translator imagines, is told, or constructs the audience to be. Any explications made by the T/Is in the TL aim to yield greater relevance to a broad section of the Deaf community constructed as the target audience or "pragmatic other." The interpreters construct this target audience according to their experiences, the goal they give to their translations, and, perhaps within a Deaf community context, whether or not the T/I is a community member. The T/Is who are core members of the Deaf community target the pragmatic other in a way they perceive eases the comprehension of the TL by the constructed audience. This in turn licenses the explicit rendering of internal enrichments, which become interlingual enrichment. Sequeiros (2002, 1083) explains that, "interlingual enrichment is more acceptable to readers that are willing to trade some loss of faithfulness in the translation for ease of comprehension and interpretation." The pragmatic other has an influence on the contextual assumptions the interpreters make (Gutt 1991). This, in turn, should also mean differences between the Deaf and hearing T/Is in their TL output and may well be something that can be changed through training or dissemination of this finding.

When asked about the ideal audience, Rebecca, one of the Deaf T/I informants in the interviews said, "the audience I aim for is those that don't understand English at all . . . it is better that they watch the information in BSL so it is clear." The T/Is have no influence on stories chosen and little power over the length of time given to ensure an effective translation. Within these constraints, they rank clarity as the most important goal. The T/Is are also aware that non-Deaf people are watching the television; they cannot afford to offend their sensibilities. This is well expressed by Kat's comment on the first interpretation of the Queen's Christmas speech in the 1980s, "the Queen was very solemn and the Deaf person had lots of facial expression because it was BSL and it was slated really. . . it was the hearing audience that disapproved of it so who is right or wrong?"

Even so, the space inhabited by the Deaf T/Is during televised broadcasts is used so the Deaf constructed audience can have their language, culture, and values reinforced; viewers who understand the language are able to see a clear act of resistance against the wider world that increases the status of sign language and maintains community and ethnic values. Identity plays a clear role in this, although it is not clear as yet that the exact nature of that role.

> I've seen some Deaf interpreters on TV, and you can tell by watching they are not native BSL users sometimes, hearing people sign better than Deaf people sometimes, it depends on the individual and how well they have mixed and acquired the language, there are some Deaf interpreters I'm not comfortable watching. (Kat)

Kat identifies that, for the Deaf T/Is, there are problems with the language of non-native users of BSL and also possibly identity; Rebecca represents the other informants' opinions on hearing interpreters, "hearing interpreters really shouldn't be on TV . . . when a Deaf person can do the job."

Taken together, this shows the complex nature of who is seen to be desirable as a T/I on television: just to be a Deaf person is not the answer. Both skills and attitudinal factors are important. Moreover, if the traditional role of native BSL users within school is to ensure BSL is passed on to further generations (Denmark 2002), Deaf T/Is may also understand the public role of the T/I on television to be a continuance of this goal. Ultimately, the Deaf community does not choose who works as a T/I on television, hearing institutions exercise control over BSL when seen publicly on the television.

## DEAF AND HEARING CONCEPTUALIZATION OF THE TL

Georgina speaks for the Deaf T/Is when she mentions she doesn't "know how hearing interpreters create their mental pictures. I can talk about Deaf interpreters as one of them, or how I understand/receive information from hearing interpreters." The Deaf T/Is rely on their ability to think as Deaf people and use this to construct the TL. Georgina expresses how empathy based on shared experience is crucial and often found in "high context cultures" like the Deaf community (Mindess 1999).

> I read the script . . . put in my head . . . try to think of them [the audience], Deaf people . . . I have to output a clear mental picture [conceptualization] . . . means me have to [take on board] all information, try to

[create a] mental picture . . . that's it, then output [sign] that . . . I want Deaf [audience] same growing mental picture, not bit by bit by bit themselves make own picture. (Georgina)

The reading of the English script appears to occur as a contact phenomenon. When the script is read, the Deaf T/Is assess whether the script can be transferred as it is, in that order, and with minimal enrichment and change. The script may be used as a gloss for a BSL text or further changes needed for coherence and clarity. These changes include adding more information and enrichments.

If the news story says, "a boy was found fell in drowned Steven what ever his name" that needs to be restructured and how old is the boy, so I found out the boy was 21 months old, then sign BOY 21 MONTHS OLD SMALL -S-T-E-V-E-N- IX FALL DROWN FOUND so I do a little research and add some background information hearing interpreters don't. (Rebecca)

The additional information established the agent and then follows the chronological order of the story. This act becomes especially important during the headlines when little or no time exists to allow the structure to be changed.

Been one block of flats, had a fire, three people died and then, on the next line of the script, someone was babysitting their niece, they died and then later again [died]. Really it's [the script] talking about the same people, so you don't need to restructure information on the next line but add, three people died, there was a fire in the flat, two of them, babysitter and niece, they were inhaling smoke, their nephew aged twenty-five tried to save them, but the three of them all died. (Kat)

As Kat's example demonstrates, after the script is read, the information is judged to be ordered in a relevant way to the constructed audience, and the English order works in BSL. But the information has to be made cohesive in order to prevent wrong inferences from the TL; in the English it is not clear how many people died because there is no explicit relation between the three people that died and the babysitter and niece, etc. To ensure the information is clear for the constructed audience, "three people died" is signed, then a description of how they died is given, constructed following chronological order congruent with an unwritten language (Ong 1982). That "three people died" is repeated at the end so the constructed audience knows the babysitter, niece, and nephew are the people in question.

The Deaf T/Is also enrich the TL by making explicit underdetermined references, for example, adding BEATLES before discussing Paul McCartney. In the following example (the) Paul McCartney is showing his artwork and is an underdetermined reference not easily recovered by a Deaf audience; (the) Paul McCartney being famous for music. The Deaf T/Is feel names often need enrichment to ensure their relevance is maximized for the Deaf audience. Context is added so the reference is more fully determined. The Deaf T/Is use the enrichments to make the TL relevant to their constructed audience.

> If you are talking about a person, you need to establish them, saying, "a man, himself aged [whatever age], then his name, but in English this happens the other way round, the name [of the man] comes first, but I don't do that order in BSL, I put his name at the end, if it were John etc. the audience would think "what?" You need to set them up, saying a man aged twenty-one, from wherever, whose name is whatever, then if his name is repeated throughout the story, I can reference him with an index using placement, or pointing at the video footage picture and point at that [the video footage] throughout. (Clark)

Information is reordered to be relevant to the constructed audience and minimize their effort: an enrichment of discourse relations. Once this referent is established, the indexing of the referent (rather than naming) is maximally relevant to the Deaf audience. An index is also more explicit than the name John and points toward the image of John on the screen, creating a determined reference.

Some Deaf T/Is suggest interpreter training does not stress creating a fully enriched TL.

> Hearing mental picture concept where . . . some interpreters, you watch them nodding, uncertain, they are still fixed English structure, English way of thinking, needs Deaf way of thinking. (Georgina)

Kim describes the mental picture mentioned by all of the Deaf T/Is.

> As I read down the text I pick out what my mental picture is, which is automatically the same as Deaf people . . . Deaf people need the information to flow/to be smooth, like when you look at a picture, after you have turned a page it becomes clear as your eyes scan the page, from side to side, and up and down, not as you turn the page, with [hearing] interpreters it's like seeing isolated [jigsaw] pieces of the picture, gradually filling up and it becoming a picture, so the [Deaf] audience looks and then finally understands, like holding the picture, seeing each isolated piece one at a time and only understanding at the end, it shouldn't be

like that, it should be more fluid, more interconnected with each piece running/flowing into each other, so that you know what information to expect next. (Kim)

Within this framework, this English way of thinking stems from little pragmatic knowledge of BSL usage. The language is not optimally relevant and requires the audience to make more cognitive effort to understand the TL, potentially relying on the audience's bilingual skills to understand a contact variety of BSL, or a marked translation.

For the T/Is some Deaf people act as sufficient enough of a language role model to be presenting on television. Deaf people do misunderstand each other, so there can be no guarantee Deaf T/Is and Deaf people automatically have the same "mental picture." But within a high-context culture (Mindess 1999; Smith 1996), the community is used to drawing upon similar references. Deaf T/Is clearly feel they are able to draw upon these references to create a relevant TL that requires less reprocessing for the audience than hearing interpreters' TL.

The T/Is looking at the video footage shown alongside the script aids the conceptualization process. The visual information can be incorporated in the BSL TL for the Deaf audience to have a clearer picture.

I always have to see the pictures [video footage]. I can read the script without watching the video footage, I can, but I strong [try to ensure that I] watch the footage, and I often use that information, and bring it into my BSL [TL]. It becomes important, like there might be a building on fire upstairs, in whatever room [that you can see in the footage and use], or a car in a multiple collision, with another vehicle along its side [and the footage shows exactly], where left or right, I bring that in [to the TL], it's reality shown there. I strong sign that information, it's not made up or an assumption, it's the information being shown, and that creates better rapport with the audience. . . because it's information in the visual mode [shown from the footage], the audience strong take on board that information. (Clark)

The Deaf T/Is believe hearing interpreters construct a TL using the inference system of English and do not maximize the use of the shared cognitive environment. Ostensive communication is achieved by using the community norms for cognitive constructions of events and categories of information. If nonnative T/Is are unable to change the way they portray information to reflect the thinking of a primarily oral culture, they are merely bringing the audience to the source culture's literate way of thinking.

The shared cognitive environment includes cultural knowledge and can be used to identify the inferences in the SL that need explication and the information that can be reduced to inference. This includes the visual information available to both the T/Is and the constructed Deaf audience. The Deaf T/Is reduce the level of cognitive effort required to understand the information: they explicate inferences from the SL requiring excessive processing by the audience by enriching the TL.

The Deaf T/Is also make information implicit in order to reduce the excessive processing required to infer the intended meaning of the SL if left explicit.

> The script was talking about NATO, people being sent off, right. If formal it should be, "NATO," they say, "-N-A-T-O- LEAD ALL-OF-THEM," but leads all of them, well some interpreters would use that, unfortunately, with "all of them," what's that [mean]? I would sign, "-N-A-T-O- LEADER ALL-OF-THEM," which means "leaders of NATO," which means you quickly realize who "all of them" are, by spelling NATO that gives a clear mental picture, then "leader all-of-them," so you know there are lots of them, right. Then it said, "are meeting," "meeting-each-other," whatever, "at lunchtime," so practically that means now, it's half past one, now [while being broadcast], lunchtime, so they [the NATO leaders] are there now, which means when I'm reading the text I could say, "meeting-each-other all-of-them, now meeting." That means now, you don't have to say lunchtime, right, so that means if the interpreter signs "now meeting all-of-them lunchtime" the audience will think, "what did you add that for?" That means it's really [best to sign] "-N-A-T-O- LEADER ALL-OF-THEM MEETING NOW THERE TALKING-ABOUT." (Kim)

Some concepts are naturally expressed in a more "impoverished" (Sequeiros 1998) way due to grammar or the implicature of BSL. From a RT perspective,

> ostension is the Speaker's manifestation of his intent to communicate a relevant meaning to a hearer at a proportionate effort, and is further realised locally in devices (like focus and other distributors or emphasis) which guide listeners to relevant contexts for inference. (Setton 1998)

The previous chapter discussed how the Deaf T/Is use focus and emphasis from nonmanual feature arrays (blinking and head movements) to segment the information for the audience. Kim's quote (above) identifies BSL and English package information differently (Talmy 2000a, 2000b). If the information is packaged from an L1 perspective without L2 influence, the cognitive effort of the Deaf audience is reduced.

Furthermore, evidence of pragmatic inference can be found by the presence of the enrichments. The Deaf translators demonstrate their understanding of the English text after the subsequent viewing of the videotape footage by their segmentation of the TL. Within each subject and predicate segment, we can see to what extent the Deaf and hearing T/Is have enriched the TL with respect to the source language and identify whether this enrichment stems from the video footage, is grammatically required, or comes from a predominantly visual cultural root.

## THE TRANSLATION AND INTERPRETATION PROCESS

The simultaneous interpreting process affects the formation of the TL (Leeson 2005a; Shlesinger 1994, 1995). Setton (1998) says the processing by the interpreter, when interpreting simultaneously, does not follow subject-predicate units. Instead, interpreters follow many different clues from the SL and adopt a variety of strategies. The TAPs allow the T/Is to use the same strategies they would use when translating or interpreting for television. The TAPs also allow for analysis of the T/Is' process. This process includes online, simultaneous processing of information; the reading and re-reading of the script; and the watching and re-watching of the video footage accompanying the news stories. These elements enable a cohesive TL product suitable for the multimedia environment.

The T/Is do not have a view of themselves in-vision, and this was one of the limitations of the TAPs since they were unable to see how their TL interacted within the multimedia environment. This limitation was countered by allowing the T/Is to take as long as they required to render the SL into the TL. Removing some time constraints allowed for maximal enrichment and reduced the need for efficiency (Hatim and Mason 1990, 93). The TAP also facilitated a translation approach, of which the T/Is could take advantage.

### The Process

Analysis of the similarities and differences between the Deaf and hearing T/Is rendering and cognitive processes provides rich information. The T/Is were asked to approach the task as if undertaking the job in the real world. The TAPs differed from the real world by giving additional rendering time to the T/Is, but only the hearing T/Is commented on this aspect.

The Deaf T/Is have more experience, which gives them more chance to develop their expertise (Ericcson 2000/01; Gile 1995a). The Deaf T/Is also said they approached the TAPs in the same way they approached the news-review format. The hearing T/Is, however, commented on not taking advantage of the greater length of time for the translation to occur.

The hearing T/Is read the script before seeing the video and then proceeded with the final rendering of the TL while listening to the English SL. Of course listening is not an option available for the Deaf T/Is, but hearing T/Is chose to listen rather than approaching the task in the same way as the Deaf T/Is. Hearing T/Is work on a daily basis with the spoken word and rarely have time to prepare a TL. Unsurprisingly, the hearing T/Is approached this task with the skills they have honed for their jobs. The Deaf T/Is approached this task with the skills they have honed, including greater rehearsal and externalized editing of the TL product before the final rendering of the TL. The Deaf T/Is signed the translation they wanted, judging it motorically, internally monitoring and adjusting the BSL TL if it did not feel right, or if they could adopt another translation strategy to express the information in the SL.

Consider Kade's (cited and translated in Pöchhacker 2004, 11) definition of interpreting as a subset of translation (quoted previously and repeated here for convenience), "a form of Translation in which a first and final rendition in another language is produced on the basis of a one-time presentation of an utterance in a source language." As this implies, other forms of translation have more than one rendition of the TL; the first and final renditions are not the same. This series of renditions would then be part of the translation process. Similarly, the SL can be presented to the translator on more than one occasion. In the case of written languages, this would suggest the TL is written. The Deaf T/Is approach BSL, an unwritten language, in a similar way.

Within the news, both the newsreader and the Deaf T/Is are given the same script, then the newsreader and the Deaf T/Is offer rehearsed presentations. In the case of reports, a difference concerns how reporters present unscripted reports and yet the Deaf T/Is only have access to the written English script without any of the intonation that is present in the news report. The hearing T/Is have access to both the written script and the intonation of the newsreader and reporter. The hearing T/Is use this intonation as additional information to understand and interpret the SL, highlighting at least one difference in their approach to the task.

Kade's (in Pöchhacker 2004, 11) definition does not account fully for the translation activity from English into BSL. This activity differs in two ways. With regards to the one time presentation of the SL, the English SL is in a scripted form the T/Is can review and re-read on more than one occasion. The video has a soundtrack the hearing T/Is can re-hear. As such, the utterance or text is continuously present for the T/I within the news broadcast domain and yet the TL is presented as a "live" performance.

The first and final rendition of the language is not applicable to some of the T/Is. The length of time taken to process the meaning of the sentences, accompanied with the explanation of understandings by the T/Is, is taken to mean the rendition of the translation/interpretation has been mentally rehearsed more than once. The Deaf T/Is also physically rehearse the rendition, going through several iterations until arriving at the final rendition (see table 6.1).

This opens up a continuum with "pure" translation at one end and "pure" interpretation at the other (see figure 6.1). From Kade (2004), interpreting involves a single presentation of the SL, and the TL is a first and final rendering. In translation, the SL is always present as a reference text, and the process of translation facilitates many renderings of the TL text to achieve the final product. The final presentation of the TL in translation is a fully edited TL text, whereas in interpreting the TL is performed live and unedited as a product. Interpreters still monitor their TL output to ensure it makes grammatical sense and conveys equivalence of information from the SL to the TL.

In the case of the TAPs, both the Deaf and hearing T/Is had access to the English script at all times. The SL was ever-present before they presented the TL to camera. When reading and re-reading the script, the Deaf T/Is manually rehearsed the TL and made changes according to whether they found a better way of translating the SL. These multiple manual renderings parallel the many renderings found in written translation. The

TABLE 6.1. *Translation and Interpretation Features of T/Is*

|  | Translation | Deaf T/Is | Dh & H T/Is | Interpretation |
|---|---|---|---|---|
| SL | ever present | ever present | ever present | one presentation |
| Renderings | many | many | internal | first and final |
| TL | fully edited | performed | performed | live performance |

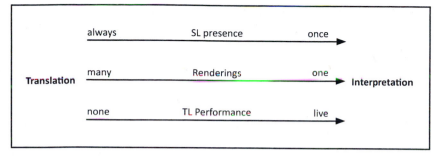

FIGURE 6.1. *Translation to interpretation continuum*

hearing T/Is did not produce multiple manual renderings of the TL and as such did not externally "edit" their TL. The time taken by the hearing T/Is to think about the TL indicates some level of translation activity. I have called this "internal rendering," and note this difference between Deaf and hearing T/Is. Finally, both the Deaf and hearing T/Is presented a live performance of the TL. At the moment there is no way of editing BSL at this minute level of detail, and it would not be undertaken in the television studio even if it were possible.

Within this continuum we see Deaf T/Is closer to the translation end and hearing T/Is closer to the interpretation end. The Deaf T/Is rehearse until they are satisfied with the TL, bearing in mind time constraints. The possibility of performance errors occurs when the SL is finally presented in BSL, as it is done live to camera (discussed previously).

**Reading the Script**

The script-reading process follows a definite path along which certain options exist. First, the script was given to the T/Is, and they read the script in a variety of different ways. One of the Deaf T/Is signed the script while reading, creating a token-for-token translation to disambiguate polysemic words. This act enabled the Deaf T/I to make greater sense of the English script. The other Deaf T/Is only signed BSL when sections were difficult.

> I'm thinking how to sign it, what is it and how to sign it . . . commercial what is that means publicity . . . oh okay business that makes sense now . . . the business of the area affected . . . yeah. (Georgina)

This manual manifestation of BSL occurred after a pause, with the misunderstood section being revisited, which allowed the Deaf T/Is to make sense of the English script. The hearing T/Is read the scripts silently until they reached a difficult section. Then they partially read aloud.

> [With the] final story thinking it could be complicated [to translate] because of seaweed, and seaweed spreading, and words like the environmentalists, I do not want to fingerspell that, people who are experts in the environment . . . (is this live) . . . so maybe I would say, "the environmentalist is worried as they cannot stop this," and I would use some facial expression, and then I would indicate WJ [the reporter, Willy Johnson], he gives it different names, that I would fingerspell . . . don't know if it is algae, or kelp seaweed, so that would be different [in BSL], whether it spreads out or is floaty, I wouldn't want to guess. (David)

David's comments mirror the example from the Deaf T/I above, the difference being the hearing T/Is read aloud in English. This important difference reflects how the thinking for the translating occurs in English for the hearing T/Is. The Deaf T/Is try to make sense of the information in BSL; the hearing T/Is make sense of the information in English (although this could be because of my presence). This very process grounds all the T/Is in their first language and culture, and reveals the translation of the English into BSL starts further along in the process for the hearing T/Is.

After the initial reading of the script, the T/Is were asked to provide a first rendering of the information. The Deaf T/Is were happy to do this, although normally they would wait for the visual information before starting to rehearse the BSL TL product. The hearing T/Is produced some manual information while talking in English about how they would create the BSL TL, and the Deaf (hearing) T/I spoke in English about the strategies he would use without showing any BSL at all.

Newsreaders rehearse what they are going to say before live broadcast. They practice both the pronunciation of words and their intonation. The Deaf T/Is appear to do something analogous. They practice the BSL TL text, using this text to make sense of the information and then editing their rendering of the English text, which explains the dominance of boundary sensitive. The Deaf T/Is prepare the BSL text rather than use a spontaneous text, whereas the hearing T/Is' text falls between the two extremes.

## Video Footage

All of the T/Is wanted to see the video footage associated with each of the news stories in order to gain additional information over and above that contained in the English script. This supported more specific lexical choices and greater enrichment of discourse relations (in this case, cause and effect). For the scripts for these stories, refer to appendix A. In the first story, no further information is supplied from the video footage, and the language of the English text provides enough information about the process.

> Hunger strike, the pictures didn't help. There's just a video of him walking along and then into the parliament, and I know what that looks like, it is typical footage and nothing is shown of his hunger strike, so that is fairly straight forward and there is no influence on the language. (Rebecca)

> Had injections and then became ill, the injection before the war, so the principal thing is sorting out the chronological order. (Georgina)

The second story was judged to be difficult by all but one of the T/Is.

> "Protesters," I think that I have a concept of that, there is a bit that I do not understand here, there are paragraphs that I do not understand, and it is not clear to me, so that [headline] means they are talking about three protesters at a naval base on the Clyde, then the Scottish Parliament, they were protesting for peace, I do not understand why there was a conviction, and then they are being charged, I do not understand. (Kim)

> Second story problem understanding the SL – have failed to have their breach of the peace convictions overturned . . . so basically it is about an appeal, so if it were live then that would be stumbled over . . . about the arguments in relation to the appeal . . . okay well if under pressure to do this quicker I think it would be miserable because the SL is in a way I do not understand. (David)

One Deaf T/I found it unproblematic.

> I think that it doesn't make sense, and how to make sense [of it], so the protest happened at Faslane, and something to do with the peace things, the process of the law is unclear, and then there are the five judges . . . still seems something failed and previously it was okay . . . okay so there are three protesters who were imprisoned, and then want an inquiry, but usually there is an appeal, they needed to decide whether to change the conviction or not, and they decided that it was to continue, right, okay, next story. (Georgina)

The Deaf T/Is wanted more visual information about the story to be grammatically encoded into the TL. Arthur, the Deaf (hearing) T/I, also wanted more information, "[it] would be interesting to know what form the protest took visually." In this case the Deaf (hearing) T/I also acts like the Deaf T/I, seeking to find further information about the SL (as mentioned by Rebecca earlier). While the video footage showed a group of protesters, this information was not deemed to be useful as it did not clarify the information contained in the script. Kim explains, "the picture shows a group, but it was three protesters, so I do not know who is in breach of the peace and who the argument is happening with."

One of the Deaf T/Is, who had problems with the second story, commented on being able to refer to the video.

> I could have pointed at the picture and said that people gathered for a demonstration and three of them were arrested, but demonstration will be clear from the picture, and then said the three were appealing against the decision. (Rebecca)

This interaction with the screen information ensures information written in the script is not repeated if redundant when viewed in conjunction with the visual information.

None of the T/Is (neither Deaf nor hearing) rendered into BSL that the protesters had protested in the Scottish Parliament. It would appear none of the T/Is understood this from the SL. It would have been more useful for the T/Is if the footage had shown the three protesters in the parliament rather than a group of protesters at the Faslane Naval Base.

Kim notes, "the picture of the protesters was of a group rather than three even though that was the aim of the story." This information could have been a contextual assumption of the journalists and news writers when preparing the script. The mainstream audience might have heard some of the story before, in which case the script assumed prior knowledge, and the footage served as a reminder and an update. In this one-off task, however, this news story was not previously known to the T/Is.

All the T/Is judged the third story to be easy; it just needed rearrangement into chronological order.

> Families . . . fishing boat sink with seven in and it sank thirty years ago. Now they want an inquiry, but the government said fine and they want to know when. . . . That one only has a little rearrangement and is easier. (Georgina)

> The third story is straightforward. (Kim)

> Interestingly, I found this SL easier to understand. (David)

One of the Deaf T/Is foregrounds the chronological ordering of the information in the news story with the families meeting that night.

> So change the order slightly, so changed from my original thought before seeing the picture, what happened in the past, then the family gathering because the government has ignored them, so then with the picture this means that I can refer to that briefly, then follow the chronology, and that they are angry and want to petition the government. (Rebecca)

Rebecca's decision was made because of video footage showing the families meeting at a venue. Other than that no reference was made to the footage.

In the final longer story, all of the T/Is said they wished they had greater general knowledge of the topic. The story explains that alien seaweed spreading around the world has now arrived in Loch Ryan (Scotland) and could cause commercial damage to the West Coast shellfish industry as well as environmental damage. In the other examples the T/Is already had an understanding of the story and watched the visual presentation for any additional information. In this example they used the information to understand much of the story.

> There is also a problem, because it says the seaweed will grow to twenty six to thirty feet, but the picture shows that it is flat [on the beach], so are they the oyster beds or are they [the oyster beds] in the water, that depends on knowledge. I don't know quite enough about this, so I expected the oysters to be on the bottom [of the sea bed], but with that picture, with the man talking, I not sure where [it is], so I want to do a bit more investigating into the script and the pictures to confirm whether I'm right, hearing news readers get away with just reading it, but I want to make sure. That it is to do with depth and that the seaweed will grow from the surface down and entangle the oysters, and those long strings [of seaweed] become entangled with fishing lines, it's about how to explain it. (Rebecca)

The footage is useful because it showed what the seaweed looked like. This information was used to select an appropriate handshape for the seaweed. But the Deaf T/Is did not prioritize the shape of the seaweed.

> Now wire weed, the pictures help alongside the autocue, so I might point to the picture and then say this is bad, pointing at holding the seaweed and that will reduce the influence of English so it is more implicit. (Rebecca)

The Deaf T/I uses the multimedia environment to create greater explicature in the TL. By relying on the shared cognitive environment between the T/I and their constructed audience, the TL moves away from a token-for-token translation. The translation follows a similar style of presentation as the reporter, mirroring the reporter holding the seaweed in his hands before beginning the news story. Here the Deaf T/I presents the information just as the reporter does in the video footage.

One of the Deaf T/Is mentioned that after seeing the footage she realized there were reporters on location, and it was not just read by a newsreader. When they rendered the SL again after viewing the video footage, they commented,

> It was not clear that different people were talking. (Georgina)

> First reaction, the influences working backwards, didn't realize that it was a different person saying twenty-six feet and eight meters. (Arthur)

But this is not seen as problematic, rather the re-telling could be clearer by showing different interviewees and the reporter speaking by indexing or pointing at the people as they appear on the video footage. The hearing T/Is mention role shift as a linguistic feature to use. David explains, "for Andrew, the interviewee, a bit of a role shift—there are two other people right, okay, so I'm starting to get the picture." However, this linguistic feature is not mentioned by any of the Deaf T/Is. Although there was no clear differentiation between who was talking, the Deaf T/Is did not explain how they would have shown this difference.

The Deaf T/Is criticized the TAP process for the lack of subtitles on the television footage showing the news program. They use subtitles to judge the pace of the information, and the start and end of each story. It was also noted that although the interpreters get to watch the screen, they do not see a Chroma-Key version of their rendering into BSL in conjunction with the news story.

> So also I need to keep checking with the pictures to know the pace, in [the television company] we always have the pictures, and the script, so that we can check the speed of the [presentation of] information, so that if there is a name then the picture can make that clear, which means that the name can be dropped [not fingerspelled], and the picture referred to [instead], and an explanation be visually motivated rather than fingerspelling names and nouns if you don't know it, you have to know everything and that is the problem, and this [script] is the same, so if you look at the script saying that, "the weed can cause environmental and commercial damage, and that's a concern," which means they are worried that it will cause damage to the area, you don't sign commercial, as

this is not relevant [is the wrong sign] for the situation, there is a lot to think about and it needs more time. (Rebecca)

The long story in the TAPs is over 120 seconds and yet only one of the Deaf T/Is mentions pointing to the screen. In the TL of the television broadcast headlines (not the TAPs data), there is no indexing of the video footage being rendered into BSL. In the television broadcast weekly news review, two of the hearing T/Is made eight indexed references to the screen in 275 seconds of footage. Of the Deaf T/Is, only one Deaf T/I made indexed references to the screen during a longer story of 176 seconds. In total, there are 375 seconds of Deaf T/Is doing longer story footage, and only in the story over 120 seconds does indexing to the screen occur. This is the same for the hearing T/Is, in that only the stories of over 120 seconds include indexing to the screen.

The hearing T/Is point to the video footage when someone is being interviewed, their indexes point to people appearing in the footage, who are then introduced by the hearing T/Is who also render what the introduced person is saying. The Deaf T/Is point toward visual information such as the footage of a traffic jam. There is one incidence of the Deaf T/I indexing someone who is talking and then rendering what the person says without an additional introduction.

## THE PROCESS OF A DEAF TRANSLATION NORM

The TAPs illustrate similarities and differences in the approach to the translation/interpreting by the Deaf, Deaf (hearing), and hearing T/Is. Generally, in terms of the process itself, the Deaf T/Is render the SL into BSL straight away and then re-render the information in BSL many times, until it makes sense. This fulfills the historical need of the Deaf T/Is to domesticate the TL as unmarked TL. It also enables the Deaf T/Is to gain greater ownership of the information and create greater presence in their translations by rehearsing the information much like newsreaders.

The Deaf (hearing) and hearing T/Is explain the process in English, thinking and reformulating in English, before singularly rendering the information in BSL. The TL is not rehearsed. The T/Is were not asked to comment on this, but my presence as a hearing researcher could mean they felt more comfortable conversing in English. Both the T/Is are my colleagues; we have often had conversations in BSL both when alone and in the presence of other hearing people who can sign so this only partially explains the lack of multiple renderings in BSL. Moreover, they were asked to follow the same process that they use in the television studio.

Both the Deaf T/Is and the hearing T/Is use the video footage to make additions to the TL. This video footage informs the T/Is about the specific types of activities going on in the news stories and allows them to make specific grammatical choices. The Deaf T/Is also use the speed of the autocue to check the pace of the information and to inform themselves of the ways in which they can use the information on the screen to produce a more relevant text. While an initial glance at the script leads to the T/I deciding on following a particular chronological order, the video footage can change this decision. Generally, the Deaf T/Is pay more attention to the interaction between the images on the screen and the information to be delivered to the constructed audience.

## Enrichment and Impoverishments

Part of the translation and interpretation process include the enrichments and impoverishments made by the T/Is. These types of translation shifts are reported by written language translation theorists (Gutt 1998; Sequeiros 2002, 1998) and spoken language interpreting theorists (Gile 1995a; Setton 1999). Padden (2000/01) also touches on this type of translation shift when commenting on the differences between interpreting between two languages and two modalities.

The TAPs and the television data provide examples of enrichments and impoverishments. The incorporation of visual information, enrichment, and impoverishment will be examined in the next sections as will be the differences between Deaf and hearing T/Is. Finally, the similarities and differences in the translation shifts between the Deaf, Deaf (hearing), and hearing T/Is will be discussed.

Evidence of enrichment happens in all the categories of enrichment although not all categories appear in all of the data types (see table 6.2). If we follow Sequeiros's categories (1998, 2002), the first example presents a temporal enrichment.

English: this afternoon

BSL: AFTERNOON AT-THE-MOMENT

In this example, the Deaf T/I has temporally enriched the concept of the order, this afternoon [right now at this very moment] (the enrichment can be found in the square brackets: [ ] ). So while the SL leaves this enrichment for the audience to make, the TL explicates the time frame so it is more specific. This requires less cognitive effort by the constructed audience, as it is more relevant.

The next example presents a thematic agent enrichment, where the agent of an event is explicitly stated in the TL and not in the SL.

English: a former soldier

BSL: BEFORE PERSON-CL HIMSELF SOLDIER

This example shows an enrichment of the order, a former soldier [a soldier is a person] that is re-ordered in the TL to become, a former [person][this person is a] soldier. While this may not be required in the English, all of the T/Is enriched the concept of soldier with a person classifier suggesting in this instance BSL can exploit a greater level of explicature than English without becoming marked.

The following example presents an enriched thematic source.

English: a planning application over six windows has cost

BSL: APPLICATION FOR SIX WINDOW+ FROM BLACK-PERSON BUILDER

In this example we see that the source of the application is enriched in the TL. This enrichment is fairly straightforward for the Deaf T/I. The enrichment is of the order, a [planning] application for six windows [from a black builder]. The video footage on the screen is of a black man and the story later mentions a judge's decision about discrimination against the black man by planning officers' story. It is never made explicit that the black man made the application; this is left as an implicature but enriched as a thematic source in the TL.

Some of the enriched discourse information is derived from the use of spatial prosody as discussed in chapter 5. The following example also demonstrates an example of a lexically enriched discourse relation.

English: in the British youth parliament. Carole Stone has succeeded

BSL: IN BRITISH YOUTH PARLIAMENT NAME
-C-A-R-O-L-E-S-T-O-N-E- ACHIEVE

To preserve the anonymity of the Deaf T/I, the name of the youth elected into the youth parliament has been changed. In the English SL there is an implicit connection between the first sentence, which introduces a girl aged fourteen who was elected in the British youth parliament and Carole Stone. This discourse relation is left for the audience to enrich. By explicating the sentence with the sign NAME, the Deaf T/I enriches the discourse relation between the first and second sentence. The enrichment is of the order, elected in the British youth parliament [called] Carole Stone.

The final example presents an enriched implicature.

English: meet tonight in Peterhead

BSL: FAMILY MEETING TONIGHT IX −P-E-T-E-R− HEAD IX WILL DISCUSS

The information stated as an explicature is of the families meeting tonight. The visual information in the video footage shows the families discussing or debating something. The Deaf T/I has combined the information from the script and from the video footage by way of an enriched implicature in the TL with respect to the SL script. The enrichment is of the order, the [family] come together [to have a meeting] tonight in Peterhead [where in Peterhead they will have discussions].

The first category of enrichment found in addition to Sequeiros' categories (1998, 2002) is locational enrichments.

English: on the Clyde

BSL: -C-L-Y-D-E- SCOTLAND

In this example we see in the English script the location *on the Clyde* is an underdetermined reference presumably because of the shared cognitive environment; the broadcast is from *Scotland Today* and the most relevant understanding of *on the Clyde*, the one requiring the least cognitive effort, would be in terms of the Scottish river. So the SL is enriched to the order, on the Clyde [which is in Scotland]. The T/Is enrich this by adding information about the location of the place, thereby reducing the cognitive effort on the part of the constructed audience.

The next example is of a thematic enriched goal.

English: a vote of no confidence

BSL: VOTE NOTHING CONFIDENCE IX-R PERSON-CL-R

In this example the SL leaves, "person for whom the vote of no confidence is called for" implicit, to be explicated by the audience from information previously given. In the TL the Deaf T/I uses the same right hand locus previously established by gaze to reestablish the goal of the action. The IX-R reestablishes the locus, and the PERSON-CL-R enriches the thematic goal of the action. The enrichment is of the order, a vote of no confidence [in the previous reference][the person]. It is still not as explicit as it could be, but a higher level of explicature exists in the TL than in the SL.

The final example illustrates an impoverishment.

English: resumed passenger flights this morning

BSL: PASSENGER FLY+ TODAY

This example shows a temporal impoverishment. The time frame in the TL is less explicit than in the SL. The shared cognitive environment of the T/I and the audience is that of a news broadcast at lunchtime, so the impoverishment is of the order: this morning [less specifically today bearing in mind the program is broadcast at lunchtime and therefore the flights would either be now at lunchtime or today would be understood to be this morning][today]. I presume that the Deaf T/I uses the pragmatic system of BSL to construct an impoverished TL minimizing the cognitive effort on the part of the constructed audience.

## Incorporating Visual Information

T/Is also use visual information to disambiguate English tokens. An example of this approach can be seen when the T/Is wanted to know the form of protest that took place at the Faslane Naval Base. The protest could be by sitting, marching, picketing, etc., and all of these actions could be specifically encoded into BSL, and the T/Is hoped to find out this information from the video footage. Kim explains, "The picture of the protesters was of a group rather than three, even though that was the aim of the story."

For the long story in the TAP, the image of the seaweed helped in understanding what the seaweed looked like and this information was used to visually motivate the manual lexicon selected for the seaweed handling classifier. Rebecca notes, "I will follow the picture and say this oh bad." She then signs, BAD IX PICK-UP (squashed O-hand) IX BAD. She decided on the squashed O-hand handling classifier after looking at the picture of the seaweed. Differently shaped seaweed would require different handshapes to represent it. This example shows how T/Is also relate the information on the screen to the information being rendered in BSL, both in terms of specific grammatical encoding of the shape of the seaweed as well as relating the action of the reporter picking up the seaweed to the BSL text. Not only does this reduce the cognitive effort of the constructed audience, it creates greater connection between the video footage and the TL.

One of the Deaf T/Is also used the visual information to encode the spreading, from the bottom of the loch bed or across the surface.

English: this stuff is gonna be possibly up to eight meters in length

BSL: WILL GROW(-5-HAND-L-5HAND-R-MOVE-APART) ABOUT EIGHT METER DEEP LONGER-LENGTH CIRCUMFERENCE EXPAND

The Deaf T/I explicates the implicatures, "this stuff [the seaweed] is gonna be [by growing] up to eight meters in length." Using the 5-hand, we explicitly know it is something of that (5-hand) shape growing, and so this is more explicit than the phrase "this stuff." Unsure of how the seaweed will grow, the Deaf T/I covers both possibilities of growth: not only the seaweed floating on the surface and growing down, but also its expansion across the surface of the water.

All of the other T/Is perform similar enrichments of the SL, using specifically chosen handshapes to encode visual properties of the seaweed disambiguating "this stuff." The handshapes differ between T/Is but are internally consistent for each T/I. And for each T/I, the handshape selected for the growing verb is also enriched.

## ENRICHMENT

Looking specifically at the categories discussed by Sequeiros (1998, 2002), the TL text contains a variety of enrichment examples. The first category Sequeiros discussed is temporal enrichments. An example can be found in the television data of a Deaf T/I.

English: Cells are cultured in a laboratory before being transplanted back into patients

BSL: -C-E-L-L-S- BEEN PICK-OUT+ IX-C LAB IX-C CYLINDER STAY+ BECOME
CREATE FROM-LAB-TAKE-TO-PATIENT PERSON-CL

In this example, the English words "cells are cultured in a laboratory before being transplanted back" are enriched to "cells are cultured
in a laboratory [that takes some time] before being transplanted back
into patients." The BSL TL makes this temporal notion of taking some
time explicit.

The next category of enrichment is the thematic agent. In the data,
these enrichments principally manifest as person classifiers.

English: Three protesters

BSL: 3 PERSON-CL++ PROTEST OBJECT

The BSL increases the level of explicitness when compared to the
English. In the example, one of the Deaf T/Is did not include this enrichment although all of the other T/Is did. Having shown the example without enrichment to a native BSL user, she judged the unenriched sentence
to be grammatical, which shows that while this enrichment might be
expected (four out of the five T/Is did it), it is not obligatory.

In the following example, signed by the Deaf (hearing) T/I, the enrichment is from "this stuff is native to water in Japan but gradually it's
spreading round the world" to "this stuff [the seaweed] is native to water
in Japan but gradually [over time] it's [the seaweed] spreading [from
Japan] round the world." The thematic source of the spreading is added
to the verb by moving the verb from the location in which the T/Is have
placed Japan.

English: This stuff is native to water in Japan, but gradually it's spreading
round the world.

BSL: KNOW START JAPAN-R IX-R BEEN START SPREAD-OUT-FROM-JAPAN

The other T/Is articulate the sign spread from the center of their chest
in "neutral" space, showing spreading without adding location information other than grammatically required by the sign SPREAD: s-hand to
5-hand moving forward. We can also see from the example of temporal
enrichment how the thematic source is enriched, "transplanted [from the
laboratory] back into patients." This further confirms the "oral" nature
of BSL showing BSL is "copious" (Ong, 1982) when compared with

the scripted English. It is also close to the human experience, describing actions we expect to see.

No examples of thematic possessor enrichment were found in the data, possibly because BSL shows less explicit possessive information than English, in much the same way that Spanish has less explicit possessive than English (Sequeiros 1998, 2002). Examples of possessor impoverishment will be discussed later.

Examples of enriched discourse relations were located, although not many examples, because while the T/Is are concerned with the balance between effectiveness and efficiency, the "live" nature of the translated news means that information must be concisely and efficiently produced. The head movement contours described in the previous chapter add prosodic information to the news stories and relate different phrases (and hence different information), therefore reducing the need to show it lexically. In the second news story of the TAPs, the second sentence and third sentence are,

> They'd argued the law and the way it's been interpreted by the courts over the centuries is too vague. But in a landmark ruling five judges at the court of appeal in Edinburgh decided that the convictions should be upheld.

In the BSL of one of the Deaf T/Is we see,

> English: They'd argued the law . . . the convictions should be upheld

> BSL: THEM-S FEEL IX-R THEIR −L-A-W- . . . AGREE TURN-DOWN THEIR −L-A-W-

The reiteration of THEIR −L-A-W- enriches the discourse relation between one sentence and the next in a more explicit way than in the English. We have examples of enriched implicature from one of the Deaf T/Is in the TAPs too.

> English: Here's Willy Johnson

> BSL: HAVE REPORTER−W-I-L-L-Y-J-O-H-N-S-O-N- TALK MORE

The enrichment is from "here's Willy Johnson," to "here's Willy Johnson [the reporter] [[reporters report information]] [[the reporter Willy Johnson will now tell you more information about what we have just been introducing]]. The assignment of the reference, Willy Johnson as a reporter, is the enriched explicature in square brackets and the enriched implicature is shown in double-square brackets. In the BSL, we have an enriched implicature although it is not as enriched as it could be (that Willy Johnson is a man for example) and so still expects some contextual assumptions (from watching the accompanying video footage) on the part of the audience, albeit less than the English SL.

Two other categories of enrichment are found in the data: locational enrichments and thematic goal enrichments. In locational enrichments, the location information is enriched.

English: in the seas off Scotland

BSL: SCOTLAND –S-E-A- WEST-COAST

Three of the T/Is added information (West Coast) from later on in the English to the beginning of the story. This add not only reordered information, it also added a locational enrichment, since additional information was added to the TL congruent with the intention the speaker wished to communicate.

In the thematic goal enrichments, the TL by one of the hearing T/Is from the television data enriches the goal of the verb.

English: armed police have shot a man dead

BSL: POLICE WITH GUN BEEN MAN IX POLICE-FIRE-GUN-AT-MAN AREA DIE IX

Apart from the anomalous use of the sign AREA, we can see the firing of the gun has the goal of the shot added to it. The index (IX) points toward a location that had previously been established, called location X for informant anonymity. The enrichment becomes, "armed police have shot [their guns at] a man [in location X] dead [the man in location X]." The verb of shooting the gun, which could also be glossed as PULLED-THE-TRIGGER-OF-A-GUN-WHILE-POINTING-THE-GUN-AT-THE-MAN-IN-LOCATION-X, enriches the goal of the verb. This example contains two locational enrichments.

Enrichment provides a useful theoretical framework for categorizing some of the decisions the Deaf and hearing T/Is made when rendering English into BSL. The next section will tease apart the differences between Deaf and hearing T/Is to better understand what constitutes a Deaf translation norm.

## Impoverishment

Some examples of impoverishments fall into the categories above. The impoverishments mean the BSL audience has to draw upon contextual assumptions and implicatures in order to enrich the language and arrive at the same equivalent propositional semantic representation.

English: earlier this year

BSL: RECENTLY

If relevant enough for the audience, this sign will provide enough information for the audience to arrive at the enriched form with the least cognitive effort. The hearing and Deaf (hearing) T/Is produced this example, which was given in the TAPs, but none of the Deaf T/Is did. Two of the Deaf T/Is had THIS-YEAR in their TL and one of them had EAR-LIER THIS-YEAR. The two Deaf T/Is judged that their constructed audience would spend less cognitive effort if they minimally added the time frame of "this year," since "recently" was not pragmatically relevant enough for the constructed audience.

The following example shows a proposition impoverished from explicature to implicature rendered by all the T/Is in the TAPs.

English: being given vaccines

BSL: BEEN INJECT-IN-ARM-PUSH-PLUNGER

The more explicit notion of being given a vaccine [a substance used to stimulate the production of antibodies and provide immunity against one or several diseases] moves to an implicature of the order, "being given a vaccine" to [an injection in the arm]. Here we see how the level of contextual assumptions is raised, and yet the T/I deems it to be optimally relevant for the audience to be able to cognitively enrich the implicature to arrive at the communicative intention. This level of implicature is always present when discussing vaccines in BSL. The iconically motivated lexical choice, of one specific example of the many ways a vaccine could be administered, needs to be enriched by the audience to be understood. But when comparing the SL to the TL, there is a move from explicature to implicature in much the same way Spanish is less explicit than English with regards to thematic possessors (Sequeiros 1998, 2002).

## Differences in Translation Shifts

The number of enrichments and impoverishments made by the Deaf, Deaf (hearing), and Hearing T/Is differ. Table 6.2 details the different types of data and the total time length of each type.

These data are not directly comparable since the clips have different lengths and the Deaf and hearing T/Is performed different tasks. The categories do, however, show trends in the type of interlingual enrichments occurring in each type of data and the number of interlingual impoverishments across the different data types.

TABLE 6.2. *Different Translation Shifts*

| Data Type | Loc | Temp | Agent | Goal | Source | Enriched Discourse Relations | Enriched Implicature | Impover |
|---|---|---|---|---|---|---|---|---|
| D-H | 1 | | | 1 | 1 | 2 | 15 | 4 |
| H-H | 2 | | | 3 | | | | |
| D-WRA | 1 | 1 | 5 | | | | 7 | 3 |
| D-WR | 9 | 2 | 5 | 2 | | 1 | 11 | 20 |
| H-WR | 3 | 3 | 5 | 4 | 1 | 2 | 23 | 14 |
| D-TAP | 5 | | 5 | | | 1 | 14 | 5 |
| DH-TAP | 2 | | 2 | | 1 | | 7 | 6 |
| H-TAP | 1 | | 2 | | | 2 | 3 | 2 |

TABLE 6.3. *Data Types and Data Length*

| Data Type (Acronym) | Length of Data (Seconds) |
| --- | --- |
| Deaf Headlines (D-H) | 347 |
| Hearing Headlines (H-H) | 71 |
| Deaf Weekly Review in-Vision (D-WR) | 420 |
| Deaf Weekly Review Anchor (D-WRA) | 99 |
| Hearing Weekly Review in-Vision (H-WR) | 468 |
| Deaf TAPS (D-TAP) | 658 |
| Deaf (Hearing) TAPS (DH-TAP) | 239 |
| Hearing TAPS (H-TAP) | 210 |

Table 6.2 shows all of the types of enrichments and impoverishments that occur in all of the data. The acronym for the type of data is taken from table 6.3, for example, D-TAP is the acronym for the data from the Deaf T/Is during the TAPs.

Generally the Deaf and hearing T/Is make enrichments in the same categories, although the ranking of the categories tends to differ. For instance, temporal enrichments only occur in the weekly. An example taken from one of the hearing T/Is,

English: it will be several weeks before doctors can assess

BSL: DOCTOR NEED ONE-WEEK TWO-WEEK THREE-WEEK ASSESS

This example shows how the proposition "several weeks" is enriched to a specific time frame of between one and three weeks. We have a similar length of data for the Deaf and hearing weekly review in-vision T/Is, and a similar number of temporal enrichments. The longer the stories, the more likelihood of temporal enrichment, and both Deaf and hearing T/Is demonstrate this enrichment. As BSL uses aspect rather than tense, it establishes a time frame and then maintains that time frame until a new time frame is introduced (Padden 1988). This characteristic appears to account for the lack of temporal enrichments generally.

Thematic goal enrichments do not occur in the TAP data and are generally used more by the hearing T/Is than the Deaf T/Is. The hearing T/Is may overgeneralize this rule as late learners, or in interpreter training they may add the thematic goal as an explication when left implicit by Deaf T/Is. The data support the idea that the hearing T/Is do not have the same conceptualization of the in SL and render the information differently in the TL.

The largest category of translation shifts for the Deaf T/Is concerns enriched implicatures, except for in-vision weekly review where it is impoverishment. With shorter news stories, the Deaf T/Is aim to enrich the TL by explicating implicatures for their constructed audience. Their aim is to ensure the constructed audience has the same mental picture as the Deaf T/Is achieved by enriching implicatures.

Explicating implicatures is also something hearing T/Is aim to achieve, but they seem less able to achieve this goal when the news stories are shorter, for example in the news headlines. It is something they then prioritize in long stories, over and above the use of impoverishments. The Deaf T/Is are able to be more efficient by undertaking translation shifts that result in impoverishments; the hearing T/Is are less able to do this. The difference with shorter stories is the Deaf T/Is explicate implicatures and, to a lesser extent, realize impoverishments. And with longer stories, they focus on realizing a higher number of impoverishments.

One explanation for this difference might be that the Deaf T/Is are working into their L1, and they can draw upon different conceptual representations than the hearing T/Is because of their age of acquisition (Fabbro 2001, Halverson 2003). These different conceptual representations result in the Deaf T/Is judging a higher degree of impoverishment than can be realized in the longer stories.

Table 6.4 shows the number of enrichments found in the TAPs and the total length of data per group. For these data, all of the T/Is rendered the same English information into BSL. The Deaf and Deaf (hearing) T/Is enriched the TL more than the hearing T/I. Moreover, by examining

TABLE 6.4. *Data from the TAPs*

|  | No. of Enrichments | Total Length (Seconds) | Enrichments Per 10s |
|---|---|---|---|
| Deaf T/Is | 25 | 658 | 4 |
| Deaf (hearing) T/I | 12 | 239 | 5 |
| hearing T/I | 6 | 210 | 3 |

the enrichments each ten seconds, the data show how the Deaf (hearing) T/I has included a higher number of enrichments than the Deaf T/Is. The Deaf (hearing) T/I follows a similar pattern to the hearing in-vision T/Is in the news-review data. Despite a mixture of short and long stories, the Deaf (hearing) T/I made decisions similar to those made by the hearing T/Is when working on longer stories with more information.

The type of news story might influence the number of translation shifts. The headlines and the weekly review anchor both consist of short stories. The TAPs are a mixture of three short stories and one long story. As seen in table 6.5, the long story in the TAPs does not, however, show the same pattern of translation shifts as the weekly review program.

TABLE 6.5. *TAP Translation Shifts*

| News Story | Deaf T/Is | Deaf (Hearing) T/I | Hearing T/I |
|---|---|---|---|
| TAP 1 (short) | 11 | 6 | 3 |
| TAP 2 (short) | 8 | 5 | 2 |
| TAP 3 (short) | 7 | 4 | 1 |
| Total for short stories | 26 | 15 | 6 |
| TAP 4 (long) | 4 | 5 | 2 |

We might expect a greater frequency of translation shifts in longer stories with a greater length of preparation. With longer preparation the text can be maximally domesticated, but time constraints appear to inhibit this. Although in the TAPs the T/Is were able to take their time, this is not the same as having a longer time to undertake the task. It was more akin to a sight translation than a translation with a longer turn-around time. Further exploration of different types of preparation time would be interesting.

Table 6.6 shows the total number of translation shifts, both enrichments and impoverishments. When comparing the headlines and the

TABLE 6.6. *Translation Shifts*

| Data Type | Enrichments Plus Impoverishments | Shifts Per 10s |
|---|---|---|
| D-H | 24 | 7 |
| H-H | 5 | 7 |
| | | |
| D-WRA | 12 | 12 |
| D-WR | 50 | 12 |
| H-WR | 55 | 12 |
| | | |
| D-TAP | 30 | 5 |
| DH-TAP | 18 | 8 |
| H-TAP | 8 | 4 |

weekly review, it becomes evident that the longer the time given to prepare (both in terms of receiving the script and having background knowledge), the more translation shifts occur.

In the TAPs, both the Deaf and hearing T/Is make fewer shifts, suggesting less knowledge to be able to handle these shifts. The Deaf T/Is mentioned this aspect when talking about the final long story. They remarked that they do not have enough background information to render the information about oysters effectively into BSL.

> Oysters they are not born but come from shells so that background knowledge is needed, do they grow, they grow, well the area is strong in oysters that would be sufficient, I need a greater concept of the information. (Georgina)

When I extrapolate from the figures above, in the TAPs the Deaf (hearing) T/I rendered a similar frequency of shifts to the Deaf and hearing T/Is when rendering the headlines.

With such a small number of T/Is it is impossible to draw statistically significant conclusions from the data, but the trend is for the Deaf (hearing) T/I to be able to draw upon his bilingual and bicultural heritage to shift between English and BSL in such a way that lack of knowledge does not reduce the effectiveness of the TL. But this is noticeably different from Deaf T/Is and potentially marks the Deaf (hearing) T/I as coming from the community, but being audiologically hearing.

It would be highly unusual for a current affairs program to be either presented or interpreted by a L2 presenter/interpreter. And within the translation and interpreting professions, there exists a common belief that ideally T/Is should work into their first language (Donovan 2004). The assumption is that by working into their L1, T/Is have maximal idiomatic fluency. This can also be explained on the level of conceptual representation (Grosjean 1997; Halverson 2003). The T/Is are influenced not so much because of lexical choice, but rather in the relationships they build within the TL text and how this cohesion is maintained on a discourse level.

Chapter 5 shows how hearing (and Deaf (hearing)) T/Is are able to produce smaller units of phrasal and discoursal cohesion. These T/Is are not, however, able to create the overarching discourse units to relate different themes together. This chapter shows how on an inferential level of *ostentation*, the hearing T/Is render enriched implicature but only during the longer stories. The Deaf T/Is render enriched implicature in the shorter stories and then high levels of impoverishment in the longer stories thereby enabling larger discourse units to be related to each other inferentially.

## Chapter 7

# The Deaf Translation Norm

This study examines the Deaf translation norm from a variety of different perspectives. Chapter 4 examines notions of identity and community and how the experiences of the T/Is inform the roles they take when rendering English into BSL. Chapter 5 examines the creation of the TL and describes the prosodic features of the TL, and chapter 6 examines the process of creating the TL, including the linguistic enrichments and impoverishments that occur to minimize cognitive effort for the TL audience. This final chapter draws together these different facets to describe the Deaf translation norm. Some notions of the Deaf translation norm are concerned with identity politics and the continuance of community values in a colonized context. Other notions of the Deaf translation norm are concerned with fluency and relating information to a constructed audience.

The Deaf community has existed as an historical entity for some time. While this community may have been hidden from the mainstream, and in recent years has developed under the shadow of colonizers (oralists, missioners, welfare officers, etc.) (Ladd 2003), historical values have been passed down from generation to generation. The Deaf translation norm is born from a heterogeneous collective community where different members contribute skills to the collective and where the T/I is a member of the community.

## THE DEAF TRANSLATION NORM FROM
## THE PAST TO THE PRESENT DAY

Deaf bilinguals have always contributed to their community by telling other Deaf people about wider society and by translating English documents (ranging from letters and newspapers to official correspondence and subtitled television broadcasts). These Deaf bilinguals would have been, and still are, members of the community, socialized within its norms.

Deaf bilinguals witnessed other Deaf bilinguals contributing within the Deaf club, and Deaf individuals acted as role models. The skopos of the translation (Vermeer 1989) is to provide greater access to information in a way understandable to Deaf monolinguals. The preliminary norm (Toury 1978/1995) of the Deaf bilinguals and monolinguals involves choosing what is translated/retold.

While the Deaf translation norm is something community-grown, the preliminary norm has changed somewhat. The interviews clearly show that the Deaf T/Is see the inclusion of Deaf people as T/Is within the media as a political process. The community does not select who is on television, whereas they would have selected whom they chose to translate their letters. Furthermore, many parts of television are judged to be areas where Deaf T/Is can work and should be working in preference to hearing T/Is, but hearing T/Is are chosen by mainstream institutions.

## The Changing Role of the Deaf Translation Norm

Historically, the Deaf bilingual shared information and ensured Deaf monolinguals understood relevant information from the mainstream—the information being chosen either by the Deaf monolingual themselves or by the Deaf bilingual. In the television studio, the Deaf T/Is do not control which stories are chosen and have no control over the relevance of the stories to the community. But the role of the Deaf T/I within this environment is clearly different from that of a simple newsreader.

The Deaf T/Is try to prepare as much as possible by watching the full news stories and video footage so they can edit the TL to be relevant and comprehensible in a domesticated TL (Venuti 1998). Often, more information is needed than what is contained in the English script to ensure an optimally relevant translation by the Deaf T/Is. They draw upon their knowledge of the Deaf audience to reflect the language the Deaf audience uses and to add relevant information.

## Presence in the Deaf Translation Norm

The Deaf translation norm incorporates greater presence during the rendering of the information into the TL than other mainstream translation norms. This value contrasts to the mainstream notion of neutrality (Rudvin 2002). For the Deaf T/Is, they are not in a neutral environment because they experience the power of the hegemony on a daily basis.

Being more than just an interpreter reinforces and maintains a Deaf cultural space.

The initial norm (Toury 1978/1995) is to create a domesticated TL text that does not look like a translation by being present in the re-telling of the information. The Deaf translation norm achieves this in several ways. First, the Deaf T/Is do not translate their introductions in the broadcast program and instead greet the audience directly. Second, the blinking frequency of the Deaf T/Is in the TL product is of the same frequency of conversation (Sze 2004), which helps to create greater rapport with the audience. Both of these actions corroborate the importance of the Deaf audience identifying with the Deaf T/Is, as they stated in the interviews.

## The Constructed Audience

Part of the Deaf translation norm involves producing equivalence in relation to a constructed audience or pragmatic other (Ruuskanen 1996). Despite the TL being broadcast with accompanying subtitles, the Deaf T/Is do not cater to an audience that reads English. The presumption is the Deaf reading audience can read the subtitles and have other ways of accessing the information.

The Deaf translation norm operates outside of the English SL. The Deaf T/Is present the concepts from the SL coherently and cohesively, and they also enrich the concepts. By presenting in this way, Deaf people with limited fluency in English (their L2) will understand the TL with the least cognitive effort.

The Deaf translation norm draws upon the Deaf T/Is' ability to think as other Deaf people think, relying primarily on their visual experience of the world and visual conceptualization of information to construct the TL as cultural insiders. The construction of an easily comprehensible TL is achieved through the experience the Deaf bilinguals have of re-telling, modifying, and reformulating information for the Deaf community.

## A Deaf Cultural Space

The Deaf T/Is expressed the importance of having a space to allow a Deaf translation style to develop, with the further aim of having it becoming a norm. If there is no space for the Deaf T/Is to take onboard information and reformulate it, the Deaf T/Is are merely being used as pawns by the hearing institutions (although possibly through lack of awareness) to fulfill legal requirements for sign language on television; they are unable to fulfill their aim of ensuring the audience has access to information that is relevant and delivered in a way that reinforces the audience's own language, culture, and way of being in the world.

National initiatives and/or guidelines created by Deaf T/Is (by the Deaf Interpreter Network and/or the national registration body, the NRCPD) and implemented by major broadcast companies could facilitate a greater on-screen presence for the Deaf T/Is. As a consequence, the historical role with which the Deaf T/Is connect could become fully present in this public space. At present, all the T/Is need to be mindful of the sensibilities of the mainstream audience, mediating this potential Deaf space by mainstream values.

## THE LANGUAGE OF THE DEAF TRANSLATION NORM

As discussed by the Deaf T/Is interviewed, lexical choice does not differ greatly between Deaf and hearing T/Is. Both Deaf and hearing T/Is are able to work toward a TL and adhere to a Deaf translation norm. The difference occurs predominantly in the use of prosody. The language of the Deaf translation norm exhibits some linguistic features in common with prepared language. The blinking behavior in a Deaf translation norm exhibits the same distribution as prepared sign language (Sze 2004, Wilbur 1994). The blinking also exhibits the same levels of frequency as dialogue (Sze 2004).

Cohesion in English uses a variety of different features (Halliday and Hasan 1976) and sign languages use body movement and space (Jouison 1985; Metzger and Bahan 2001). The data clearly show, however, differences in the use of prosody both between genres (headline news and weekly review) and between groups of T/Is with respect to the nonmanual segmentation of the BSL text. These differences can, at least partially, be accounted for by the different processes the Deaf, Deaf (hearing), and hearing T/Is undertake. Text cohesion is something created by the use of spatial prosody and the interrelation of segments within nested structures. The operational norms (Toury, 1978/1995) of the Deaf translation are such that blinks and head movements are used cumulatively to create discoursal prosodic cohesion. Different types of head movements can be combined together at a lexical and discourse level.

## Prosodic Control

The Deaf translation norm predominantly uses boundary sensitive blinks (80 to 90 percent) to segment the TL. The other blink category being voluntary blinks (around 10 percent). The lack of other types of blinks shows the language is prepared rather than spontaneous (Sze 2004) and supports the idea of the TL being a translation rather than an interpretation.

The blinking frequencies are of dialogue rather than monologue frequencies (Sze 2004). This suggests greater visual attention on the part of the Deaf T/Is either to the constructed audience or to the process of reading the autocue as a memory aid. Both may contribute to the TL, and the TL still exhibits dialogue frequency in the TAPs when the prepared nature of the text suggests a monologue frequency could be achieved. Based on intuitive judgments from the informants, this lower frequency of blinking enables audience rapport and is part of the Deaf translation norm.

## Discoursal Prosodic Cohesion

Head movements are found exhibiting echo phonology as well as phrasal and larger discourse head movements. These head movements form superarticulatory arrays in conjunction with boundary sensitive blinks to create nested structures. The Deaf translation norm uses this spatial prosody, with the head moving on the x, y and z axes, to create cohesion in the TL text. This cohesion reduces the cognitive effort of the constructed audience in understanding the TL information. This spatial prosody provides one of the ways that the Deaf translation norm makes the TL domesticated and relevant to the constructed audience.

## THE PROCESS OF THE DEAF TRANSLATION NORM

The translation activity from a written to an unwritten language enables us to expand the view of interpreting as a specific type of translation activity and take the view that translation and interpretation exist at either end of a continuum. The process undertaken by the Deaf T/Is is different from the process undertaken by the hearing T/Is. The Deaf translation norm incorporates a performed translation rather than an interpretation facilitated by a different process.

One of the fundamental things the Deaf translation norm adheres to, as an initial norm, is that the SL is read rather than listened to. The Deaf T/Is read the script and then the autocue information; neither of these texts have any SL prosody. Watching the video footage then enables the Deaf T/Is to see the facial expressions and body movements of the interviewees within news reports in order to understand emotional information. This ensures the T/I is not influenced by the prosody and emphasis of the SL, and instead experiences the information in the same way the Deaf constructed audience will experience the information. This process reduces the influence of the mainstream culture on the TL. It ensures the T/I is able to create a Deaf cultural-centered TL. It does, however, differ from the retellings in the Deaf club because the news studio is mainstream space and the news broadcast is institutionally hearing.

Using a Sense Model approach (Finkbeiner et al. 2004) on bilingual lexical access for translation, it would appear the Deaf T/Is are using the script (written in their L2) to construct a semantic concept of the news stories. These scripts are then realized syntactically and rehearsed to ensure the influence from the L2 is reduced (Agrifoglio 2004). The video footage is used for specific lexical decisions, including culturally appropriate deixis to reduce the cognitive effort of the audience. This allows for a mental blend between the image on the screen and the language being presented (Fauconnier 1997; Fauconnier and Turner 2002; Liddell and Metzger 1998).

## The Performed Translation of the Deaf Translation Norm

As the data show, the TL of the Deaf T/Is exhibits linguistic features of a prepared language. By using Kade's (cited and translated in Pöchhacker 2004, 11) definition, we are able to see how the Deaf translation norm adopts a process that facilitates the operational norms of prepared language, dialogue blinking frequency, and spatial prosody. The SL is present for the T/Is to refer to and to use as a memory aid when presenting the TL in front of the camera. The Deaf T/Is try to find out more information from the fuller English scripts and include this information in the TL, being mindful that this information will not be present on the autocue.

The Deaf translation norm includes a process of practice by which the Deaf T/Is move immediately into BSL and re-tell the information, rendering this information many times until a satisfactory TL text has been created. This includes some re-ordering of information, as well as having a kinesthetic sense of an appropriate TL. This kinesthetic (or proprioceptive) sense comes from a robust internal linguistic model of a fluent, and preferably native, BSL user.

As BSL is an unwritten language, the final translation still has to be performed. In this regard, the translation of unwritten languages differs from that of written languages. Written languages can be rendered multiple times and then fully edited to create the final text. BSL is prepared in much the same way, but with the multiple renderings happening by signing and then having to be remembered by the T/I. This is where the importance of fluency in the Deaf translation norm is paramount.

## Use of the Multimedia Environment

The rendering of the news happens in a multimedia environment where information is delivered from the English script and from the video footage broadcast simultaneously. The Deaf translation norm takes on board this shared cognitive environment between the T/I and the constructed audience.

The TL incorporates visual information available from the video footage. This happens both in terms of referencing the information on the screen and by incorporating specific information into the TL by way of choosing specific handling classifiers. The referencing of information on the screen and the choice of a specific, consistent manual lexicon reduce the cognitive effort on the part of the constructed audience. This process also maximizes the relevance of the TL for the constructed audience.

Similarly, within the news studio, the video footage is shown with subtitles. This informs the Deaf T/Is of the pace of information delivery. When performing the translation, this pace is reflected by the speed of the autocue. By judging the pace of the information, without being influenced by the prosody of the SL, the Deaf T/Is are able to make "in" and "out" decisions (Vuorinen 1995). These decisions relate to the effectiveness and efficiency of the TL (Hatim and Mason 1990).

## Making the TL Relevant in the Deaf Translation Norm

The Deaf translation norm aims to create an effective TL, understood by the constructed audience, while being efficient, that is, taking no more or less time than needed to ensure understanding. This construction of relevance occurs by several means.

1. the prosodic construction of the language that interrelates different idea units within the TL
2. encoding information from the video footage into the TL
3. enriching and impoverishing the information so that it is optimally relevant within the shared cognitive environment of the T/I
   and the constructed audience. This ensures that the constructed
   audience has the lowest cognitive processing effort for the information being presented.

The enrichments and impoverishments fall into the same categories as
those described by Sequeiros (1998, 2002) but also include locational
enrichment and thematic goal enrichment. The Deaf translation norm
aims principally to enrich implicature within the text so the information
is relevant to the constructed audience. It also aims to use the implicatures occurring in BSL by impoverishing the TL, which increases both
efficiency and effectiveness. While each subcomponent could be present
separately, all three are needed to meet the Deaf translation norm.

## IMPLICATIONS AND APPLICATIONS OF THIS RESEARCH

This work shows, although underexplored, that a translation norm
exists within the Deaf community. The training of interpreters has not
included community translation norms, and as such could benefit from
the inclusion of much of this information. This includes all of the univer-
sities that currently teach undergraduate and postgraduate sign language
interpreting, as well as other training institutions. Further exploration
should allow for the understanding of when a text should be translated
rather than interpreted and to understand the process by which this can
be achieved.

Furthermore, more training institutions give Deaf T/Is access to training
courses to become trained/qualified interpreters. These training courses
have in the past focused on mainstream models of translation and interpretation, none of which are based in the Deaf community. This research
allows for the introduction of a Deaf community translation model. This
could facilitate T/Is, both Deaf and hearing, in relating to the Deaf audience (television or otherwise) and situating themselves as understanding
and presenting Deaf thinking in their signed language TL.

The translation model not only allows for hearing students to follow a Deaf model of translation, but also to think more critically about when to use the consecutive interpreting mode rather than the simultaneous interpreting one (Russell 2005), regardless if the consecutive mode should be used more frequently by T/Is than it is at the moment. The consecutive mode allows the T/Is more space to and time to prepare a TL understood by the constructed Deaf audience and increases the presence of the T/I.

## Applications for Media Translation

Hearing T/Is, journalists, newsreaders, and reporters need to afford Deaf T/Is greater agency so programs, DVDs, Web sites, etc., can truly be rendered into signed languages, following the Deaf translation norm. Deaf T/Is need to be involved in the selection of the news stories and other materials to be translated, as well as in the arrangement of the stories and information.

A consequence would be that the Deaf T/Is' role would include other roles such as journalist or producer. Similarly, more Deaf news with Deaf people as anchors and English voice-over would prioritize signed languages as the SL. This would enable a full journalist role on the part of the Deaf T/Is. Even though translation would still be used as part of the job, this would take place in the preproduction phase as with other news broadcasts (Vuorinen 1995).

## Further Areas for Study

For this research, data was explored from interviews, from available television data, and from TAPs. This data enabled a Deafhood-led research methodology to explore a Deaf translation norm. The interviews provided rich descriptions of perceived differences between Deaf and hearing T/Is, the television data allowed the exploration of these rich descriptions in broadcast data, and the TAPs allowed the exploration of the process and translation of an identical sample script.

In trying to achieve catalytic validity, a lunchtime seminar in BSL, presented to interpreting students, researchers, and informants, was filmed and has been circulated by DVD to Deaf people who work as interpreters. A similar presentation was also made at the ASLI conference in May 2005 with the DVDs also distributed to participants who were members of DIN. Further dissemination of this work needs to occur within Deaf organizations and broadcasting organizations so they engage with Deaf T/Is in such a way that effective rendering of English scripts can occur. This book is part of that journey.

These data provide an interesting starting point for an analysis, from a Deaf-centered perspective, of the differences between Deaf and hearing T/Is. A larger data set would need to be examined in order to arrive at findings that could be statistically significance. Further TAPs preferably would use a full autocue and Chroma-Key facilities to create an atmosphere closer to the studio environment and one that would allow the T/Is to fully reference the information on the screen. By seeing how the T/Is interact with the video footage, we can better explore the construction of presence within the TL.

Partway through this research Deafstation.org was launched. This Internet-based daily news broadcast is produced and presented by Deaf people for Deaf people in BSL. It would be interesting to explore its discourse style and understand the process by which the Deaf presenters construct their BSL texts.

Hopefully, the future will see further examination of the Deaf translation norm. This research distinguishes Deaf and hearing T/Is sufficiently to warrant further investigation. If Deaf T/Is are interpreting into their first language and for their own community, certainly there is much that hearing interpreters can learn and benefit from as a result of such investigations. As the practice of Deaf interpreting continues to grow, a definite need for additional research grows.

Even though Deaf professionals are paid as T/Is, they clearly do not want to follow hearing/mainstream-centered models of interpreting. The Deaf T/Is would not be following the Deaf translation norm they observe in action in the community and are trying to role model in public on broadcast television. If the Deaf T/Is cast themselves as "just interpreters," then they do their community a disservice.

## Reporting Scotland TAPs News Scripts

A former soldier has gone on hunger strike to force a public enquiry into Gulf War Syndrome. Alexander Iset, a former Lance Corporal from Cumbernauld, says he's ready to die to force the military to come clean. Mr. Iset became ill after being given vaccines in the run up to the 1990 Gulf War. Earlier this year he took his case to the Scottish Parliament and he says he's become frustrated with the slow progress.

Three protesters who took part in antinuclear demonstrations at the Faslane Naval Base on the Clyde and in the Scottish Parliament have failed to have their breach of the peace convictions overturned. They'd argued the law and the way it's been interpreted by courts over the centuries is too vague. But in a landmark ruling, five judges at the court of appeal in Edinburgh decided that the convictions should be upheld.

The families of seven fishermen killed in a fishing disaster thirty years ago meet tonight in Peterhead. They want to know when a public enquiry will be held into the sinking of the *Trident*, which went down in the Pentland Firth in 1974. The wreck of the vessel was discovered three years ago. The government has promised a full inquiry, but the families are saying that they are growing impatient that a date is still to be set.

An alien species is lurking in the seas off Scotland. It's a fast spreading seaweed that's made an unwelcome first appearance in our waters. Environmentalists say that once established there will be no stopping it, and they fear the consequences. Here's Willy Johnson.

WJ: *Sargasum nuticum*, or Japweed or wireweed. Call it what you will but by any name it shouldn't be here. This stuff is native to waters in Japan but gradually it's spreading round the world. And now it's arrived in Scotland here in Loch Ryan in Gallaway.

It's not a welcome discovery.

Andrew: It doesn't look terribly impressive at the moment, or even threatening, but later on in the year this stuff is gonna be possibly up to eight meters in length. Erm and the problem is that it could shade out a lot of the species that are here, the native seaweeds that make this place such an important area.

WJ: The weed can cause commercial as well as environmental damage, and that's a worry. Loch Ryan has Scotland's most important commercial oyster beds. The whole West Coast shellfish industry is on the doorstep.

Andrew: It could get an impact on the shellfisheries in the loch, especially the oysters beds if it was to get really stuck in there it could shade out species. But also it has a nuisance value in that it could get tangled up in fishing gear generally, and if it was to get out of Loch Ryan into the Clyde and maybe further up the West Coast it could have a wider impact on fisheries there as well.

Robert: It seems that it grows to quite a considerable length about twenty-six to thirty feet. This obviously can damage commercial shipping pleasure shipping getting caught in propellers and such like. And we're also looking at the development of Loch Ryan so anything that's a threat has obviously got to be dealt with seriously.

WJ: The alien seaweed is spread on the hulls of ship and almost certainly came in on the ferries from Northern Ireland where it was found some time ago. It's probably here to stay.

Wherever wireweed has taken hold so far it's proved impossible to shift. Further spread within Scotland is now felt to be almost inevitable. If you see some on a shore near you SNH would like to hear about it. Willy Johnson reporting, Scotland Loch Ryan.

# References

Agrifoglio, Marjorie. 2004. Sight translation and interpreting: A comparative analysis of constraints and failures. *Interpreting* 6:43–67.

Ahrens, Barbara. 2005. Prosodic phenomena in simultaneous interpreting: A conceptual approach and its practical application. *Interpreting* 7:51–76.

Akmajian, Adrian. 1995. *Linguistics: An introduction to language and communication.* London: MIT Press.

Alexander, Claire, Rosalind Edwards, and Bogusia Temple. 2004. Access to services with interpreters' user views. York: Joseph Rowntree Foundation.

Álvarez, Román, and M. Carmen-África Vidal, eds. 1996. *Translation, power, subversion.* Topics in Translation 8. Clevedon, U.K.: Multilingual Matters.

Anders, Ericcson K. 2000/01. Expertise in interpreting: An expert-performance perspective. *Interpreting* 5:187–220.

Arber, Sara. 2001. Designing samples. In *Researching social life,* ed. Nigel Gilbert, 58–82. London: Sage.

Austin, J. L. 1962. *How to do things with words.* Oxford: Clarendon.

Bach, K., and R. M. Harnish. 1979. *Linguistic communication and speech acts.* Cambridge, Mass.: MIT Press.

Bahan, Ben. 1989. Notes from a "seeing" person. In *American Deaf Culture,* ed. Sherman Wilcox, 29–32. Silver Spring, Md.: Linstok Press.

Baker, Charlotte, and Carol Padden. 1978. *American Sign Language. A look at its history, structure, and community.* Silver Spring, Md.: Linstok Press.

Baker, Mona. 1992. *In other words: A coursebook on translation.* London: Routledge.

Baker-Shenk, Charlotte L., Robbin Battison, and William C. Stokoe. 1980. *Sign language and the deaf community : Essays in honor of William C. Stokoe.* Silver Spring, Md.: National Association of the Deaf.

Baker-Shenk, Charlotte L. 1986. Characteristics of oppressed and oppressor peoples: Their effect on the interpreting context. In *Interpreting: The art of cross cultural mediation,* ed. M. McIntire, 59–71. Silver Spring, Md.: RID Publications.

Bassnett, Susan, and Harish Trivedi. 1999. *Post-colonial translation: Theory and practice.* London; New York: Routledge.

Bell, Allan. 1999. News stories as narratives. In *The discourse reader,* ed. Adam Jaworski and Nikolas Coupland, 236–51. London: Routledge.

Bernard, H. R., P. Killworth, D. Kronenefeld, and L. Sailer. 1984. The problem of informant accuracy: The validity of retrospective data. *Annual Review of Anthropology* 13:495–517.

Bishop, Michele, and Sherry Hicks. 2005. Orange eyes: Bimodal bilingualism in hearing adults from Deaf families. *Sign Language Studies* 5 (Winter):188–230.

Blakemore, Diane. 1987. *Semantic constraints on relevance.* Oxford: Blackwell.

———. 1992. *Understanding utterances.* Oxford: Blackwell.

Bourdieu, P. 1993. *Sociology in question.* London: Sage.

Boyes-Braem, Penny. 1999. Rhythmic temporal patterns in the signing of Deaf early and late learners of Swiss German Sign Language. *Language and Speech* 42:177–208.

Brien, David, Richard Brown, and Judith Collins. 2002. *The organisation and provision of British Sign Language/English interpreters in England, Scotland and Wales.* London: Department for Work and Pensions, HMSO.

Bulwer, J. 1648. *Philocopus, or the deaf and dumbe mans friend.* London: Humphrey Moseley.

Carmel, S, and L. Monaghan. 1991. An introduction to ethnographic work in deaf communities. *Sign Language Studies* 73:410–20.

Carston, Robyn. 2002. *Thoughts and utterances: The pragmatics of explicit communication.* Oxford: Blackwell.

———. 2004. Explicature and semantics. In *Semantics: A reader,* ed. S. Davis and B. Gillon. Oxford: Oxford University Press.

Catford, J. C. 1965. *A linguistic theory of translation: An essay in applied linguistics.* London: Oxford University Press.

Coates, Jennifer, and Rachel Sutton-Spence. 2001. Turn-taking patterns in Deaf conversation. *Journal of Sociolinguistics* 5:507–29.

Cohen, L., L. Manion, and K. Morrison. 2000. *Research methods in education.* London: Routledge Falmer.

Cokely, Dennis. 1986. The effects of lag time on interpreter errors. In *Sign language interpreters and interpreting,* ed. Dennis Cokely, 39–70. Burtonsville, Md.: Linstok Press.

———. 1992. *Sign language interpreters and interpreting.* SLS Monographs. Burtonsville, Md.: Linstok Press.

Cook, Ian, and Mike Crang. 1995. *Doing ethnographies.* Concepts and Techniques in Modern Geography, vol. 58. London: Institute of British Geographers.

Cronin, Michael. 2002. The empire talks back: Orality, heteronomy and the cultural turn in interpreting studies. In *The interpreting studies reader,* ed. Franz Pöchhacker and Miriam Shlesinger, 386–97. London: Routledge.

Dalgarno, G. 1661. *Ars signorum, vulgo character universalis philophica et lingua.* London: J Hayes.

Danks, Joseph H. 1997. *Cognitive processes in translation and interpreting.* Thousand Oaks, Calif.: Sage.

de Saussure, Ferdinand. 1922. *Course de linguistique générale.* Paris: Payot.

———. 1916/1974. *Course in General Linguistics*. London: Fontana/Collins.

Denmark, Clark. 2002. The domino effect: Changing values = changing language = new styles of training. In *DeafWay II*. Washington, DC.

Donovan, Clare. 2004. European masters project group: Teaching simultaneous interpretation into a B language. *Interpreting* 6:205–16.

Duncan, Bob. 1997. Deaf people interpreting on television. *Deaf Worlds* 13:35–9.

Edwards, Rosalind, Temple Bogusia, and Claire Alexander. 2005. Users' experiences of interpreters: The critical role of trust. *Interpreting* 7:77–95.

Engberg-Pedersen, Elisabeth. 1993. Space in Danish sign language: The semantics and morphosyntax of the use of space in a visual language. In *International studies on sign language and communication of the deaf*. Hamburg: Signum.

Fabbro, Franco. 2001. The bilingual brain: Cerebral representation of languages. *Brain and Language* 79:211–22.

Fauconnier, Gilles. 1997. *Mappings in thought and language*. Cambridge: Cambridge University Press.

Fauconnier, Gilles, and Mark Turner. 2002. *The way we think: Conceptual blending and the mind's hidden complexities*. New York: Basic Books.

Finkbeiner, Matthew, Kenneth Forster, Janet Nicol, and Kumiko Nakamura. 2004. The role of polysemy in masked semantic and translation priming. *Journal of Memory and Language* 51:1–22.

Frishberg, N. 1990. *Interpreting: An introduction*. Silver Spring, Md.: RID.

Furniss, Graham. 2004. *Orality: The power of the spoken word*. Basingstoke: Palgrave Macmillan.

Gannon, Jack R. 2004. A tribute to Roy J. Stewart: He helped make our sign language immortal. *Sign Language Studies* 4 (Spring): 225–30.

Gile, Daniel. 1995a. *Basic concepts and models for interpreter and translator training*. Amsterdam: Benjamins.

———. 1995b. Interpretation research: A new impetus. *Journal of Linguistics* 14:15–30.

———. 2001. *Getting started in interpreting research: Methodological reflections, personal accounts and advice for beginners*. Benjamins Translation Library, vol. 33. Amsterdam: Benjamins.

Goodley, Dan. 1999. Disability research and the "researcher template:" reflections on grounded subjectivity in ethnographic research. *Qualitative Inquiry* 5:24–46.

Green, Karen. 2001. ASLI fees and salaries report: ASLI.

Gresswell, Emilie. 2001. How applicable to BSL are contemporary approaches to translation? *Deaf Worlds* 17:50–62.

Grice, H. P. 1975. Logic and conversation. In *The philosophy of language*, ed. A. P. Martinich, 159–70. Oxford: Oxford University Press.

————. 1978. Further notes on logic and conversation. In *Syntax and semantics 9: Pragmatics*, ed. P. Cole, 113–28. New York: Academic Press.

————. 1981. Presupposition and conversational implicature. In *Radical pragmatics*, ed. P. Cole, 183–98. New York: Academic Press.

Groce, Nora Ellen. 1985. *Everyone here spoke sign language: Hereditary deafness on Martha's Vineyard*. Cambridge, Mass.: Harvard University Press.

Grosjean, François. 1997. The bilingual individual. *Interpreting* 2:163–87.

————. 1998. Studying bilinguals: Methodological and conceptual issues. *Bilingualism: Language and Cognition*1:131–49.

Gutt, Ernst-August. 1991. *Translation and relevance: Cognition and context*. Oxford: Blackwell.

————. 1998. Pragmatic aspects of translation: Some relevance-theory observations. In *The pragmatics of translation*, ed. Leo Hickey, 41–53. Clevedon, U.K.: Multilingual Matters.

————. 2005. On the significance of the cognitive core of translation. *The Translator* 11:25–49.

Hadar, U, T. J. Steiner, and F. C. Rose. 1984. Involvement of head movements in speech production and its implications for language pathology. *Advances in Neurology* 42:247–261.

Halliday, M. A. K., and R. Hasan. 1976. *Cohesion in English*. London: Longman.

Halverson, Sandra. 2003. The cognitive basis of translation universals. *Target* 15:197–241.

Harris, Margaret. 2001. It's all a matter of timing: Sign visibility and sign reference in Deaf and hearing mothers of 18-month-old children. *Journal of Deaf Studies and Deaf Education* 6:177–85.

Hatim, B., and Ian Mason. 1990. *Discourse and the translator*. London: Longman.

Hatim, B. 2001. *Teaching and researching translation*. Applied Linguistics in Action. Harlow: Longman.

Hermann, Alfred. 1956. Interpreting in antiquity. In *The interpreting studies reader*, ed. Franz Pöchhacker and Miriam Shlesinger, 15–22. London: Routledge.

Home Office. 2005. Police and Criminal Evidence Act 1984 (s.60(1)(a), s.60A(1) and s.66(1)) Codes of Practice A-G: TSO.

Hinnenkamp, Volker. 2005. Semilingualism, double monolingualism and blurred genres - on (not) speaking a legitimate language. *Journal of Social Science Education* OSD 1. http://www.jsse.org/2005–1/semilingualism_hinnenkamp.htm.

Hymes, Dell. 1964. Introduction. In *Language in culture and society*, ed. Dell Hymes, 3–14. New York: Harper & Row.

Inghilleri, Moira. 2003. Habitus, field and discourse: Interpreting as socially situated activity. *Target* 15:243–68.

Isham, William P. 1984. The role of message analysis in interpretation. In *Interpreting: The art of cross cultural mediation*, ed. M. McIntire, 111–22. Silver Spring, Md.: RID Publications.

Jääskeläinen, Riitta, and Sonja Tirkkonen-Condit. 2000. *Tapping and mapping the processes of translation and interpreting*. Benjamins Translation Library, vol. 37. Amsterdam; Benjamins.

Janzen, Terry. 2005. Interpretation and language use. In *Topics in signed language interpreting*, ed. Terry Janzen, 69–105. Amsterdam: Benjamins.

Johnston, Trevor, Miriam Vermeerbergen, Adam Schembri, and Lorraine Leeson. 2007. Real data are messy: Considering the cross-linguistic analysis of constituent ordering in Australian Sign Language (Auslan), Vlaamse Gebarentaal (VGT) and Irish Sign Language (ISL). In *Sign languages: A cross-linguistic perspective*, ed. Pamela Perniss, Roland Pfau, and Marcus Steinbach, 163–206. Berlin: Mouton de Gruyter.

Jouison, Paul. 1985. The role of the body in the organization of signed expressive discourse. Paper presented at Signs of Life, second European congress on sign language research, Amsterdam.

———. 1989. Analysis and linear transcription of sign language discourse. Paper presented at the Third European Congress on Sign Language Research, Hamburg, July 26–29.

Kendon, Adam. 1988. *Sign language of Aboriginal Australia: Cultural, semiotic, and communication perspectives*. Cambridge [Cambridgeshire]: Cambridge University Press.

Lewis, Margaret S. Jelinek, and Dorothy W. Jackson. 2001. Television literacy: Comprehension of program content using closed captions for the Deaf. *Journal of Deaf Studies and Deaf Education* 6 (Winter): 43–53.

Kyle, Jim, and Lorna Allsop. 1982. Deaf people and the community: Final report to Nuffield Foundation. Bristol: Bristol University, School of Education.

Kyle, Jim, and Bencie Woll. 1985. *Sign language: The study of deaf people and their language*. Cambridge: Cambridge University Press.

Labov, William. 1973. Some principles of linguistic methodology. *Language in Society* 1:97–120.

Ladd, Paddy. 1998. In search of Deafhood towards an understanding of British Deaf culture. PhD diss., Centre for Deaf Studies, University of Bristol.

———. 2003. *In search of Deafhood*. Clevedon, U.K.: Multilingual Matters.

———. Forthcoming. Signs of change—sign language and televisual media in the U.K. In *Minority language media*, ed. M. Cormack and N. Hourigan. Clevedon, U.K.: Multilingual Matters.

Lather, P. 1986. Research as praxis. *Harvard Educational Review* 56:257–77.

Leeson, Lorraine, and Susan Foley-Cave. 2004. MEAN^DEEP BUT DEPEND^SITUATION: Some reflections on the challenges of interpreting semantics and pragmatics in an Irish context. Paper presented at Supporting Deaf People, online 2004.

Leeson, Lorraine. 2005a. Making the effort in simultaneous interpreting: Some considerations for signed language interpreters. In *Topics in signed language interpreting*, ed. Terry Janzen, 51–68. Amsterdam: Benjamins.

———. 2005b. Vying with variation. In *Topics in signed language interpreting*, ed. Terry Janzen, 251–91. Amsterdam: Benjamins.

Lerum, Kari. 2001. Subjects of desire: Academic armor, intimate ethnography, and the production of critical knowledge. *Qualitative Inquiry* 7:446–83.

Li, Defeng. 2004. Trustworthiness of think-aloud protocols in the study of translation processes. *International Journal of Applied Linguistics* 14:301–13.

Liddell, Scott K. 1990. Four functions of a locus: Re-examining the structure of space in ASL. In *Sign language research: Theoretical issues*, ed. Ceil Lucas, 176–98. Washington, DC: Gallaudet University Press.

Liddell, Scott K, and Melanie Metzger. 1998. Gesture in sign language discourse. *Journal of Pragmatics* 30:657–97.

Liddell, Scott K. 2000. Indicating verbs and pronouns: Pointing away from agreement. In *The signs of language revisited: An anthology to honor Ursula Bellugi and Edward Lima*, ed. Karen Emmorey and Harlan Lane, 303–20. London: Lawrence Erlbaum.

———. 2003. *Grammar, gesture, and meaning in American Sign Language.* Cambridge: Cambridge University Press.

Macfarlane, A. H. 2002. Restoring the individual: The cultural dimension of special education in three Te Arawa sites. *He Puna Kōrero: Journal of Māori and Pacific Development* 3:82–89.

Mandel, M. 1977. Iconic devices in ASL. In *On the other hand: New perspectives on American Sign Language*, ed. L Friedman, 57–107. New York: Academic Press.

Matthews, P. H. 1997. *The concise Oxford dictionary of linguistics.* Oxford: Oxford University Press.

Mayberry, Rachel I. 1995. Mental phonology and language comprehension, or what does that sign mistake mean? In *Language, gestures, and space*, ed. Karen Emmorey and J. Reilly. Hove, U.K.: Lawrence Erlbaum.

McNeill, D. 1992. *Hand and mind: What gestures reveal about thought.* Chicago: University of Chicago Press.

Metzger, Melanie. 1995. Constructed dialogue and constructed action in American Sign Language. In *Sociolinguistics in Deaf Communities*, ed. Ceil Lucas, 255–71. Washington, DC: Gallaudet University Press.

———. 1999. *Sign language interpreting: Deconstructing the myth of neutrality.* Washington, DC: Gallaudet University Press.

Metzger, Melanie, and Ben Bahan. 2001. Discourse analysis. In *The sociolin-guistics of sign language*, ed. Ceil Lucas, 112–44. Cambridge: Cambridge University Press.

Mindess, Anna. 1999. *Reading between the signs: Intercultural communication for sign language interpreters*. Boston: Intercultural Press.

Mitchell, Ross E. 2004. Chasing the mythical ten percent: Parental hearing status of Deaf and hard of hearing students in the United States. *Sign Language Studies* 4:138–63.

Munday, Jeremy. 2001. *Introducing translation studies*. London: Routledge.

Napier, Jemina. 1998. Free your mind—the rest will follow. *Deaf Worlds* 14:15–22.

———. 2002. Sign language interpreting: Linguistic coping strategies. Coleford, U.K.: Douglas McLean.

Napier, Jemina, and Rachel Locker McKee. 2002. Interpreting into international sign. *Sign Language and Linguistics* 5:27–54.

Naples, Nancy. 1996. The "outsider phenomenon" in rural Iowa. In *The field: Readings on the field research experience*, ed. Carolyn S. Smith and William Kornblum, 139–49. New York: Praeger.

Nespor, Marina, and Wendy Sandler. 1999. Prosody in Israeli Sign Language. *Language and Speech* 42, 2–3:143–76.

Newport, E. 1984. Constraints on learning: Studies in the acquisition of American Sign Language. *Papers and Reports on Child Language Development* 23:1–22.

———. 1990. Maturational constraints on language learning. *Cognitive Science* 14:147–72.

Ong, W. 1982. *Orality and literacy—Technologising the word*. London: Routledge.

Padden, Carol. 1988. *Interaction of morphology and syntax in American sign language*. Outstanding Dissertations in Linguistics. New York: Garland.

Padden, Carol, and T. Humphries. 1988. *Deaf in America*. Cambridge, Mass.: Harvard University Press.

Padden, Carol. 1989. The culture of Deaf people. In *American Deaf Culture*, ed. Sherman Wilcox, 1–16. Silver Spring, Md.: Linstok Press.

———. 1990. The relation between space and grammar in ASL verb morphology. In *Sign language research: Theoretical issues*, ed. Ceil Lucas, 118–32. Washington, DC: Gallaudet University Press.

———. 2000/01. Simultaneous interpreting across modalities. *Interpreting* 5:169–85.

Pöchhacker, Franz, and Miriam Shlesinger, eds. 2002. *Interpreting studies reader*. London: Routledge.

Pöchhacker, Franz. 2004. *Introducing interpreting studies*. London: Routledge.

Preston, Paul. 1996. Chameleon voices: Interpreting for Deaf parents. *Social Science & Medicine* 42:1681–90.

Quinto-Pozos, David. 2007. Can constructed action be considered obligatory? *Lingua* 117(7): 1285–314.

Robinson, Douglas. 1997. *Translation and empire postcolonial theories explained*. Manchester: St. Jerome.

Romaine, S. 1995. *Bilingualism*. Oxford: Blackwell.

Roy, Cynthia B. 1989. Features of discourse in an American Sign Language lecture. In *The sociolinguistics of the Deaf community*, ed. Ceil Lucas, 231–51. San Diego: Academic Press.

———. 1993. The problem with definitions, descriptions, and the role metaphors of interpreters. In *The interpreting studies reader*, ed. Franz Pöchhacker and Miriam Shlesinger, 344–53. London: Routledge.

Rudvin, Mette. 2002. How neutral is "neutral"? Issues in interaction and participation in community interpreting. In *Perspectives on interpreting*, ed. M. Viezzi and G. Garzone, 217–33. Bologna: CLUEB.

———. 2004. Cross-cultural dynamics in community interpreting: Troubleshooting. In *Claims, changes and challenges in translation studies: Selected contributions from the EST congress*, 271–83. Amsterdam: Benjamins.

Ruuskanen, D. D. K. 1996. The effect of pragmatic factors on the definition of equivalence in translation. *Language Sciences* 18:883–95.

Russell, Debbie. 2005. Consecutive and simultaneous interpreting. In *Topics in signed language interpreting*, ed. T. Janzen, 135–64. Amsterdam: Benjamins.

Sandler, Wendy. 1999a. The medium and the message. *Sign Language and Linguistics* 2:187–215.

———. 1999b. Prosody in two natural language modalities. *Language and Speech* 42:127–42.

Scott-Gibson, Liz. 1991. Sign language interpreting: An emerging profession. In *Constructing deafness*, ed. Susan Gregory and Gillian M. Hartley, 253–58. London: The Open University.

Searle, John R. 1979. *Expression and meaning: Studies in the theory of speech acts*. Cambridge: Cambridge University Press.

Seleskovitch, D. 1978. *Interpreting for international conferences*. London: Pen & Booth.

———. 2002. *Interpreting for international conferences*. London: Pen & Booth.

Senghas, Richard, and Leila Monaghan. 2002. Sign of their times: Deaf communities and the culture of language. *Annual Review of Anthropology* 31:69–97.

Sequeiros, Xavier R. 1998. Interlingual impoverishment in translation. *Bulletin of Hispanic Studies* 75:145–57.

———. 2002. Interlingual pragmatic enrichment in translation. *Journal of Pragmatics* 34:1069–89.

Setton, Robin. 1999. *Simultaneous interpretation: A cognitive-pragmatic analysis*. Amsterdam: Benjamins.

Shlesinger, Miriam. 1994. Intonation in the production and perception of simultaneous interpretation. In *Bridging the gap: Empirical research in simultaneous interpretation*, ed. Sylvie Lambert and Barbara Moser-Mercer. Amsterdam: Benjamins.

———. 1995. Shifts in cohesion in simultaneous interpreting. *The Translator* 1:193–214.

Shoemaker, Pamela J. 1991. *Gatekeeping*. London: Sage.

Simon, R. I., and D. Dippo. 1986. On critical ethnigraphic work. *Anthropology and Education Quarterly* 17:195–202.

Simpson, Stewart. 1991. A stimulus to learning, a measure of ability. In *Constructing deafness*, ed. Susan Gregory and Gillian M. Hartley, 217–26. London: The Open University.

Skelton, Tracey, and Gill Valentine. 2003a. "It feel like being Deaf is normal:" An exploration into the complexities of defining D/deafness and young D/deaf people's identities. *The Canadian Geographer* 47:451–66.

———. 2003b. Political participation, political action and political identities: Young D/deaf people's perspectives. *Space and Polity* 7 (August): 117–34.

Skutnabb-Kangas, Tove. 1981. *Bilingualism or not: The education of minorities*. Clevedon, U.K.: Multilingual Matters.

Smith, Theresa B. 1996. Deaf people in context. PhD diss., University of Washington.

Sperber, Dan, and Deirdre Wilson. 1981. Pragmatics. *Cognition* 10:281–86.

———. 1986. *Relevance: Communication and cognition*. Oxford: Blackwell.

———. 1995. *Relevance: Communication and cognition*. Oxford: Blackwell.

———. 2002. Pragmatics, modularity and mind-reading. *Mind & Language* 17(February/April): 3–23.

Spindler, G., and L. Spindler. 1992. Cultural process and ethnography: An anthropological perspective. In *The handbook of qualitative research in education*, eds. M. D. LeCompte, W. Milroy and J. Preissle, 53–92. London: Academic Press.

Steiner, Ben. 1998. Signs from the void: The comprehension and production of sign language on television. *Interpreting* 3:99–146.

Stolze, Radegundis. 2004. Creating "presence" in translation. In *Claims, changes and challenges in translation studies selected contributions from the EST Congress*, 39–50. Amsterdam: Benjamins.

Stone, Christopher A. 2001. An examination of the register and discourse of two BSL texts and the subsequent rendering of those texts into spoken English by BSL/English interpreters. Master's thesis, Centre for Deaf Studies, University of Bristol.

———. 2005. ASLI fees and salaries report 2005/6: ASLI.

Stone, Christopher, and Bencie Woll. 2008. Dumb O Jemmy and others: Deaf people, interpreters and the London courts in the 18th and 19th centuries. *Sign Language Studies* 8(Spring): 226–40.

Strauss, Anselm, and Juliet Corbin. 1990. *Basics of qualitative research: Grounded theory and procedures and techniques.* London: Sage.

Strong, Michael, and Philip M. Prinz. 1997. A study of the relationship between American Sign Language and English Literacy. *Journal of Deaf Studies and Deaf Education* 2 (Winter): 37–46.

Sutton-Spence, Rachel, and Linda Day. 2001. Mouthings and mouth gestures in British Sign Language (BSL). In *The hands are the head of the mouth: The mouth as articulator in sign languages,* ed. Penny Boyes-Braem and Rachel Sutton-Spence, 69–85. Hamburg: Signum.

Sze, Felix. 2004. Blinks and intonational phrasing in Hong Kong Sign Language. Paper presented at *Theoretical Issues in Sign Language Research*, Barcelona.

Talmy, Leonard. 2000a. *Toward a cognitive semantics.* Vol. 1 of *Language, speech, and communication.* London: MIT Press.

———. 2000b. *Toward a cognitive semantics.* Vol. 2 of *Language, speech, and communication.* Cambridge, Mass.: London: MIT Press.

Taub, Sarah F. 2001. *Language from the body: Iconicity and metaphor in American Sign Language.* Cambridge: Cambridge University Press.

Tavner, S. 2008. Celebrating 180 years of deafness. *Guardian*, May 31.

Taylor, Philip. 1998. Looking for Thomas . . . a search for my roots. In *See-Hear*, at 26 minutes, 27 seconds. United Kingdom: BBC.

Temple, Bogusia. 1997. Watch your tongue: Issues in translation and cross-cultural research. *Sociology* 31:607–18.

Temple, Bogusia, and Alys Young. 2004. Qualitative research and translation dilemmas. *Qualitative Research* 4:161–178.

Tirkkonen-Condit, Sonja. 1989. Theory and methodology in translation research. In *Empirical studies in translation and linguistics*, ed. Sonja Tirkkonen-Condit and S. Condit, 3–18. University of Joensuu, Faculty of Arts.

Toury, Gideon. 1978/1995. The nature and role of norms in translation. In *The translation studies reader*, ed. Lawrence Venuti. London: Routledge.

Toury, Gideon. 1995. *Descriptive translation studies and beyond.* Benjamins Translation Library, vol. 4. Amsterdam: Benjamins.

United Kingdom Parliament. 1996. The Broadcasting Act: HMSO.

Veinburg, L., and Ronnie B. Wilbur. 1990. A linguistic analysis of the negative headshake in American Sign Language. *Sign Language Studies* 68:217–44.

Venuti, Lawrence. 1995. *The translator's invisibility: A history of translation.* Translation Studies. London: Routledge.

Venuti, Lawrence. 1998. *The scandals of translation: Towards an ethics of difference.* London: Routledge.

Vermeer, Hans J. 2000. Skopos and commission in translational action. In *The translation studies reader*, ed. Lawrence Venuti, 221–32. London: Routledge.

Vuorinen, E. 1995. News translation as gatekeeping. In *Translation as intercultural communication*, ed. Mary Snell-Hornby, 325–38. Amsterdam: Benjamins.

West, Donna. 2001. "Here forever" the importance of ethnographic research in the search for an understanding of Deaf children's identity development. Master's thesis, Centre for Deaf Studies, University of Bristol.

Wilbur, Ronnie B. 1994. Eyeblinks and ASL phrase structure. *Sign Language Studies* 84:221–40.

Wilbur, Ronnie B., and C. G. Patschke. 1997. Body leans and the marking of contrast in American Sign Language. *Journal of Pragmatics* 30:275–303.

Wilbur, Ronnie B. 1999. Stress in ASL: Empirical evidence and linguistic issues. *Language and Speech* 42:199–250.

Wilbur, Ronnie B., and C. G. Patschke. 1999. Syntactic correlates of brow raise in ASL. *Sign Language and Linguistics* 2:3–41.

Wilbur, Ronnie B. 2000. Phonological and prosodic layering of nonmanuals in American Sign Language. In *Signs of language revisited*, ed. Karen Emmorey and Harlan Lane, 213–41. Hove, U.K.: Lawrence Erlbaum.

Wilson, Deirdre, and Dan Sperber. 1993. Pragmatics and time. In *Working papers in linguistics*, ed. J. Harris, 277–98. London: University College Department of Phonetics and Linguistics.

———. 2002. Relevance theory. Paper presented at Working Papers in Linguistics 14, University College London, London.

Wilson, Deirdre. 2005. New directions or research on pragmatics and modularity. *Lingua* 115:1129–46.

Winsa, Birger. 1998. Language attitudes and social identity: Oppression and revival of a minority language in Sweden, ed. Pauline Bryant. Canberra: Applied Linguistics Association of Australia.

Winston, E. A. 1991. Spatial referencing and cohesion in an American Sign Language text. *Sign Language Studies* 73:397–410.

———. 1995. Spatial mapping in comparative discourse frames. In *Language, gesture and space*, ed. Karen Emmorey and J Reilly, 87–114. Hove, U.K.: Lawrence Erlbaum.

Woll, B. 2000. Exploring language, culture and identity: Insights from sign language and the Deaf community. Paper presented at the Language Across Boundaries Conference, Anglia Polytechnic University, Cambridge.

———. 2001. The sign that dares to speak its name: Echo phonology in British Sign Language. In *The hands are the head of the mouth: The mouth as articulator in sign language*, ed. Penny Boyes-Braem and Rachel Sutton-Spence, 87–98. Hamburg: Signum.

Young, Alys. 1995. Family adjustment to a deaf child in a bilingual, bicultural framework. PhD diss., Centre for Deaf Studies, University of Bristol.

Zaitseva, Galina, Michael Pursglove, and Susan Gregory. 1999. Vygotsky, sign language and the education of Deaf pupils. *Journal of Deaf Studies and Deaf Education* 4 (Winter): 9–15.

# Index

*Figures and tables are denoted by "f" and "t" following page numbers.*

additions in linguistic transfer, 2. *See also* enrichment
adult learners of BSL, 27
Allsop, Lorna, 61
Álvarez, Román, 34
American Sign Language (ASL), 24, 55
ancient Egypt and use of translators, 31
arrays, 52, 169
Arthur (Deaf/hearing interview participant), 59t
  blinking activity of, 124t, 130f
  envisioning Deaf parents when signing, 98
  head movement of, 130f
  on video footage's usefulness, 145–46, 148
ASLI affiliation of interpreters, 33, 173
assimilation, 34–35, 44, 45
audience considerations, 41–44. *See also* constructed audience (or "pragmatic other")
  blinking frequency and audience rapport, 167, 168, 169
  causing audience to reach, 43–44
  Deaf T/Is' focus on, 81, 84–85, 94, 97, 98, 102, 134–36
  ease of Deaf audience to understand T/Is, 138–39
  how to reach, 42–43, 102
  mainstream audience's influence, 37–38
  target audience, 133–35
authenticity and domestication, 37

autocue, use of, 25, 89–90, 96–97, 170, 171
  as memory aid, 113, 119, 169

Bahan, Ben, 50
Baker, Mona, 1, 49, 56
balanced bilingualism, 27–28, 29
Bassnett, Susan, 5, 5f
Beaugrande, 4, 5f
"Behind the News" feature on *See Hear*, xiii
bilingualism. *See also* Deaf bilinguals; hearing bilinguals; *specific languages*
  balanced bilingualism, 27–28, 29
  levels of, 26–30, 104
Blakemore, Diane, 14
blinks
  boundary sensitive. *See* boundary sensitive blinks
  cohesion created by use of, 168
  comparison of news review and headlines blinking activity, 121t, 168
  co-occurring with head movements. *See* co-occurring blinks with head movements
  in Deaf translation norm, xi, 114
  frequency of Deaf T/Is and audience rapport, 167, 168, 169
  glossing of, 69–70
  in headlines, 115–18
    Deaf headlines blinking categories, 115, 115t, 116–17f
    hearing headlines blinking categories, 118, 118t

blinks (*continued*)
  hesitations and false starts. *See*
    hesitations and false starts
    (blink type)
  in news review, 119–20*f*, 119–22,
    123*t*
  physiological. *See* physiological
    blinks
  preparedness and, 7, 114
  superarticulation in sign language
    and, 52
  in TAPs, 122–25, 124–25*t*
  types of blinking activity, 55–56,
    115–19
  voluntary. *See* voluntary blinks
boundary sensitive blinks, 55, 56, 69,
    69*f*, 115–19, 115*t*, 116–17*f*, 121,
    121*t*, 123–25*t*, 125, 129, 169
boundary sensitive head movements,
    126
Boyes-Braem, Penny, 53, 54
British Sign Language (BSL)
  cognitive effort of audience and,
    139
  enrichment and relevance theory,
    20–21
  referencing in, 112
  television use of, xiv–xv, 79. *See
    also* television
  translation and interpreting into.
    *See* translation/interpreting
  translation norm for, ix, 98, 171.
    *See also* Deaf translation norm
    process
  translators and interpreters into. *See*
    Deaf translators/interpreters
    (T/Is); hearing translators/
    interpreters (T/Is)
  visual motivation in, 23–24
Broadcasting Act of 1996, x, xiii

CA (constructed action), 47, 91
catalytic validity, 60

Catford, J. C., 2, 4, 5*f*, 40
CD (constructed dialogue), 47, 91
choice of interpreter, 33–34, 98–100,
    135, 166
Clark (Deaf interview participant),
    59*t*
  on adding background information,
    85–86, 89
  on advantages of Deaf T/Is, 94
  on audience considerations, 81,
    85–86
  Deaf community membership,
    133
  enrichment for constructed
    audience, 101, 137
  cohesion and, 110–11
  considered excellent T/I by other
    study participants, 90, 110–11
  on Deaf readers' role to impart
    information to Deaf
    community, 84
  on eye gaze, 111
  on interpreting preferences, 106–8
  on lack of standardization in news
    signing, 92–93
  on processing by Deaf T/Is, 108
  on role of T/Is, 83
  on video footage as aid in
    translation, 138
code-based comprehension models, 11
cohesion
  defined, 46
  discoursal prosodic cohesion, 169
  in English vs. BSL, 46–49, 168
  prosody in sign language creating,
    110–11
  spatial cohesion in sign languages,
    49–52
  in translation/interpretation, 56–57
Cokely, Dennis, 2
colonial context, 38, 43
commas, compared to blinking and
    head movements, 114

community. *See* Deaf community

"complementary principle" (Grosjean), 28–29

conceptualization competency, 110, 135–40, 138, 161

consecutive mode of translation, 173

constructed action (CA), 47, 91

constructed audience (or "pragmatic other"), ix, 9, 42, 44, 98, 101, 134, 167

constructed dialogue (CD), 47, 91

contact phenomenon of reading of English script, 136

continuum of "pure" translation to "pure" interpretation, 142–43, 142t, 143f

co-occurring blinks with head movements, 55, 115, 115t, 121t, 123–24t

cooperative principle, 11

covert translation, 16, 84, 91, 95, 101, 110

critical ethnography, 59–60

Cronin, Michael, 3

cultural identity, xii, 7, 31, 34, 36–38

culture. *See also* Deaf culture equivalence

cultural appropriateness, 8

cultural competence, 10

cultural relevance and equivalence, 39

cultural vs. linguistic transfer, 3

differences and norms, 35, 43

intentionality and, 6–8

David (hearing interview participant), 59t

blinking activity of, 124t

on script-reading process, 144

on video footage's usefulness, 145, 146, 148

Deaf bilinguals

compared with hearing bilinguals, 30–31

levels of bilingualism within Deaf community, 26–30

power of, 32

as translators for Deaf monolinguals, ix, 83, 165–66

Deaf children of Deaf parents, 26

Deaf clubs, x

Deaf community

Deaf bilinguals' role in, 165–66

membership in, xii

commitment of T/Is to, 110

study participants, 30

nature of, 37

shared cognitive environment of, 139, 147–48

Deaf culture equivalence, 38–46

audience considerations, 41–44

authorship in translation, 40–41

constructing equivalence, 39–40

gatekeeping in translation, 44–46

intercultural communication, 42

sense-for-sense rendering, 38–39

subtitles, 41–42

Deaf Interpreter Network (DIN), 33, 168, 173

Deaf jobs, 98–100, 166

Deaf-led research, 60

Deaf monolinguals as constructed audience. *See* constructed audience (or "pragmatic other")

Deaf residential schools, 42

Deafstation.org, 174

Deaf translation norm process, xi–xii, 95, 109, 149–54, 165–74. *See also* Deaf translators/interpreters (T/Is)

changing role of, 166

constructed audience and, 167

Deaf cultural space and, 167–68

difference from process of hearing T/Is, 112–14, 169–72, 174

Deaf translation norm process
    (*continued*)
  enrichment and impoverishment,
      150–53
  existence of norm, validation of,
      172
  history of, 165–66
  language of, 168–69
  multimedia environment, use of,
      171
  performed translation of, 170–71
  presence in, 166–67
  prosodic control, 169
  reducing influence of mainstream
      culture in, 170, 174
  relevance in, 171–72
  visual information incorporated
      into BSL, 153–54. *See also*
      video footage, use of
Deaf translators/interpreters (T/Is),
    xi–xii. *See also* Deaf translation
    norm process
  advantages of using, 80–81, 91–92,
      94–95, 98, 103, 110, 137, 141
  cohesion of, 111
  constraints on, xiv, 29
  cultural identity of, 36–38, 93–95
  ease of Deaf audience to
      understand, 138–39
  influence of hearing T/Is on, 95,
      106
  interpreter's role, 80–81
    news company's failure to consult
        Deaf T/Is, 96
    presence, 88–89
  journalist role of, 40, 86, 88, 173
  language differences from hearing
      T/Is, 101–64. *See also* Deaf
      translation norm process;
      interpreted/translated
      language features; translation/
      interpreting
  memory skills of, 90, 97, 111

participatory perspective of, 104–5
power of, 32
preferences of, 105–8
processing by, 107–8
professional employment
    possibilities for, xii–xiii, xiv,
    32–33, 104, 173. *See also*
    choice of interpreter
  hearing T/Is in job of, 98–100,
      166
  role or identity of, 76–79
  selection from multigenerational
      Deaf families, xii, 37
  study participants, 30–31, 59*t*
  training of. *See* training
  view of hearing T/Is, 98–99, 135,
      138
DIN. *See* Deaf Interpreter Network
directionality, 7, 29, 31, 35, 39
discoursal prosodic cohesion, 169
disjointedness, 131
domestication, 37

early vs. late acquisition of sign
    language, 26–27
echo phonology, 55, 130
ellipsis, 49
empathy. *See* audience considerations
employers choosing hearing vs. Deaf
    T/Is. *See* choice of interpreter
English-to-Finnish translation, 44
enrichment, 6, 17–22, 137, 150–
    64, 172. *See also* pragmatic
    enrichment/impoverishment
  translation shifts, differences among
      types of T/Is, 159–63*t*, 159–64
equivalence, 4, 8–22, 38–46, 134. *See*
    *also* Deaf culture equivalence
  constructing, 39–40
  explicature and implicature, 13–16.
      *See also* explicature and
      implicature

impoverishment and enrichment, 17–22. *See also* enrichment; impoverishment

inference-based comprehension models, 11–12

pragmatic theory, 10–11

relevance theory, 12–13. *See also* relevance theory (RT)

search for, 31–34

translation and, 16–17

ethics for interpreters, 32

evaluation of translation, 7

explicature and implicature, 13–16, 152, 154, 157, 158, 161

eye gaze, use of, 52, 111–12

facial expression, use of, 38, 52, 53, 92, 103–7, 110–13, 134

faithfulness, 9, 10

false starts. *See* hesitations and false starts (blink type)

feminist translation style, 4

fingerspelling, 102–3

first language, advantages of T/Is working into, 164

*For Deaf Children* (television program), xiii

foregrounding, 105, 147

Frishberg, N., 1

future research needs, 173–74

Gaboriau, Linda, 4

gatekeeping in translation, 44–46

Georgina (Deaf interview participant), 59t

on adding extra information, 111

advantages of using Deaf T/Is, 80–81, 110

on audience considerations, 81, 84–85, 94, 98, 135–36

blinking activity of, 119–20f, 123, 124t

on facial expressions use by Deaf T/Is, 111, 112

head movements in TAPs, 128f

on interpreter training, 137

on job of interpreters, 80

on mainstream control of how Deaf T/Is do their job, 91

on memory vs. use of autocue, 90, 97

needing more information to know what script means, 78, 163

on NMF, 112

on participatory perspective of Deaf T/Is, 104–5

on presence, 88

on processing by Deaf T/Is, 97, 107

on script-reading process, 143

on video footage's usefulness, 145, 146, 148

gestural vs. linguistic aspects, 51

glossing, 68–71

Grice, H. P., 11, 12

Grosjean, François, 28–29

Gutt, Ernst-August, 9, 16, 22

Halliday, M. A. K., 47, 49, 56

Hasan, R., 47, 49, 56

Hatim, B., 3–4, 6, 7

headlines and blinking. *See* blinks

head movements

cohesion created by use of, 168, 169

co-occurring with blinks. *See* co-occurring blinks with head movements

Deaf translation norm's use of, xi, 114, 130–32, 131t

enrichment and, 156

glossing of, 70

nested. *See* nested head movements

superarticulation in sign language and, 52

types of, 125–30, 126–30f

hearing bilinguals compared with
    Deaf bilinguals, 30–31
hearing translators/interpreters (T/Is),
    32–33
  bias of employer to hire, 33–34, 99.
      See also choice of interpreter
  conceptualization competency of,
      110
  constraints on, 29
  disadvantages of using. See Deaf
      translators/interpreters
      (T/Is), subheading: advantages
      of using
  formulaic interpreting by, 104
  influence on Deaf T/Is, 79, 95, 106
  "internal rendering" of, 143
  in jobs of Deaf T/Is, 98–100, 135,
      166
  language differences from Deaf
      T/Is, 101–64. See also Deaf
      translation norm process;
      Interpreted/translated
      language features; translation/
      interpreting
  listening to English while
      translating, 114, 141
  overcompensation by, 108, 109
  presenting like Deaf people, 108–22
  study participants, 30–31, 59t
  training of. See Training
hegemony, 34–35. See also
    assimilation
hesitations and false starts (blink
    type), 55, 114, 115t, 118t, 121t,
    123–24t
Holmes, 5, 5f
Hong Kong Sign Language (HKSL),
    55
hybrid texts, 44–45

ideal translation, 34
identity
  cultural bias and, 25–57

of interpreter, translator, or
    newsreader, 76–79
ideology of translation, 3
implicature, 13–16, 42, 152, 154,
    157, 158, 172
impoverishment, 6, 17–22, 139,
    150–53, 158, 172. See also
    pragmatic enrichment/
    impoverishment
indexation, 48, 137, 148
inference-based comprehension
    models, 11–12
Inghilleri, Moire, 37, 61
initial norms, x–xi, 82, 167, 170
institutional limits of television news
    company, 96–97, 103
intentionality, 6–8
intercultural communication, 42, 45
interlingual impoverishment, 17
"internal rendering" of hearing T/Is,
    143
International Sign (IS), 89, 91
Internet. See Web translation/
    interpretation
interpreted/translated language
    features, 101–32
  bilingualism, levels of, 104
  language construction, 101–5
  NMF (nonmanual features), 103–4
  participatory perspective of T/Is,
      104–5
  preferences of interpreters, 105–8
  presenting like Deaf T/Is,
      108–32. See also blinks;
      head movements
  referencing, 103, 111
interpreter paradox, 36
interpreting. See translation/
    interpreting
inter-subjective truths, 63, 67
intonation
  hearing T/Is using, 141
  newsreaders practicing, 144

irony, 11–12
IS (International Sign), 89, 91

jargon, 102
Jerome (Saint), 38
journalist role of Deaf T/Is, 40, 86, 88, 173
judgment sampling, 60

Kade, 1, 141, 142, 170
Kat (Deaf interview participant), 59t
  on advantages of Deaf T/Is, 91, 92
  on audience considerations, 82
  on bilingual skills required of T/Is, 104
  blinking activity of, 116f, 120f
  on cohesion, 136
  on comparison of Deaf and hearing T/Is, 135
  feelings about hiring of hearing T/Is, 135
  head movements in TAPs, 128f
  on hearing T/Is' need to be supportive to Deaf T/Is, 99
  on hearing T/Is presenting like Deaf people, 108, 109
  on influence of hearing T/Is on Deaf T/Is, 79, 95
  on lack of standardization in news signing, 93
  on mainstream control of how Deaf T/Is do their job, 91, 109
  on NMF, 103
  on participatory perspective of Deaf T/Is, 105
  on processing by Deaf T/Is, 107–8, 136
  on Queen's Christmas speech interpretation, 134
  on referencing and eye gaze, 103
  on role of T/Is, 87
Kim (Deaf interview participant), 59t
  on acceptance of T/I, 110
  on audience considerations, 102, 105
  blinking activity of, 116f, 123, 124t
  on difference between working on television and working from BSL to International Sign (IS), 89, 91
  on disadvantage of using hearing T/Is, 78, 82–83, 87, 94
  head movements of, 127, 127f, 129f
  on hearing T/Is presenting like Deaf people, 108–10
  on implicature, 139
  on lack of standardization in news signing, 92
  on language differences of Deaf vs. hearing T/Is, 113
  on mainstream control of how Deaf T/Is do their job, 96
  on mental picture, 137–38
  on NMF, 113
  on preferences in interpreting, 106, 107
  on processing by Deaf T/Is, 90
  on role of T/I, 80
  on simultaneous interpreting, 88
  on television's effect on T/I, 92–93
  on video footage's usefulness, 146, 153
kinesthetic sense of appropriate BSL translation, 171

Labov, William, 36
Ladd, Paddy, 43
language construction, 101–5
late vs. early acquisition of sign language, 26–27
length of story and translation shifts, 162, 162t
lexical head movements, 126, 126f, 131
linguistic analysis, 67–68

listening by hearing T/Is vs. Deaf reliance on autocue, 113–14

*Listening Eye* (television program, later *Sign On*), xiii

locational enrichment, 152, 157, 172

locus, use of, 48

mainstream motivations and control of translation/interpretation, 37–38, 44, 82, 91, 99, 167–68

Mandel, M., 23

Mary Hare Grammar School, 32

Mason, Ian, 35

Matthews, P. H., 46

Mayberry, Rachel I., 26

memory skills of Deaf T/Is, 90, 97, 111. *See also* autocue, use of

mental pictures, 85, 94, 98, 137–38, 161, 170

message model, 11

methodology of study, 7, 58–75, 59*t*, 173. *See also individual participants by name*
  author's background, 60–61
  catalytic validity, 60
  critical ethnography, 59–60
  Deaf-led research, 60
  glossing, 68–71
  inter-subjective truths, 63, 67
  judgment sampling, 60
  participants, 68–71
  reflexivity, 60–62
  reliability of coding, 70–71
  respondent validation, 59, 65, 66–67
  semistructured interviews, 58, 62–68
    informants and sampling, 64
    interviews, 64–65
    linguistic analysis, 67–68
    memos, use of, 66
    open coding, 66
    translation issues, 65–66

think-aloud protocols (TAPs), 58, 60, 71–75

triangulation, 59–60

typicality, 60

Metzger, Melanie, 36, 50

monolingual monologue and dialogue, 56

multigenerational Deaf families in the study, xii, 37

multimedia environment, use of, 171

Napier, Jemina, 8, 38

naturalness, 7, 19, 24, 41, 95

negative headshakes, 53, 129

nested head movements, xi, 128–29, 128–29*f*

neutrality in translation/interpreting, 35–36, 82–83, 166

Newport, E., 27

news (hearing) anchors, Deaf T/Is engaging with, 77–78

news programs. *See* television

*News Review* (television program), xiii

news-review blinks, 119–20*f*, 119–22, 123*t*
  comparison of news review and headlines blinking activity, 121*t*
  hearing T/Is, 122, 122*t*

NMF (nonmanual features), 103–4, 112

normalization, 43, 45

norms. *See* Deaf translation norm process; translation norms

NRCPD (formerly CACDP)
  directory, 33
  role possible in developing national guidelines for on-screen translation/interpreting, 168

omissions in linguistic transfer, 2, 17. *See also* impoverishment

Ong, Walter, 46–47
open coding, 66
operational norms, xi, 128, 168, 170
oral cultures, 47
oralism and power, 32, 43, 45
ostentation, 12, 139, 164
overcompensation of hearing T/Is
　　trying to present like Deaf people,
　　108, 109

Padden, Carol, 150
participatory perspective of Deaf T/
　　Is, 104–5
periods, compared to blinking and
　　head movements, 114
phrase-for-phrase parity. *See* word-
　　for-word parity
physiological blinks, 55, 115, 115*t*,
　　116–17*f*, 117, 118*t*, 119, 119*f*,
　　121*t*, 122, 123–24*t*
point of saturation, 63
politics of translation, 34–38, 97–100
　　hegemony and assimilation, 34–35
postcolonial context, 43
power
　　cultural identity and, 34
　　differentials between majority and
　　　　minority languages, 35
　　translation and, 31–32
pragmatic enrichment/
　　impoverishment, 6, 17, 74, 140
"pragmatic other." *See* constructed
　　audience
pragmatic theory, 10–11
preferences of Deaf T/Is, 105–8
preliminary norms, ix–x, 87, 166
preparedness, 7–8, 56, 114
　　rehearsing by newsreaders, 144
　　rehearsing of translation, 142, 170
presence, 88–89, 109
　　in deaf translation norm, 166–67
　　eye gaze, use of, 112

profession of sign language
　　interpreting, xii–xiii, xiv, 32–33,
　　104, 173
prosodic control, 169
prosodic marking, xi, 129, 131
prosody, 53, 110, 112–13
　　intonation and, 114
punctuation, compared to blinking
　　and head movements, 114

Rebecca (Deaf interview participant),
　　59*t*
　　adding background information,
　　　　86, 136
　　on advantages of using Deaf T/Is vs.
　　　　shortcomings of hearing T/Is,
　　　　95, 98, 103, 137
　　on audience considerations, 97,
　　　　102, 134
　　blinking activity of, 116, 116*f*, 123,
　　　　124*t*
　　feelings about hiring of hearing T/
　　　　Is, 98–99, 135
　　on fingerspelling, 102
　　head movements of, 126–27*f*, 127
　　on lack of Deaf choice in news, 85,
　　　　88
　　on lack of standardization in news
　　　　signing, 92
　　on NMF, 103
　　on video footage's usefulness,
　　　　145–46, 147, 148–49, 153
referencing, 103, 111
reflexivity, 60–62
register, 6
rehearsing. *See* preparedness
relevance theory (RT), 5–6, 9, 12–13,
　　24
　　author's choice to use, 62
　　ostention and, 139
　　pragmatics and, 10–11
　　translation and, 16–17, 171–72
respondent validation, 59, 65, 66–67

restructuring of news stories by
T/Is, 78, 97, 107, 170. *See also*
audience considerations
role of translators/interpreters (T/Is),
76–79
Deaf identity, 93–95
definition of job, 80–81
first language, working into, 164
historical roots of, 83–85
television standards, 92–93
translation act, 81–83
Romaine, S., 27–28
Rudvin, Mette, 36, 61
Ruuskanen, D. D. K., 9

Sandler, Wendy, 52–53
Schäffner & Adab, 44, 45
Schleiermacher, 16
script-reading process, xi, 77, 114,
136, 143–44
TAP process and, 72–74
secondary orality, 47
*See Hear* (BBC television program),
xiii, xiv, 79, 102
semilanguage peoples, 41
semistructured interviews, 58, 62–68
informants and sampling, 64
inter-subjective truths, 63, 67
interviews, 64–65
linguistic analysis, 67–68
memos, use of, 66
open coding, 66
respondent validation, 59, 65,
66–67
themes of, 66
topics of, 63
translation issues, 65–66
sense-for-sense translation/
interpreting, 38–39
Sense Model approach, 170
Sequeiros, Xavier R., 17, 18, 22, 150,
152, 154, 172
Shlesinger, Miriam, 8, 56

Shoemaker, Pamela J., 44
Signature (formerly CACDP), 43
sign languages. *See also* British Sign
Language (BSL); *specific sign
languages*
recording of, xiii
spatial cohesion in, 49–52
superarticulation in, 52–55
translation/interpreting into. *See*
translation/interpreting
*Sign On* (television program), xiii, 79
SignStream™, 68
simultaneous interpreting process, 88,
140–49, 173
"skewing," 36
Skopos (goal of translation), 5, 85,
166
Spanish-to-English translation, 17–22,
35, 158
spatial cohesion in sign languages,
49–52, 168, 169
spatial mapping, 50
spectrum of texts in study, 7
Sperber, Dan, 12, 13, 15, 17, 23
Steiner, Ben, 53
Stolze, Radegundis, 6, 40–41
subtitles, 41–42, 148, 171
superarticulation in sign languages,
52–55
Swiss German Sign Language, 53
Sze, Felix, 53, 55–56, 70, 114, 115,
118, 125

TAPs. *See* think-aloud protocols
Taub, Sarah F., 23–24
television
BSL provided on, x–xi, xiv–xv
Deaf T/Is on. *See* Deaf translators/
interpreters (T/Is)
failure to consult Deaf community
about validity of BSL
translation/interpreting, 25

hearing T/Is on. *See* hearing
    translators/interpreters (T/Is)
institutional limits of television
    news company, 96–97, 103
preference in hiring hearing over
    Deaf T/Is. *See* choice of
    interpreter
programming aimed at Deaf
    audience, xiii
spectrum of texts in study, 7
standards advocated for, 92–93
translation/interpreting process,
    23–24
Temple, Bogusia, 34
temporal enrichment, 150–51,
    154–55, 160
temporal shifts, 18
text linguistics, 46–57
    blinking. *See* blinks
    cohesion, 46–49
    cohesion in translation/
        interpretation, 56–57
    spatial cohesion in sign languages,
        49–52
    superarticulation in sign languages,
        52–55
thematic enrichment, 19, 151, 152,
    155–56, 160, 172
theoretical saturation, 63
think-aloud protocols (TAPs), 71–75
    analysis of translation shifts, 74–75,
        74t
    blinking activity in, 122–25,
        124–25t
    head movements in, 129, 129f
    in prior research, 60
    process of, 58, 72–74, 114
    script for, 72–74, 175–76
    strategic use of, 140
    translation shifts and enrichment in,
        161–62t, 161–63
time constraints, removal of, 140, 141

T/Is (Translators/interpreters). *See*
    Deaf translators/interpreters
    (T/Is); Hearing translators/
    interpreters (T/Is); Role of
    translators/interpreters (T/Is)
Toury, Gideon, 5, 5f, 39, 79
training, xiv–xv, 32–33
    Deaf translation norm,
        recommendation to
        incorporate in, 172
    Deaf translators/interpreters (T/
        Is), recommendations for
        programs for, 62, 93, 134,
        137, 172
    Deaf vs. hearing translators/
        interpreters (T/Is), 29, 104,
        137
    on purpose of translation, 85
"Translationese," 45, 46, 106, 107
translation/interpreting
    authorship in, 40–41
    blinking, use of. *See* blinks
    cohesion in, 56–57. *See also*
        cohesion
    comparison of Deaf and hearing
        T/Is, 140–49
    continuum of "pure" translation to
        "pure" interpretation, 142–43,
        142t, 143f
    cultural vs. linguistic transfer, 3
    equivalence, 8–22. *See also*
        equivalence
    facial expression. *See* facial
        expression, use of
    gatekeeping in, 44–46
    head movements, use of. *See* head
        movements
    ideal translation, 34
    influence of translating on
        interpreting, 2
    interpreting vs. translation, 1, 141,
        169

translation/interpreting (*continued*)
  neutrality in, 35–36. *See also*
      neutrality in translation/
      interpreting
  performance, 89–92
  politics of, 34–38
  power and, 31–32
  relevance theory and, 16–17
  script-reading process, 143–44. *See*
      *also* script-reading process
translation norms, ix–xii, 2–8. *See*
    *also* Deaf translation norm
    process
  initial norms, x–xi, 82, 167, 170
  operational norms, xi, 128, 168,
      170
  preliminary norms, ix–x, 87, 166
translation shifts, 6, 20, 22, 74–75,
    74*t*, 133, 150, 159–63*t*,
    159–64. *See also* enrichment;
    impoverishment
translators/interpreters (T/Is). *See*
    Deaf translators/interpreters
    (T/Is); hearing translators/
    interpreters (T/Is); role of
    translators/interpreters (T/Is)
triangulation, 59–60

typicality, 60

Veinburg, L., 53
Venuti, Lawrence, 1, 4, 5*f*, 16, 31,
    34–35, 37, 38, 43
Vidal, M. Carmen-África, 34
video footage, use of, 23, 73, 138,
    145–49, 152–54, 170, 171
visual motivation in sign languages,
    24
voluntary blinks, 55, 69, 69*f*, 115*t*,
    116–17*f*, 116–22, 118*t*, 120*f*,
    121*t*, 123–25*t*, 169
Vuorinen, E., 44

Web translation/interpretation
  equivalence and, 9
  Internet-based daily news
      (Deafstation.org), 174
  preparation possible due to advance
      receipt scripts, 29–30
Wilbur, Ronnie B., 53, 55, 56, 70
Wilson, Deirdre, 12, 13, 15, 17, 23
Winston, E. A., 50–51
word-for-word parity, 2, 40, 96

Young, Alys, 34